Lecture Notes
in Business Information Processing   275

More information about this series at http://www.springer.com/series/7911

Boris Shishkov (Ed.)

Business Modeling and Software Design

6th International Symposium, BMSD 2016
Rhodes, Greece, June 20–22, 2016
Revised Selected Papers

 Springer

Editor
Boris Shishkov
Bulgarian Academy of Sciences,
   Institute of Mathematics and Informatics/
Interdisciplinary Institute for Collaboration
   and Research on Enterprise Systems
   and Technology - IICREST
Sofia
Bulgaria

ISSN 1865-1348   ISSN 1865-1356   (electronic)
Lecture Notes in Business Information Processing
ISBN 978-3-319-57221-5   ISBN 978-3-319-57222-2   (eBook)
DOI 10.1007/978-3-319-57222-2

Library of Congress Control Number: 2017937152

Printed on acid-free paper

This Springer imprint is published by Springer Nature
The registered company is Springer International Publishing AG
The registered company address is: Gewerbestrasse 11, 6330 Cham, Switzerland

Preface

BMSD (http://www.is-bmsd.org) – the International Symposium on Business Modeling and Software Design – is an annual event that brings together researchers and practitioners interested in looking into both enterprise engineering and software engineering, inspired by the goal of proposing innovative ideas and solutions about a better utilization by enterprises of the current technical (IT) possibilities.

The above-mentioned goal is reflected in the evolution of business processes: Considered as an essential enterprise asset, business processes used to receive much attention, for the sake of improving the enterprise performance, decreasing the enterprise costs, increasing the satisfaction of customers, and so on. Hence, it was widely agreed that by improving business processes, enterprises could substantially increase their value. Many years ago, improving business processes was a matter of enterprise engineering – then the big challenge was how to organize ordering, accounting, shipping, etc., such that all the different tasks are in synch while the business processes are as simple as possible, leading to effectiveness and efficiency in serving the customer. Nevertheless, changes in business processes came when computers first appeared on the scene and it was possible to replace paper streams by databases, to re-use document constructs, and to search faster through information – then the big challenge was how to make better use of computers heavily dependent, in turn, on corresponding software: this was a matter of software engineering. Initially these two disciplines developed separately because the so-called computerization was simply about automation – the same tasks realized by human entities had to be "given" to computers. Indeed, this allowed many companies to tremendously bring down their workforce but the quality of the IT support delivered to enterprises used to be low exactly for that reason: Enterprise engineers would only superficially re-design their business processes because they lacked deep IT knowledge while software engineers would only partially respond to the business requirements because they lacked deep domain knowledge. This was labeled as a "mismatch between enterprise modeling and software design," and since the new millennium we have been witnessing more and more efforts directed toward bringing together enterprise engineering and software engineering, for the sake of bridging the above-mentioned gap. This would de facto mean bringing together: (a) social theories, such as enterprise ontology, organizational semiotics, theory of organized activity, etc., and (b) computing paradigms, such as component-based software development, service-oriented computing, model-driven engineering, etc. However, this appeared to be a non-trivial task because:

- Enterprise engineering has delivered knowledge on how to create enterprise models usefully restricting the software system-to-be, but this only reached the level of software functionality specification, leaving ambiguity with regard to the implementation choices, platform choices, networking choices, and their impact with regard to the business processes.

– Software engineering has delivered knowledge on how to develop software based on computation-independent models or how to compose software services at high level (not being burdened by the underlying technical complexity), but all these issues stem from a view on the software itself, not assuming an enterprise modeling-driven derivation of software.

Bringing together all those enterprise engineers and software engineers who acknowledge the challenge and are working (from their perspective) toward new ideas and solutions on further bridging business modeling and software design is of key importance to the BMSD community.

Since 2011, we have enjoyed six successful BMSD editions. The first BMSD edition (2011) took place in Sofia, Bulgaria, with the theme "Business Models and Advanced Software Systems." The second BMSD edition (2012) took place in Geneva, Switzerland, under the theme "From Business Modeling to Service-Oriented Solutions." The third BMSD edition (2013) took place in Noordwijkerhout, The Netherlands, and the theme was "Enterprise Engineering and Software Generation." The fourth BMSD edition (2014) took place in Luxembourg, Grand Duchy of Luxembourg, with the theme "Generic Business Modeling Patterns and Software Re-use." The fifth BMSD edition (2015) took place in Milan, Italy, and had the theme of "Towards Adaptable Information Systems." The sixth BMSD edition (2016) took place in Rhodes, Greece, under the theme "Integrating Data Analytics in Enterprise Models and Software Development." In 2017, BMSD is going to Barcelona, Spain, with the theme "Modeling Viewpoints and Overall Consistency."

The Rhodes edition of BMSD demonstrated for a sixth consecutive year a high quality of papers and presentations as well as a stimulating discussion environment.

In 2016, the scientific areas of interest to the symposium were: (a) enterprise modeling and elicitation of requirements; (b) enterprise engineering and service-oriented computing; (c) enterprise modeling-driven software generation; and (d) information systems architectures. Further, there was an application-oriented special session, namely, the special session on "Green IT Solutions."

BMSD 2016 received 59 paper submissions from which 27 papers were selected for publication in the symposium proceedings. Of these papers, 17 were selected for a 30-minute oral presentation (full papers), leading to a full-paper acceptance ratio of 29% – an indication of our intention to preserve a high-quality forum for the next editions of the symposium. The BMSD 2016 authors and keynote lecturers were from Austria, Belgium, Bulgaria, Colombia, Greece, Finland, Germany, Japan, The Netherlands, Poland, Portugal, Sweden, Switzerland, Tunisia, UK, and USA (listed alphabetically); this indicates the strong international spirit of the sixth edition of BMSD.

The high quality of the BMSD 2016 program was enhanced by three keynote lectures, delivered by distinguished guests who are renowned experts in their fields: Paris Avgeriou (University of Groningen, The Netherlands), Jan Jürjens (University of Koblenz-Landau/Fraunhofer ISST, Germany), and Mathias Kirchmer (University of Pennsylvania/BPM-D, USA). Their lectures inspired the audience for interesting discussions touching upon software development, and in particular technical debt and security certification, and also touching upon business process management and strategy execution. Further, Mathias's and Paris's participation (together with Dr. Cordeiro from Portugal and Dr. Mitrakos from Greece) in the BMSD 2016 panel was of additional value.

BMSD 2016 was organized and sponsored by the Interdisciplinary Institute for Collaboration and Research on Enterprise Systems and Technology (IICREST), being technically co-sponsored by BPM-D. Cooperating organizations were the Aristotle University of Thessaloniki, Delft University of Technology, University of Twente – Center for Telematics and Information Technology (CTIT), Bulgarian Academy of Sciences – Institute of Mathematics and Informatics (IMI), the Dutch Research School for Information and Knowledge Systems (SIKS), and AMAKOTA Ltd.

This book contains revised and extended versions of 11 BMSD 2016 papers (selected as a result of additional post-symposium reviewing considering both the quality of the papers and the way they were presented), covering a large number of BMSD-relevant research topics: from business-processes-related topics, such as business process management, variability of business processes, and inconsistencies in risk detection (here it should be mentioned that several papers consider and analyze particular business process modeling formalisms and tools), through system engineering-related topics, such as conceptual modeling, enterprise architectures, human-centered design, sign modeling, and idiosyncrasies capturing, to service-oriented software engineering-related topics, such as service orchestration and e-services design.

I would like to take this opportunity to express our gratitude to Springer for the inspiring collaboration on six books (including the current book), namely, LNBIP 109, LNBIP 142, LNBIP 173, LNBIP 220, LNBIP 257, and LNBIP 275, and to extend my compliments to Ralf Gerstner, Viktoria Meyer, Eleonore Samklu, and Christine Reiss, with whom we have collaborated brilliantly over the years!

We hope that you will find the current LNBIP volume interesting. We believe that the 11 selected papers will be a helpful reference with regard to the aforementioned topics.

March 2017   Boris Shishkov

Organization

Chair

Boris Shishkov   Bulgarian Academy of Sciences/IICREST, Bulgaria

Program Committee

Hamideh Afsarmanesh	University of Amsterdam, The Netherlands
Mehmet Aksit	University of Twente, The Netherlands
Paulo Anita	Delft University of Technology, The Netherlands
Dimitar Birov	Sofia University St. Kliment Ohridski, Bulgaria
Barrett Bryant	University of North Texas, USA
Cinzia Cappiello	Politecnico di Milano, Italy
Kuo-Ming Chao	Coventry University, UK
Ruzanna Chitchyan	University of Leicester, UK
Dimitar Christozov	American University in Bulgaria – Blagoevgrad, Bulgaria
José Cordeiro	Polytechnic Institute of Setúbal, Portugal
Jan L.G. Dietz	Delft University of Technology, The Netherlands
Teduh Dirgahayu	Universitas Islam Indonesia, Indonesia
John Edwards	Aston University, UK
Boris Fritscher	University of Lausanne, Switzerland
J. Paul Gibson	T&MSP – Telecom & Management SudParis, France
Arash Golnam	Business School Lausanne, Switzerland
Rafael Gonzalez	Javeriana University, Colombia
Clever Ricardo Guareis De Farias	University of Sao Paulo, Brazil
Jens Gulden	University of Duisburg-Essen, Germany
Philip Huysmans	University of Antwerp, Belgium
Ilian Ilkov	IBM, The Netherlands
Ivan Ivanov	SUNY Empire State College, USA
Marijn Janssen	Delft University of Technology, The Netherlands
Kecheng Liu	University of Reading, UK
Leszek Maciaszek	Macquarie University, Australia/University of Economics, Poland
Nikolay Mehandjiev	University of Manchester, UK
Dimitris Mitrakos	Aristotle University of Thessaloniki, Greece
Ricardo Neisse	European Commission Joint Research Center, Italy
Bart Nieuwenhuis	University of Twente, The Netherlands
Olga Ormandjieva	Concordia University, Canada
Mike Papazoglou	Tilburg University, The Netherlands
Oscar Pastor	Universidad Politécnica de Valencia, Spain

Barbara Pernici	Politecnico di Milano, Italy
Plamen Petkov	Dublin City University, Ireland
Henderik Proper	Luxembourg Institute of Science and Technology, Grand Duchy of Luxembourg
Jolita Ralyte	University of Geneva, Switzerland
Gil Regev	EPFL/Itecor, Switzerland
Wenge Rong	Beihang University, China
Ella Roubtsova	Open University, The Netherlands
Shazia Sadiq	University of Queensland, Australia
Valery Sokolov	Yaroslavl State University, Russia
Richard Stramans	Utrecht University, The Netherlands
Coen Suurmond	RBK Group, The Netherlands
Bedir Tekinerdogan	Wageningen University, The Netherlands
Roumiana Tsankova	Technical University of Sofia, Bulgaria
Marten van Sinderen	University of Twente, The Netherlands
Roel Wieringa	University of Twente, The Netherlands
Shin-Jer Yang	Soochow University, Taiwan
Benjamin Yen	University of Hong Kong, SAR China
Fani Zlatarova	Elizabethtown College, USA

Invited Speakers

Paris Avgeriou	University of Groningen, The Netherlands
Jan Juerjens	University of Koblenz-Landau/Fraunhofer ISST, Germany
Mathias Kirchmer	BPM-D, USA

Contents

Principles of Semantically Integrated Conceptual Modelling Method

Remigijus Gustas[(⊠)] and Prima Gustiené

Department of Information Systems, Karlstad University, Karlstad, Sweden
Remigijus.Gustas@kau.se

Abstract. To obtain value from the graphical representations that are used by different stakeholders during the system development process, they must be integrated. This is important for achieving a holistic understanding about system specification. Integration can be reached via modelling process. Currently, most of information system modelling methods present different modelling aspects in disparate modelling dimensions and therefore it is difficult to achieve semantic integrity of various diagrams. In this paper, we present the principles of semantically integrated conceptual modelling method for information system analysis and design. The foundation of this modelling method is based on interaction flows. This way of modelling is critical for the identification of discontinuity and inconsistency in information systems specifications. It also provides possibility to integrate business processes and business data, which is necessary for the integration of various architectural domains and to reach the holistic view of enterprise architecture. We have explained in object-oriented terms how interactive, structural and transitional aspects are merged. We also demonstrated the interpretation of various patterns, in terms of semantically integrated conceptual modelling method. It was shown that the method has sufficient expressive power to cover some special cases, which do not match the standard pattern of transaction. The inference rules of interactions help in reasoning about system decomposition. In this method, decomposition is graphically described as classification, inheritance or composition of concepts. SICM method is based on a single type of diagram, which enables reasoning about integration with the help of a special set of inference rules. The ultimate goal of this paper is to present the generic principles for computation- neutral modeling of service interactions.

Keywords: Conceptual modelling · Modelling aspects · Service interactions · Consistency · Value flows · Inference rules · Decomposition · Object transitions

1 Introduction

Various models and methods are used to support the process of Information Systems (IS) development, but still after many years of practice, there are a lot of questions and unsolved problems that cause IS development process to fail (Moody and Sindre 2003). One of the reasons is that rapid changes in the business environment require introducing new business solutions, which should be supported by information technology (IT). Such situation increases the complexity of IS specifications and creates difficulties for

© Springer International Publishing AG 2017
B. Shishkov (Ed.): BMSD 2016, LNBIP 275, pp. 1–26, 2017.
DOI: 10.1007/978-3-319-57222-2_1

organizations to reach their business objectives (Gustiené 2010). Conventional modelling methods do not provide the guidelines how pragmatic specifications that motivate business design can be linked to structural and dynamic aspects of IS specifications, which presents business data and processes (Snoeck 2003). The lack of conceptual modelling method that helps to detect semantic integrity problems creates a communication gap between business and IT experts.

Conceptual modelling is a fundamental activity in requirements engineering (Nuseibeh and Easterbrook 2000). It is the act of abstracting a model from a problem domain (Lankhorst 2005). Requirements modelling much depends on having the knowledge of what should be modelled and how (Leite 1991). The most difficult part is to transform unclear requirements into a coherent, complete and consistent system specification of a desired information system (Gustas and Gustiené 2004). One of the main problems in conceptual modelling of Information Systems is that traditional modelling methods define different aspects of a system using different types of diagrams. The integration principles of such diagrams are not clear.

The lack of a conceptual modelling method that helps to detect semantic integrity of IS specifications is a big problem in IS development process. To capture the holistic structure of a system, it is necessary to understand how various components are related. In system development process many stakeholders with different interests are involved. These people have different viewpoints concerning the designed system (Dijkman et al. 2008). To obtain value from graphical representations that are used in an organization by different stakeholders, these representations must be integrated. Integrated enterprise models might help business and information technology experts to communicate in order to assess and trace the impact of organizational changes.

Integration can be reached via modelling process. Modelling helps system developers to visualize, specify, construct and document different aspects of the system. It is the only way to control system development process. Various aspects of the system may have many modelling projections, which are typically described by using different types of diagrams. These diagrams are critical to distinguish between disparate dimensions of enterprise architecture (Zachman 1987). The Zachman Framework (1987) can be viewed as taxonomy for understanding different types of diagrams. This framework defines separate dimensions of business application and data architecture, such as *Why, What, How, Who, Where* and *When*. Inability to detect inconsistency among different architecture views and dimensions is one of the fundamental problems in Information System methodologies.

Most conventional conceptual modelling languages are plagued by the semantic mismatch between static and dynamic constructs of meta-models. To achieve semantic integration in such a case is very difficult. Unified Modelling Language (UML) (OMG 2009) uses various types of diagrams to represent behavioral, structural and interaction aspects of the system. Every modelling approach that covers more than one type of requirements and is represented by the collection of different diagrams must contain the systematic method for the detection of inter-model inconsistency. The static aspects describe characteristics of objects, which are invariant in time. The dynamic aspects describe interactive and behavioral characteristics of objects over time. These aspects are complimentary and they cannot be analyzed in isolation.

Inter-model consistency and completeness of system specifications is hard to achieve for non-integrated model collections (Glinz 2000). Modelling techniques that are realized as collection of models are difficult to comprehend for business experts. There are often semantic discontinuity and overlapping in various specifications, because static and dynamic constructs do not fit perfectly. A number of rules are defined for UML (Evermann and Wand 2009) that are not supported by available CASE tools. Thus, working with the collections of non-integrated models causes difficulties to realize semantic quality of system specifications, which are represented on various levels of abstraction. By modelling isolated IS views and dimensions creates difficulties for business experts, who determine the organizational strategies. Consequently, this isolation increases semantic problems of communication between business experts and IT-system designers.

Semantically Integrated Conceptual Modelling Method (SICM) presented in this paper provides several advantages (Gustas 2010). Since the method is based on a single diagram type, the integrity rules can be introduced directly into one model. Particular views of specific diagram types, which define structural, behavioral or interactive aspects, can be generated by producing projections of one integrated model. In this paper, we demonstrate how the SICM method can be applied for integration of behavioral and structural aspects of conceptual representations. The central role of service concept in this study provides us with a possibility to model the most essential parts of the system, which is composed of organizational or technical components. This way of modelling is more comprehensible not just for IS designers, but also for business modelling experts, who are mostly interested in computation-neutral analysis of organizations. The presented SICM method shares many similarities with ontological foundation of service process (Ferrario and Guarino 2009). Nevertheless, the internal behavior of service is analyzed by using the basic principles of an ontological framework, which is developed by Bunge (Bunge 1979).

This paper is organized as follows. In the next section, some deficiencies of traditional conceptual modelling approaches are described. In Sect. 3, architectural framework for SICM method is presented. Value flow exchanges and interactions as well as the elements for SICM method are presented in Sect. 4. Merging of interactive, behavioral and structural aspects are presented in Sect. 5. The basic pattern of service interaction is discussed in Sect. 6. The standard and cancellation patterns of service interaction are presented in Sect. 7. The inference rules of interactions are discussed in Sect. 8. And finally, we present the conclusions of this work.

2 Deficiencies of Graphical Modeling Approaches

The quality of system specifications depends on reaching the semantic integrity of graphical representations. Semantic integrity is the degree to which graphical representations are comprehensible enough despite their complexity (Gustiené 2010). Ambiguous, incomplete and inconsistent system specifications make the verification of semantic integrity between business process and data especially difficult. Conceptual modelling provides a possibility to identify, analyze and describe the essential concepts and constraints, using modelling language, based on a set of the concepts to form a meta-model (Guizzardi et al. 2002). Conceptual models used during the modelling process should be concise and express reality perceived by system users and system designers. They should be understandable for all stakeholders involved. Conceptual modelling still lacks the methods that provide a possibility to model different aspects and perspectives from problem domain in an integrated way. Integrated graphical representation of business process and business data is very relevant for reasoning about enterprise redesign decisions.

Another problem is that traditional modelling approaches pay less attention on an 'early-phase' requirements analysis (Yu 1997). It is mandatory to early elicit the details of the goals set for the software (Leite et al. 1991). The analysis and representation of a business strategy through goal modelling is critical to achieve organizational alignment with IT subsystems. Analysis of goals is important as goals are supposed to motivate and drive the overall IS analysis and design process (Gustas and Gustiené 2008). There are number of methods that attempt to solve semantic integration problems. The Object Process Methodology (OPM) is an attempt to integrate behavioral and structural aspects of data. OPM puts into foreground the modelling of static and dynamic relationship between objects (Dori 2002). It emphasizes the difference between physical and informational objects. Physical objects can be subsystems, which are able to carry out actions and change informational objects that are understood as passive concepts. The problem is that the interactive flows in this methodology cannot be explicitly captured. Some modelling methods put into foreground the modelling of the external behavior of different actors (Dietz 2006a). One such example is ArchiMate (Lankhorst 2005) modelling language. It is an enterprise architecture modelling language for the definition of relationship between concepts of different domain. Nevertheless, the ArchiMate language is quite weak in representing the interplay between physical objects interactions and the associated changes in various classes of objects.

UML (OMG 2009) was developed with the ultimate goal to unify the best features of the graphical modelling languages and create a de facto industry standard for system development. However, the semantic integration principles of different UML diagram types are not sufficiently clear. UML models have several weaknesses, which can be summarized as follows: value flow exchanges between actors cannot be explicitly captured; system decomposition principles are ambiguous; it is unclear how to integrate interactive, structural and behavioral aspects together in a single view. UML also supports various types of associations between classes, actors, or between software or hardware components. However, these methods are not suitable for modelling the direct communication among actors that define actor interactions outside the technical system boundary. It is unclear how to visualize the rich context of actor interactions, which are important components in any system. If we have no method how to explicitly capture actors and their interactions, then this important part of specification, which may be viewed as a tacit knowledge, will be hidden from enterprise architects.

One of the benefits of enterprise modelling is the ability to analyze business processes for reaching agreement among various stakeholders on how and by whom the processes are carried out. The industrial versions of information system modelling methods that are intended for business process modelling do not explicitly use the concept of value flow. Value models, which include resource exchange activities among actors, can be viewed as design guidance. The declarative nature of value flows is very useful from the system analysis point of view for the simple reason that flows have very little to do with the dependencies between business activities. Each value flow between actors, that can play the role of service requester and service provider, can be further refined in terms of more specific coordinating interactions among organizational components. The way of modelling, which is based on interaction flows, is more comprehensible and thus more suitable to discuss changes of process architectures with business developers, enterprise architects, system designers and users. Business process modelling does not deal with the notion of value flow, which demonstrates value exchange among actors involved (Gordijn et al. 2000). Traditionally, information system methodologies are also quite weak in representing the alternative value flow exchange scenarios, which usually represent the broken commitments.

Bunge (1979) provides one of the most general ontological definitions of a system. In this paper, his definition serves as the theoretical basis for understanding the notions of organization and enterprise ontology (Dietz 2001). Bunge's ontological principles are fundamental for the justification of various conceptual modelling constructs in our semantically integrated modelling method (Gustas and Gustiené 2012). These principles are as follows: enterprise system can be decomposed into subsystems, which are viewed as interacting components; every subsystem can be loosely coupled with interactions to other subsystems; when subsystems interact, they cause certain things to change and changes are manifested via properties. Any subsystem can be viewed as an object, but not every object is a subsystem. According to Bunge, only interacting objects can be viewed as subsystems. It is quite beneficial to specify service interactions and to keep track of crosscutting concerns (Jacobson and Ng 2005) between different subsystems in order to justify their usefulness. However, a basic underlying principle in UML is to provide separate models for different aspects. It is not totally clear how these aspects can be merged back into one model. Subsystems in UML cannot be realized as composite classes. UML does not provide any superimposition principles of static and dynamic aspects. There is very little research done on how the structural aspects and state dependent behavior of objects should be combined with use case models. Classes and their associated state machines are regarded as the realization of use cases. Use case diagrams are typically not augmented with specification of state related behavior (Glinz 2000). System decomposition should be strictly partitioned. Every component partitions a system into parts, which can be loosely coupled with other components without detailed knowledge of their internal structure. Object transitions and structural aspects have to be related to one separate service, which consists of organizational or technical components. The limitation of conventional system modelling methods results in two side effects, better known as tangling and scattering in aspect-oriented software development (Jacobson and Ng 2005). The treatment of these deficiencies requires the modification of UML foundation. Introducing fundamental changes into UML syntax and semantics with the purpose of semantic integration of collections of models is a complex research activity. However, such attempts would allow using UML to provide computation-neutral type of diagrams, which are more suitable to reason about enterprise architectures. It is recognized that UML support for such task is vague, because semantic integration principles of different diagram types are still lacking (Harel and Rumpe 2004).

Conceptual modelling still lacks the methods that provide a possibility to model different problem domains in an integrated way. Integrated graphical representation of business process and business data is very relevant for reasoning about enterprise redesign decisions.

3   Semantically Integrated Conceptual Modelling Method

Semantically Integrated Conceptual Modelling (SICM) method presented in this paper challenges the existing integration and consistency problems among interactive, behavioral and structural aspects (Gustas 2010; Gustas and Gustiené 2012) of IS specifications. SICM method provides not just the modelling language, framework, but also the modelling process. The success of modelling process depends on two things; on the modelling language used to form models and on the process how these models are used. Modelling constructs should be communicated to all the stakeholders involved therefore the modelling language should be expressive enough to convey the design. It should be unambiguous and easy to use. It should facilitate the identification of contradictions that usually cause semantic problems of communication. SICM method provides an appropriate modelling way that guides the modelling process in a systematic manner among different levels of abstraction, from goal modelling to implementation. As all steps in SICM method uses the same model and the same way of modelling that is based on service interaction flows it enables enterprise architects to gradually decompose a system and to move smoothly from system analysis to design. SICM method provides a three-level architectural framework, which is presented in Fig. 1.

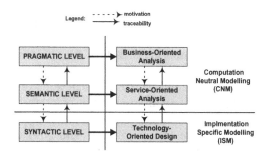

Fig. 1. Architectural framework for SICM

The fitness between these three levels is critical for the success of the final result. The fitness and consistency between levels depends much on having modelling techniques for the refinement of pragmatic entities such as goals, problems, opportunities (Gustas and Gustiené 2008) that represent their structural and dynamic aspects at the semantic level. An integrated modelling way provides a guide to support the analysis and transition from the early requirements to the design of the system. It also provides a way to map from computation-neutral to implementation-specific modelling.

The modelling process is pragmatic-driven. It starts at pragmatic level. At this level business goals and objectives are discussed. Understanding the goals is essential to guide the design of the business processes and to evaluate the operational quality of the solutions taken by business experts (Gao and Krogstie 2009). After stating goals and analyzing the possibilities and solutions at the pragmatic level, it is important to show how these goals are refined further at the semantic level. The semantic (conceptual) level provides description of the static and dynamic aspects of business processes across organizational and technical system boundaries (Gustas and Gustiené 2004). Activities at this level are prescribed by goals. The semantic specifications cannot be analyzed in isolation from the pragmatic specifications. This way of modelling provides a foundation for checking consistency and coherence between levels. Modelling at pragmatic and semantic levels is computation-neutral. It means that the modelling is not bias to any implementation details.

From a software designer's perspective, it is not enough to represent the system architecture just from a pragmatic and semantic perspective. System designers also need to understand technical system architecture, where the application is going to be implemented. The syntactic level is supposed to define the implementation-specific details. Modelling process through three architectural levels provide the techniques and guidelines from the transition from one level to another. This way of modelling enables possibilities for validation of goals started at the pragmatic level and the verification of logical design made at the syntactic and semantic levels. Integrated way of modelling provides a way for semantic traceability via three levels and enables interplay between business requirements and technical solutions, which provides the view to comprehend the modelling artefact as a whole.

4 Value Flow Exchanges and Interactions

Semantically integrated conceptual modelling paradigm is based on more rigorous interpretation of human work. A new conception helps us to develop the method of enterprise engineering that allows practitioners to see the sources of breakdowns, the connections to systems design and to guide the redesign of work processes towards greater productivity and customer satisfaction. Business process models of organizations are quite good for viewing moving material and information flows, but they provide no mechanism for ensuring that the service requester is satisfied. Service requesters deal with work processes to be done, agreements on what will be done, who will to it, and whether they are satisfied with what has been done. The movement of information or material flows is a consequence of this work. Service flow modelling is quite intuitive way of system analysis that is easy to understand for business experts and information system designers. Actions in services are required for exchange of business flows. Actions together with exchange flows can be viewed as fundamental elements for specifying business process scenarios. A scenario is an excellent means of describing the order of service interactions. Scenarios help system designers to express business processes in interplay with elementary service interactions between enterprise system components. In such a way, value flows and service interactions provide a natural way of process decomposition.

The technologies to model coordination processes and tracking events have not been available till now. There are some concepts such as commitment and contract that are present in all business scenarios. Understanding these concepts makes it much easier to design and to change systems under construction. Commitment is a promise or obligation of an actor to perform a specific action. Contract is an agreement between service requester and service provider to exchange one asset into another. Thus, the contract may specify what happens if the commitment is not fulfilled. According to McCarthy (1982), the contract consists of increment and decrement events. If an enterprise increases one resource in an exchange, it has to decrease the value of another resource. The contract includes (1) transfer of economic resources, (2) transfer of exchange rights. Any exchange is a process, in which an enterprise receives economic resource and in return gives other resources. For example, a contract contains commitments to sell goods and to receive payments. The terms of the sales order can specify penalties if goods or payments have not been received on time. The creation and termination of primary business data in these exchanges are important for an enterprise. Artefacts such as credit, debit, account balances are derived from these exchanges. Actors, actions and exchange flows are elements that are necessary for demonstration of value exchange. Economic resources are special types of concepts, which represent moving things. Rectangles with shaded background are used for denotation of moving resources and dotted line boxes are used for representation of data flows. Actors are represented by square rectangles. Actions are performed by actors, which will be represented by ellipses. Actions are necessary for transferring economic resources, data flows or decision flows between actors. Concepts may represent data stores, which represent static aspects of a system. Concepts can be moved from one state to another. Graphical notation of elements in SICM method is presented in Fig. 2.

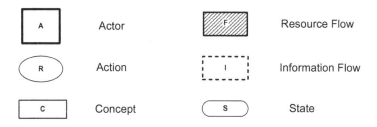

Fig. 2. Elements of SICM method

Interaction loop between two actors indicates that they depend on each other by specific actions. Service providers are actors who typically receive service requests, over which they have no direct control. They initiate service responses that are sent to service requesters. These two interacting actors can be used to define more complex interaction activities. Using interaction pattern, as the way of modelling, enables system designers to construct the blueprint of interacting components. This can be represented by different actors across organizational and technical system boundaries. Any enterprise system can be defined as a set of interacting and loosely connected components, which are able to perform specific services on request.

Increment and decrement events represent values exchanged in business processes. Value models (Gordijn et al. 2000) clarify why actors are willing to exchange economic resources with each other. Two actors and transfer of value flows into opposite directions is illustrated in Fig. 3.

Fig. 3. Value exchange

This figure illustrates that Deliver and Pay actions may happen at any time. It is not stated, which action should happen first. We just want show that a customer is exchanging a Payment flow into a Delivery flow. Deliver action is initiated by vendor, because a shipment's moving direction is from Vendor to Customer. In contrary, the payment is moving from customer to vendor through the action of pay. Action of Pay and action of Deliver represent increment and decrement events. The process of paying is essentially an exchange of Shipment for Payment from the point of view of both actors. For a Vendor, the pay action is an increment event and deliver action is a decrement event, because it decreases the value of resources under control. For a Customer, it is vice versa. The terms of increment and decrement depend on the actor, which is the focus of this model.

Our buying and selling example focuses on the core phenomenon. Most customers pay in advance of shipment, but some customers may pay later when they receive the delivered products. If we consider the case of on line sales, then customers provide credit card details before the product items are delivered. Some customers may receive an invoice later and pay for all their purchases in a certain period. All these cases are covered by the same service interaction loop, which is illustrated in Fig. 4. When the shipment is delivered, then the delivery fact is registered in a system by a newly created object with its mandatory properties. The transition arrow ($\longrightarrow$) is pointing to the class of Shipment.

Every instance of the fact of money transfer from the Customer to the Vendor is represented by Payment. If we want to represent that Deliver action precedes Pay action, then the created Shipment should be linked by the transition arrow with the Pay action, which indicates the creation of the next object. The Pay action creates the Payment from Shipment, which is the property of Payment.

We may ask for payment in advance. In this case, we show first the action of pay, which is designed to transform the concept of order to payment. The second action of deliver should be connected by transition arrow from payment to shipment. In this way, a payment flow would be exchanged to shipment.

Actors represent physical subsystems and structural changes of concepts represent static aspects of a system. In such a way, the model illustrates actions, which result in

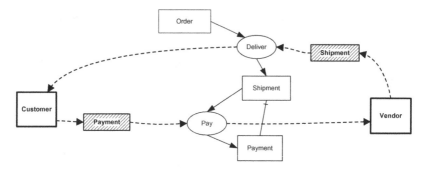

Fig. 4. Interaction loop, where deliver action precedes pay action

changes of the attribute values. All actions are used to show the legal ways in which actors interact with each other. Structural changes of objects can be manifested via static properties of objects. They are represented by the mandatory attributes. The mandatory attributes are linked to classes by the single-valued or by multi-valued attribute dependencies. One significant difference of the presented modelling approach is that the association ends of static relations are nameless. The justification of this way of modelling can be found in some other papers (Gustas 2010; Gustas and Gustiené 2012). The main reason for introducing nameless attribute dependencies is improving stability of conceptualizations. Semantics of static dependencies are defined by cardinalities, which represent a minimum and maximum number of objects in one class (B) that can be associated with the objects in another class (A). Single-valued dependency is defined by the following cardinalities: (0,1;1,1), (0,*;1,1) and (1,1;1,1). Multi-valued dependency denotes either (0,1;1,*) or (1,1;1,*) cardinality.

According to the ontological principles, which are developed by Bunge (Bunge 1977), structural changes of objects are manifested via object properties. Properties can be understood as mandatory attribute values. If diagrams are used to communicate unambiguously semantic details of a conceptualized system, then optional properties should be proscribed (Gemino 1998). The decline in cognitive processing performance that occurs, when optional attributes and relationships are used, appears to be substantial (Bodart et al. 2001). In the presented method, the mandatory attributes are defined by a single-valued ($\rightarrow$) or by a multi-valued attribute dependency ($\rightarrow\!\!\!\leftarrow$). If A $\rightarrow$ B or A $\rightarrow\!\!\!\leftarrow$ B, then concept A is viewed as a class and concept B - as a property of A. One significant difference in SICM method is that the association ends of static relations are nameless. Association ends cannot be used to denote mappings in two opposite directions. However, the attribute dependen-cies are stemming from the traditional semantic models. Their semantics is defined by cardinalities, which represent a minimum and maximum number of objects in one class (B) that can be associated to objects in another class (A). Graphical notation of an attribute dependency between A and B is represented in Fig. 5.

In the previous example (Fig. 4), a shipment is a single-valued attribute of a payment. Any passive concept can be defined as an exclusive complete generalization of two concepts. Passive concept can also be characterized by state (Dori 2002) or condition

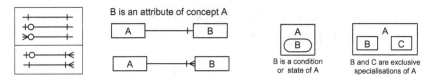

Fig. 5. Notation of attribute dependencies

(Gustas and Gustiené 2009). Notation of the exclusive generalization and notation of state are presented in this diagram as well.

5   Merging of Interactive, Behavioral and Structural Aspects

Good principles of decomposition and separation of crosscutting concerns are not suffi-cient for analysis of behavioral and structural aspects of enterprise architectures. To understand the effects of the internal service interaction between service requesters and service providers, the graphical representations of processes must be integrated with data models. The dynamic aspects of service interactions can be expressed by defining structural changes of passive concepts. Passive concepts are classes or derived entities, which can be characterized by mandatory attributes. Values of such attributes are created or consumed in service requests and service responses. Requests, responses and classes are fundamental for understanding the semantic aspects of service interaction. From an ontological perspective, when two subsystems interact (Bunge 1979) one subsystem may affect the state of another subsystem. Changes in object state are characterized in terms of object properties. Interaction dependency R(A ▪▪▪▶ B) between two active concepts A and B indicates that A subsystem can perform action R on one or more B subsystems. Actions are able to manipulate object properties. Property changes may trigger object transitions from one class to another.

We will analyze the expressive power of the main construct of semantically inte-grated conceptual modelling method from the point of view of object-oriented approach. The construct shows that it can dynamically cover six basic events, which are related to different operations of creation and termination of objects. These events are as follows (Martin and Odell 1995):

(1) Creation of an object,
(2) Termination of an object,
(3) Classification of an object,
(4) Declassification of an object,
(5) Connection of two objects,
(6) Disconnection of two objects.

The internal effects of objects can be expressed by using transition links (▬▶) between passive concepts. There are three fundamental ways for representing object behavior by using reclassification, creation and termination actions. If termination and creation action is performed at the same time, then it is called a reclassification action. Graphical notation of these three variations of actions is graphically represented in Fig. 6.

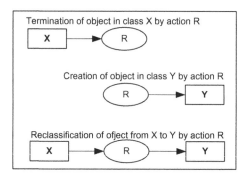

Fig. 6. Three variations of transition dependencies

Creation action is represented by a transition to an initial class. Termination action can be represented by transitions from a final class. For instance, initiation of the order delivery action is typically used to create an Order record in a Vendor database or archive, which represents data at rest. If customer Order is accepted, then it may be used for triggering the send invoice action (Fig. 7). The internal changes of objects are expressed by using the attribute dependencies between various classes of objects. For instance, the Invoice class has an Order as its attribute. Termination action may require several objects to be removed. For instance, removal of a Shipment object would require deletion of the Payment, Invoice and Order objects.

Creation and termination actions can be expressed by using object flows. Object flows are typically used together with the UML activity diagrams. A diagram showing operations and object flows with states has most of the advantages of activity diagrams without most of their disadvantages (Blaha and Rumbaugh 2005). A transition arrow to action or transition arrow from action represents a control flow. In this way, any communication action can be used to superimpose interactions and control flow effects in the same diagram. Order object is created by the Order Deliver action and then it is reclassified by the Send invoice action to Invoice object. The reclassification is defined as termination of object in one class and creation of object in another class. Sometimes, objects are created and then they may pass several classes.

A customer is sending a purchase order to a vendor by using the order delivery action, which creates an order. The invoice object is reclassified from the order object by the send invoice action, which is using an Invoice as a moving data. In the second interaction loop, a customer delivers a Payment flow to a vendor. The pay action is responsible for a creation of Invoice [Paid] and Payment objects. The deliver action corresponds to the performing act. It produces the result by using the shipment flow. This is represented by the object of shipment, which is reclassified from the object of payment. At the same time, the deliver action represents an exchange of payment to shipment. Example of two interaction loops is presented in Fig. 7.

The deliver action also creates the Shipment object with the single valued property of Payment, which is characterized by a single-valued property of Invoice[Paid]. It means that Invoice[Paid] class consists of the same kind of objects, which are found among Invoice objects. This situation in object-oriented approaches is represented by a

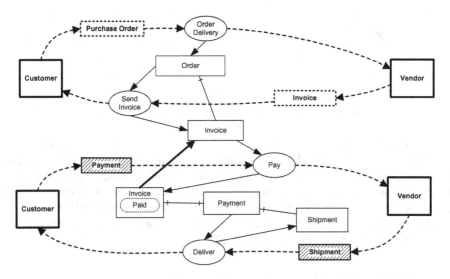

Fig. 7. Example of two interaction loops with the creation, connection, declassification and reclassification events

classification from Invoice to Invoice[Paid]. The classification and declassification events are represented in Fig. 8.

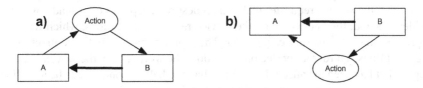

Fig. 8. Notation of classification and declassification events

Classification construct is instantiating an object from the class A to class B (see Fig. 8a). Inheritance arrow from B to A (B ➡ A) indicates creation of the same type of object. Declassification event is used for removal of object from concept B and classifying it as an object of concept A. It is presented in Fig. 8b.

The construct of connection and disconnection of two different objects is represented in Fig. 9. It shows how an object of concept B can be connected to an object of concept A (see Fig. 9a). The second construct represents disconnection of an object of class B from an object in class A, which is represented in Fig. 9b.

Connection event is performed together with the creation event of object B and disconnection event is performed together with the removal event from object B. In Fig. 7, we can see two operations of connection and one operation of classification. The first operation Send Invoice is performing connection of Invoice to Order. The second operation of Pay is a classification of Invoice to Invoice[Paid]. The third operation of Deliver is connecting the object of Shipment to Payment.

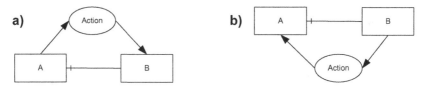

Fig. 9. Notation of connection and disconnection events

Fundamentally, two kinds of changes occur during reclassification: removal of an object from a precondition class and creation of an object in a postcondition class. Sometimes, postcondition class may require preservation of some precondition class objects. So, the static dependencies have a higher priority as compared to object removal request. It is not difficult to see that such preserved classes of objects are Order, Invoice and Payment (see Fig. 7). Quite often preserved classes are not required. Objects are passing several classes and then are destroyed.

6   The Basic Pattern of Service Interaction

The basic element of coordination processes is a closed loop between service requester and service provider. We call it a service interaction loop. Service provider promises to satisfy request of a service requester. In marketing these roles are called buyer and seller. In everyday life, they might be called customer and vendor. The loop consists of four stages. First, the service requester makes a request or accepts an offer made by service provider. Second, they negotiate on the service requester conditions, which will result in a promise made by the service provider. The promise may imply the contract to fulfil those conditions. Third, the service provider does the work. Forth, the service requester accepts what has been promised. It signifies that one half of contract has been fulfilled, which means completion of a service interaction loop.

Every communication action is able to produce new facts, which are represented by various classes of objects. For instance, the Request action between service requester and service provider stores all the details a service request object. Such concepts are representing data at rest. They are represented by rectangles. If we are talking about the hotel reservation request, then this concept can be characterized by who has requested the room, the amount of people staying in a room and the number of required rooms. If such room is expected to be delivered, then Promise object is created in the reply action. In our case, the concept of Promise is related by a single valued dependency to the Request. This means that the object of request is not removed, because it is required by the promise. In the next service interaction loop, the fact of Promise is reclassified to the Result, which is implemented by the Perform action. This result may be finally accepted by the service provider by the Accept action. It produces the Accepted Result. This fact is linked by the inheritance arrow to the concept of Result, which is produced by service provider. It signifies that the first half of the service exchange was performed. This pattern corresponds to the basic pattern of transaction (Dietz 2006b) when service requester and service provider are consenting with each other. It is represented in Fig. 10.

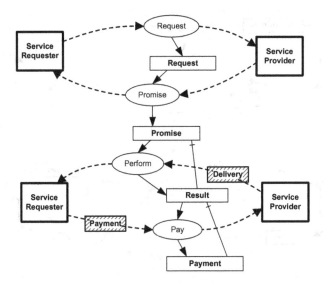

Fig. 10. The basic pattern of transaction

The idea behind a conversation for action schema can be explained by turn-taking. First, the requester initiates a request and waits for a particular promise. Then, service provision (perform) is followed by accept action. It is often the case in practice that the promise or accept actions are missing. They can be performed tacitly. Request, promise and accept are corresponding coordination actions. Coordination events are related to one production event (perform action). Coordination actions are necessary for making commitment regarding corresponding production action, which are supposed to bring value flow to service requester. Both coordination and production actions are combined together into scenarios, which can be expressed as expected sequence of interactions between service requester and service provider.

The behavioral and structural dimensions of interactions are analyzed in terms of creation, termination and reclassification effects. The internal changes of objects are expressed by using transition links between various classes of objects. The reclassification of object is defined as termination event in one class and creation of object in another class. Sometimes, objects are created, they may pass several classes, and then they are terminated. Unbroken transition arrows represent the control flow of creation and termination events. A creation event is denoted by the outgoing transition arrow to a class. A termination event is represented by the transition dependency directed from a class.

We now will demonstrate a pattern of exchange between a customer and a vendor. A customer requests a shipment from a vendor by initiating the order delivery action. This action creates an order object. A vendor promises to deliver shipment by replying with the send invoice action. This action is creating an invoice, which is data at rest object, from the moving invoice flow. The interaction loop between customer and vendor is represented in Fig. 11.

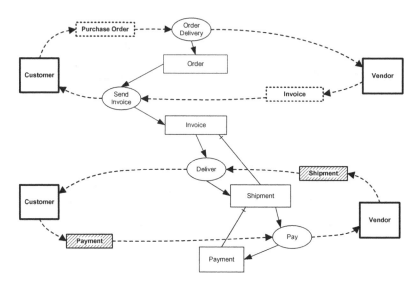

Fig. 11. Two interaction loops between service requester and service provider

In the second interaction loop, a vendor delivers the shipment to a customer. The deliver action corresponds to the perform act, which produces the result. It is represented by the object of shipment. Finally, the pay action is indicating an acceptance of the delivered result. At the same time, it is a second performing action, which represents an exchange of shipment to payment.

7   The Standard and Cancellation Patterns of Service Interaction

We have already illustrated how turn-taking, which is prescribed by the conversation for action schema (Winograd and Flores 1986), is expressed by composing two inter-action loops into a sequence. The service requester typically triggers a request and then waits for a particular promise or service response from the service provider. However, a provider may dissent. Instead of promising or delivering a requested product, a provider may respond by rejecting a request. The alternative actions are necessary to handle breakdowns in the basic pattern of a transaction.

Various interaction alternatives between two actors can also be defined by interaction dependencies, which may produce different, similar or equivalent behavioral effects. A performer may experience difficulties in satisfying a request. For example, the Hotel Reservation System may Reject request of a customer, because it is simply incorrect or incomplete. Instead of promising, the service provider may respond by rejecting the request. The requester may also express disappointment in the result and decline it. Decline is represented by the termination of Result and the creation of a Decline object. For instance, the Hotel Guest may decline the provided hotel room, which was previously assigned by the Provide Hotel Room action. The basic transaction pattern can be complemented with these two dissent patterns. This extended schema is known as the standard pattern. It is represented in Fig. 12.

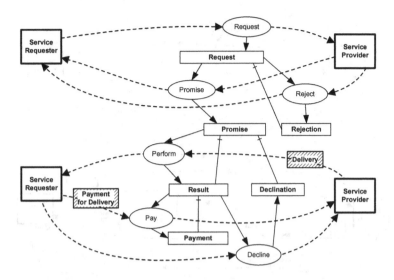

Fig. 12. The standard pattern of transaction

In practice, it is also common that either requester or provider is willing to completely revoke some events. For example, the requester may withdraw his own request. According to Dietz (2006b) there are four cancellation patterns, which may lead to partial or complete rollback of a transaction. Every cancellation action can be performed if the corresponding fact exists. For instance, the Withdraw Request action can be triggered if a request was created. The request cancellation event may be triggered when the customer finds a better or cheaper room alternative in another hotel. A Withdraw Promise action may take place if a Promise for some reason cannot be fulfilled by the Service Provider. For instance, a Hotel Room was damaged by the former room guest. The requester may agree or disagree to accept the consequences of the Withdraw Promise action. Withdrawal should terminate a Promise and preserve a Request. The third cancellation event can be represented by the option Cancel result. It should be initiated by the service provider to avoid a Decline action by the requester. The requester typically allows cancellation of the result. The forth cancellation event may take place when the whole transaction is completed, but the requester discovers some hidden problem and he regrets acceptance. For instance, a customer may try to Cancel Acceptance of the hotel room for the reason that wireless Internet access is not working properly. The standard pattern, which is superimposed with the four cases of cancellation, is presented in Fig. 13.

The possibility to extend the standard pattern with four cancellation patters is not the only advantage of the presented modelling method. The method has sufficient expressive power to cover not just four described cancellation patterns, but also other special cases, which do not match the standard pattern of transaction. For instance, the payment may take place before the delivery of goods. This is represented by a diagram, which is depicted in Fig. 14.

This pattern can be characterized by the same types of actions, which are triggered in different order:

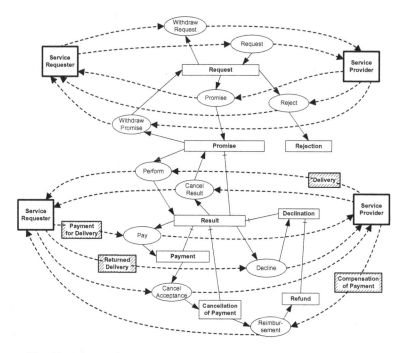

Fig. 13. The standard pattern of transaction and four cancellation patterns

(a) Request,
(b) Promise,
(c) Pay and
(d) Perform.

The first two actions are the same like in the standard transaction pattern. The service requester initiates a request and then waits for a promise. The promise may take the form of invoice, which needs to be paid. If the payment for delivery is done, then the perform action takes place. It is necessary to make a shipment of delivery, which is reclassifying payment to result.

Interaction dependencies between requester and performer can be mapped by a well-known conversation for action schema (Winograd and Flores 1986). We can represent the basic course of a conversation in a simple diagram in which each circle represents a possible state of the conversation and the lines represent actions. The purpose for introducing this schema was initially motivated by the idea of creating computerized tools for conducting conversations.

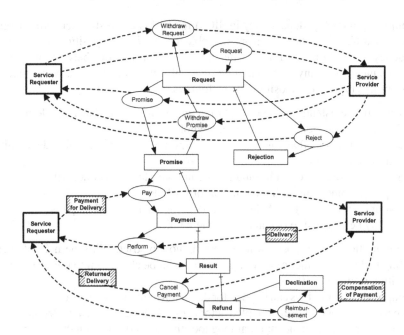

Fig. 14. Not standard pattern of transaction

8   Inference Rules of Interactions

A model of a system can be analyzed as the composition of organizational and technical components. These components represent various types of actors. Organizational components can be seen as interacting subsystems such as individuals and divisions, which denote groups of people. Technical components can be seen as interacting subsystems such as machines, software and hardware. SICM method distinguishes between two types of concepts: active and passive (Gustas 2010). Actors can be represented just by active concepts. An instance of any actor is an autonomous subsystem. Its life cycle can only be motivated by a set of interaction dependencies with other actors. Actors are represented by non-overlapping subsystems. Classes of objects, which represent persistent data, are denoted by passive concepts. Mandatory attributes characterize all passive concepts. The objects that are represented by passive concepts can be affected by various interactions. Passive concepts can be related by the static relations such as classification, inheritance and composition.

Classification dependency (●—) specifies objects or subsystems as instances of concepts. Classification is often referred to as instantiation, which is the reverse of classification dependency. Object-oriented approaches treat a classification relation as a more restrictive. It can only be defined between a class and an object. A class cannot play the role of object. In SICM method, each concept can be interpreted again as an instance (Gustas 2010). For example; MS Outlook ●— E-mail Application, E-mail Application ●— Product Type, Product Type ●— Concept.

Composition (—▶—) dependency in SICM method is much stronger form of aggre-gation, and differs significantly from the object-oriented composition. Composition dependency in SICM method allows just 1 or 1...* cardinalities between wholes and parts. This means that any part cannot be optional. The distinctive and very important features of this type of composition are as follows (Guizzardi 2007):

(a) each part is existentially dependent on a whole, if a whole has a single part, then this part has coincident lifetime with a whole,
(b) if a whole has more than one part, then creation of a first part is coincident with the creation of a whole,
(c) removal or creation of additional parts can take place any time, but removal of a last part is coincident with the removal of a whole.
(d) creation or removal of a whole can be done together with all its parts,
(e) part may belong just to one and the same whole.

The definition of composition in general is not so strict. With the help of special modelling techniques, other cases of aggregation can be changed into this strict kind of composition (Gustas 2010).

Composition hierarchies can be used for detection of inconsistent interaction depend-encies between actors. Loosely coupled actors never belong to the same decomposition hierarchy. Interaction dependencies among loosely coupled actors on the lower level of decomposition are propagated into compositional wholes. So, composition links can be used for reasoning about derived interaction dependencies between actors on the higher granularity levels of specification. Interaction dependencies between actors, which are placed on two different composition hierarchies, are characterized by the following inference rules:

(1) if Action(X ---▶ Z), Action(C1) —▶ C2 and X —▶— Y

then Action(Y ---▶ Z),

(2) if Action(Z ---▶ X), Action(C2) —▶ C3 and X —▶— Y

then Action(Z ---▶ Y).

Interaction dependency Action(X ---▶ Z) between two actors X and Y indicates that subsystem denoted by X is able to perform an action on one or more subsystems of Z. Action(X ---▶ Z) represents base interaction dependency and Action(Y ---▶ Z), which is shown in the second part of the rule, represents derived interaction dependency. For instance, if Order Delivery (Customer ---▶ DB), Order Delivery($\perp$) —▶ Order, (DB —▶— Vendor) and then Order Delivery (Customer ---▶ Vendor) where $\perp$ represents an empty class. Two subsystems of Organization, DB (Database) and Vendor together with their interaction dependencies are represented in Fig. 15.

This example is based on a well-known situation in Ford Motor Company after a radical change (Hammer 1990). Ford Motor Company plays the role of an organization, which places a purchase order into a shared database (DB). The same service interaction loop, which was discussed previously, is represented in this diagram as well. The inter-action loop between Customer and Vendor represents an exchange of Shipment for Payment. Please note that the derived interactions cannot be in conflict with the specified

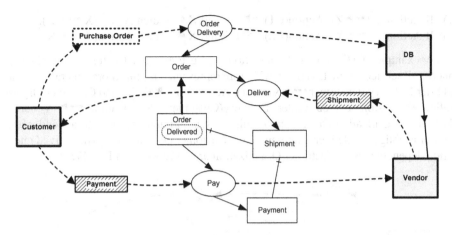

Fig. 15. Basic interactions between Customer and Vendor

dependencies in other diagrams. The interaction links, which are presented in Fig. 15, are consistent with the interaction dependencies of Fig. 16.

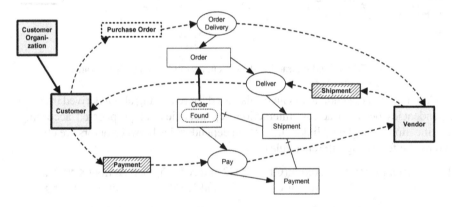

Fig. 16. Derived and basic interactions between Customer and Vendor

Static and dynamic similarities of active concepts can be shared by more specific concepts according to the following rule:

if X ➡ Y and Y ➡ Z then X ➡ Z.

For instance, if a Company is a specialization of Customer Organization, and Customer Organization is an Organization, then for a Company can be applied static and dynamic similarities of an Organization.

More specific actors inherit interaction dependencies from the more generic actors. It should be noted that in the object-oriented approaches, inheritance link is defined just for attributes and operations. Inheritance dependency is convenient for sharing service interaction loops of more general actors. Interaction dependencies are inherited according to the following inference rules:

(1)   If Action(Y $\cdots\blacktriangleright$ Z), Action(C1) $\longrightarrow\blacktriangleright$ C2 and X $\blacktriangleright$ Y then Action(X $\cdots\blacktriangleright$ Z),
(2)   If Action(Z $\cdots\blacktriangleright$ Y), Action(C2) $\longrightarrow\blacktriangleright$ C3 and X $\blacktriangleright$ Y then Action(Z $\cdots\blacktriangleright$ X).

For example, if a Customer Organization is a Customer then Customer Organization inherits all service interaction links, which are represented for this more general concept. If Order Delivery (Customer $\cdots\blacktriangleright$ Vendor), Action($\perp$) $\longrightarrow\blacktriangleright$ Order and Customer Organization $\blacktriangleright$ Customer then Order Delivery(Customer Organization $\cdots\blacktriangleright$ Vendor). Customer Organization has the opportunity to send a purchase order to a Vendor and Vendor is obliged to deliver Shipment to the Customer Organization. The derived interaction dependencies of Customer Organization are represented in Fig. 17.

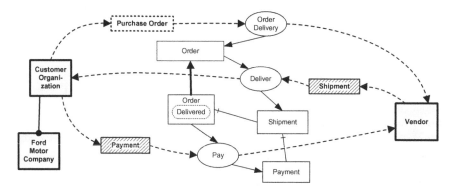

Fig. 17.   Derived interaction dependencies of Customer Organization

Classification dependencies can be also used for reasoning about derived interaction dependencies between actors. Interaction dependencies are propagated according to classification dependency links. Interaction dependencies between actors are characterized by the following inference rules:

(1)   if Action(Y $\cdots\blacktriangleright$ Z), Action(C1) $\longrightarrow\blacktriangleright$ C2 and X $\bullet\!\!-$ Y then Action(X $\cdots\blacktriangleright$ Z),
(2)   if Action(Z $\cdots\blacktriangleright$ Y), Action(C1) $\longrightarrow\blacktriangleright$ C2 and X $\bullet\!\!-$ Y then Action(Z $\cdots\blacktriangleright$ X).

For instance, if Order Delivery (Customer $\cdots\blacktriangleright$ Vendor), Order Delivery($\perp$) $\longrightarrow\blacktriangleright$ Order and Ford Motor Company $\bullet\!\!-$ Customer then Order Delivery(Ford Motor Company $\cdots\blacktriangleright$ Vendor).

This interaction loop can be replaced by simply switching from Customer to Ford Motor Company. It is represented in Fig. 18.

The responsibilities of different actors can be analyzed using conceptual models of interactions. For instance, the Order Delivery action can be viewed as an opportunity for sending a Purchase Order by Ford Motor Company to the Vendor. If a Vendor accepts it, then he is responsible to deliver a Shipment to Ford Motor Company.

Please note that the opportunities, responsibilities, commitments and obligations of these two actors must be consistent with interaction dependencies. Inconsistency can be detected by naming the conflicts between actions or flows. More specific actors must be justified by their intrinsic communication actions, which are defined in terms of the complementary interaction dependencies of these actors. The presented inference rules

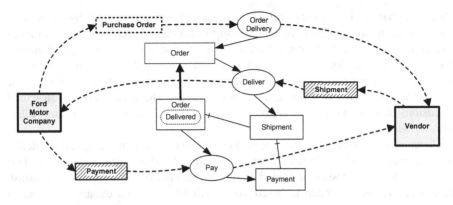

Fig. 18. Derived interaction loop of Ford Motor Company

are useful, but they are insufficient for reasoning about the consistency of interaction dependencies, which can be defined on different levels of specification. To understand the deep structure of service interactions, the behavioral and structural aspects of communication actions must be studied.

9 Conclusions

The main contribution of this paper is presenting SICM method for an integrated way of modelling. The paper presents the principles of SICM method that provides us with a holistic way of modelling. One of the goals is to demonstrate how interactive, transitional and structural aspects of conceptual modelling can be integrated. Object-oriented modelling method projects static and dynamic aspects using different diagram types. In this case, to reach sematic integration of business processes and business data is very difficult. The semantic integration principles of different UML diagram types are not sufficiently clear. Since different modelling dimensions are highly intertwined, it is crucial to maintain integrity of various diagrams. We have demonstrated the interplay of three different aspects of conceptual models.

Interactions between actors are important to follow value exchange. Increment and decrement events represent economic resources exchanged in various business processes. Value exchanges are represented by two performing actions into opposite directions. The performing actions are triggered for the reason of coordinating actions. In this way, these actions are related to one value exchange. Every communication action is able to produce new facts that can be represented by various classes of objects. Value flow and service interactions provide the natural way of system decomposition. Value models help to clarify why enterprise actors want to exchange business objects with each other.

The ultimate goal of this paper is to overview deficiencies of traditional conceptual modelling approaches and to present the principles of SICM method for the development of the holistic models of information systems. Bunge's ontological principles of decomposition are lying in foregrounded in SICM method. Actors can be seen as organizational or technical system components. Organizational components are denoted by individuals, groups, or company divisions. Technical components can be seen as software or hardware system components. Decomposition of information system is based on semantic relations of classification, composition and inheritance. Similarities of these relations are explained in comparison with object-oriented approaches. Inference rules of the semantic relations are presented in this paper as well. The behavioral and structural dimensions of interactions were analyzed in terms of creation, termination and reclassification action.

Conceptual modelling methods, which put emphasis on active concepts, typically focus on analyzing interactivity between organizational and technical components. This tradition is quite successful for modelling of external behavior of a system. In contrast, the object-oriented approach is based on modelling static and dynamic aspects of concepts, which can be represented by various classes of objects. The majority of traditional approaches in the area of systems analysis and design recommend concentrating first on domain modelling. Such methods do not put into foreground modelling of active concepts. They project the structural, interactive and behavioral aspects into totally different types of diagrams that cause difficulties to integrate static and dynamic aspects of enterprise architecture dimensions. Very few emerging modelling approaches make attempts to illustrate the deep interplay between active and passive structures. We have illustrated with simple examples how to represent integration of various aspects of information systems by using the principles of SICM method.

References

Blaha, M., Rumbaugh, J.: Object-Oriented Modelling and Design with UML. Pearson, London (2005)

Bodart, F., Patel, A., Sim, M., Weber, R.: Should optional properties be used in conceptual modelling? A theory and three empirical tests. Inf. Syst. Res. **12**(4), 384–405 (2001)

Bunge, M.: Treatise on Basic Philosophy, Ontology I: The Furniture of the World, vol. 3. Reidel Publishing Company, Dordrecht (1977)

Bunge, M.: Treatise on Basic Philosophy, Ontology II: A World of Systems, vol. 4. Reidel Publishing Company, Dordrecht (1979)

Dietz, J.L.G.: DEMO: towards a discipline of organisation engineering. Eur. J. Oper. Res. **128**, 351–363 (2001). Elsevier Science

Dietz, J.L.G.: The Deep Structure of Business Processes. Commun. ACM **9**(5), 59–64 (2006a)

Dietz, J.L.G.: Enterprise Ontology: Theory and Methodology. Springer, Heidelberg (2006b)

Dijkman, R.M., Quartel, D.A.C., van Sinderen, M.J.: Consistency in multi-viewpoints design of enterprise information systems. Inf. Softw. Technol. **50**(7–8), 737–752 (2008)

Dori, D.: Object-Process Methodology: A Holistic System Paradigm. Springer, Heidelberg (2002)

Evermann, J., Wand, Y.: Ontology based object-oriented domain modeling: representing behavior. J. Database Manage. **20**(1), 48–77 (2009)

Ferrario, R., Guarino, N.: Towards an ontological foundation for services science. In: Domingue, J., Fensel, D., Traverso, P. (eds.) FIS 2008. LNCS, vol. 5468, pp. 152–169. Springer, Heidelberg (2009). doi:10.1007/978-3-642-00985-3_13

Gao, S., Krogstie, J.: A combined framework for development of business process support systems. In: Persson, A., Stirna, J. (eds.) PoEM 2009. LNBIP, vol. 39, pp. 115–129. Springer, Heidelberg (2009). doi:10.1007/978-3-642-05352-8_10

Gemino, A.: To be or maybe to be: an empirical comparison of mandatory and optional properties in conceptual modeling. In: Proceedings of the Annual Conference on Administrative Sciences Association of Canada, Information Systems Division, Saskatoon, pp. 33–44 (1998)

Glinz, M.: Problems and deficiencies of UML as a requirements specification language. In: Proceedings of the 10-th International Workshop on Software Specification and Design, San Diego, pp. 11–22 (2000)

Guizzardi, G., Herre, H., Wagner, G.: On the general ontological foundations of conceptual modeling. In: Spaccapietra, S., March, S.T., Kambayashi, Y. (eds.) ER 2002. LNCS, vol. 2503, pp. 65–78. Springer, Heidelberg (2002). doi:10.1007/3-540-45816-6_15

Guizzardi, G.: Modal aspects of object types and part-whole relations and the de re/de dicto distinction. In: Krogstie, J., Opdahl, A., Sindre, G. (eds.) CAiSE 2007. LNCS, vol. 4495, pp. 5–20. Springer, Heidelberg (2007). doi:10.1007/978-3-540-72988-4_2

Gustas, R., Gustiené, P.: Service-oriented foundation and analysis patterns for conceptual modelling of information systems. In: Wojtkowski, W., Wojtkowski, G., Lang, M., Conboy, K., Barry, C. (eds.) Information Systems Development: Challenges in Practice, Theory, and Education, vol. 1, pp. 249–265. Springer, New York (2009)

Gustas, R., Gustiené, P.: Towards the enterprise engineering approach for information system modelling across organisational and technical boundaries. In: Piattini, M., Camp, O., Filipe, J., Hammoudi, S. (eds.) Enterprise Information Systems V, pp. 235–252. Kluwer, Dordrecht (2004)

Gustas, R., Gustiené, P.: Pragmatic-driven approach for service-oriented analysis and design. In: Johanesson, P., Söderström, E. (eds.) Information Systems Engineering: From Data Analysis to Process Networks, pp. 97–128. IGI Global, New York (2008)

Gustas, R., Gustiené, P.: Conceptual modeling method for separation of concerns and integration of structure and behavior. Int. J. Inf. Syst. Model. Des. 3(1), 48–77 (2012)

Gustas, R.: A look behind conceptual modeling constructs in information system analysis and design. Int. J. Inf. Syst. Model. Des. 1(1), 78–107 (2010)

Gustiené, P.: Development of a new service-oriented modelling method for information systems analysis and design. Doctoral thesis, Karlstad University Studies (2010)

Gordijn, J., Akkermans, H., Vliet, H.: Business modelling is not process modelling. In: Liddle, S.W., Mayr, H.C., Thalheim, B. (eds.) ER 2000. LNCS, vol. 1921, pp. 40–51. Springer, Heidelberg (2000). doi:10.1007/3-540-45394-6_5

Hammer, M.: Reengineering work: Don't Automate, Obliterate. Harvard Bus. Rev. **68**, 104–112 (1990)

Harel, D., Rumpe, B.: Meaningful modeling: what's the semantics of 'Semantics'? IEEE Comput. **37**, 64–72 (2004)

Jacobson, I., Ng, P.-W.: Aspect-oriented software development with use cases. Pearson Education, Pennsylvania (2005)

Lankhorst, M.: Enterprise Architecture at Work: Modelling, Communication and Analysis. Springer, Heidelberg (2005)

Leite, I.C.S.P., Freeman, P.A.: Requirements validation through viewpoint resolution. IEEE Trans. Software Eng. **17**(12), 1253–1269 (1991)

Martin, J., Odell, J.J: Object-Oriented Methods: A Foundation. Prentice Hall (1995)

McCarthy, W.E.: The REA accounting model: a generalized framework for accounting systems in a shared data environment. Acc. Rev. **LVII**(3), 554–578 (1982)

Moody, D., Sindre, G.: Managing complexity in object oriented analysis: adapting UML for modelling large scale information systems. In: Proceedings of the 14th Australian Conference on Information Systems, pp. 328–338. School of Management Information Systems (ECU), Perth (2003)

Nuseibeh, B., Easterbrook, S.: Requirements engineering: a roadmap. In: Proceedings of the Conference on the Future of Software Engineering: International Conference on Software Engineering, pp. 35–46. ACM Press, New York (2000)

OMG: Unified Modeling Language Superstructure, version 2.2 (2009). www.omg.org/spec/UML/2.2/. Accessed 19 Jan 2010

Snoeck, M.: Sequence constraints in business modelling and business process modelling. In: Enterprise Information System, vol. 4, pp. 194–202. Kluwer, Hingham (2003)

Winograd, T., Flores, F.: Understanding Computers and Cognition: A New Foundation for Design. Ablex, Norwood (1986)

Yu, E.: Towards modelling and reasoning support for early-phase requirements engineering. Requirements Eng. 9(4), 1–19 (1997)

Zachman, J.A.: A framework for information system architecture. IBM Syst. J. 26(3), 276–292 (1987)

Applying NOMIS - Modelling Information Systems Using a Human Centred Approach

José Cordeiro[✉]

Setúbal School of Technology, Polytechnic Institute of Setúbal, Campus do IPS,
Setúbal, Portugal
jose.cordeiro@estsetubal.ips.pt

Abstract. NOMIS is an innovative human centred information systems model-
ling approach that is based on human *observable* actions. It seeks to deliver the
desired objectivity and precision required in information systems development.
From a theoretical perspective, NOMIS offers a vision into an Information System
(IS) using different views that are complimentary, comprehensive and consistent.
Some of these views are adaptations and extensions of the theoretical IS insights
provided by the theories of Organisational Semiotics, the Theory of Organised
Activity and Enterprise Ontology. From a practical perspective, NOMIS proposes
a modelling notation that uses a set of tables and diagrams to represent NOMIS
vision and views.

In this paper, we will provide an overview of NOMIS and we will describe
NOMIS modelling elements and notation. A case study of a course system is used
to show a practical example of modelling with NOMIS that includes a real system
created using the NOMIS approach.

Keywords: Information Systems · Information systems modelling · Human-
Centred information systems · Human relativism · Organisational Semiotics ·
Theory of Organized Activity · Enterprise Ontology · NOMIS · NOMIS vision ·
NOMIS models · NOMIS modelling notation · NOMIS metamodel

1 Introduction

In spite, many years of research and practice, Information Systems (IS) are still created
with a loose understanding of information and how computers relate to human activities.
From an information perspective, data as *information*, is stored in databases per schemas
developed by technical people without sufficient business people contribution and,
without objective guidelines for its design. Often, schema elements are reproduced as
user interface terms, that are inadequately or not properly understood under the business
context. Regarding human activities, it is also common that the computer application
does not allow a human user for certain actions required or useful for a specific activity,
or does not provide the required action information.

NOMIS is an innovative human centred information systems modelling approach
based on human *observable* actions that intends to improve modelling objectivity and
precision. NOMIS proposes: (1) a vision composed by different views *inspired* by ideas

© Springer International Publishing AG 2017
B. Shishkov (Ed.): BMSD 2016, LNBIP 275, pp. 27–45, 2017.
DOI: 10.1007/978-3-319-57222-2_2

from three known socio-technical approaches namely Organisational Semiotics [1], the Theory of Organized Activity [2] and, Enterprise Ontology [3], and (2) its visual representation composed by different models shown as a set of diagrams and tables. For this representation NOMIS provides its own modelling notation.

This paper extends and complements the work presented in [4]. In this previous paper, NOMIS vision was described and, an empirical case study of a library system was presented to highlight some modelling aspects and to show a practical application of NOMIS modelling approach. In that paper, an empirical library system was modelled via a set of diagrams using UML profiles adapted from [5, 6] that are not fully suitable to express NOMIS modelling elements and their relationships.

In this paper the NOMIS metamodel and a modelling notation are presented together with a real case study of an e-learning system. This case study is modelled with some diagrams using NOMIS modelling notation. Furthermore, an implementation prototype putting into practice NOMIS Vision and ideas is given.

This paper is organized as follows: Sect. 2 gives a brief overview of NOMIS vision, Sect. 3 presents NOMIS elements metamodel and describes NOMIS modelling notation, Sect. 4 presents a case study and part of its model, Sect. 5 introduces the e-learning platform and the developed e-learning prototype and, Sect. 6 concludes and points some future research directions.

2   NOMIS Vision

2.1   Introduction

NOMIS – **NO**rmative **M**odelling of **I**nformation **S**ystems is a human centred modelling approach to information systems development (ISD). NOMIS as a social-technical approach understands information systems "as human activity (social) systems which may or may not involve the use of computer systems" [7]. Nevertheless, its main goal is the development of computerized systems suited for human use within organisations.

NOMIS kernel elements are *human actions* and *information*, both associated to the central *human* element, mandatory in any information system (IS). Human actions are present in many social approaches to ISD such as the Speech-act approach (see [8]), based on language-acts as (human) actions, or the Activity Theory approach [9] based on human collective actions, which are, both, in the roots of NOMIS.

Human actions utilized in NOMIS are human *observable* actions, those perceived by the human sensory system. This focus comes from its foundational philosophical stance – Human Relativism [10] – that sees *observable reality* as *"more consensual, precise and, therefore more appropriate to be used by scientific methods"*.

The second kernel element in NOMIS is information, the basis of all information systems, still a misunderstood concept (see, for example, [11]). NOMIS understands information as the result of an *interpretation* process coming after *perceiving* the *observed reality*. Following this idea, information is only available from data after being interpreted by a human. There is no information without a human interpreter.

Information is the subject area of Semiotics which is the *study of signs* (see, for example, [12]) where signs can be understood as information. In fact, Semiotics could be defined as the *study of meaning*: how meaning is created, represented, interpreted and communicated and, meaning is all about information. Semiotics is also in the roots of NOMIS.

From a holistic view of human actions in general, NOMIS proposes a *vision* of information systems composed by a set of views addressing human interaction, action processes and context for actions inspired and based on, respectively, Enterprise Ontology (EO) [3], the Theory of Organized Activity (TOA) [2], and Organisational Semiotics (OS) [1]. These views will be explained in the next section.

NOMIS views form a coherent and consistent vision of an IS from a human *observable* action perspective that is complemented with a fourth view related to *information* consumed, produced, stored and exchanged.

Considering the nature of human actions, NOMIS adds *Norms* as human behaviour regulators. *Norms* is a concept borrowed from OS [13] that addresses and regulates sequences of human actions. Expected (human) behaviour is derived from *systems of norms* or *information fields* (IF) as they are called within OS [13], where people tend to behave in a certain, expected and controlled way. Examples of IF are an organisation, a department, a team or even a family. IF and Norms are a *glue* connecting human actions and information.

An overall NOMIS Vision is sketched in Fig. 1.

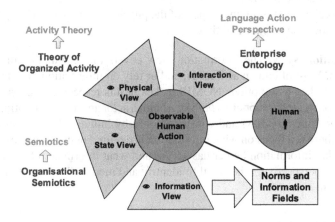

Fig. 1. NOMIS Vision – its views and foundational theories

2.2 NOMIS Views

NOMIS Vision is the way NOMIS sees and understands IS. Its central element is the human and, his/her *observable* actions. Focused in human actions it provides three different views or perspectives based on the theories of Enterprise Ontology, the Theory of Organized Activity and Organisational Semiotics as mentioned before. All of them were adapted and expanded in NOMIS. A fourth view addressing information is added. Each of these views will be briefly explained in the next subsections.

The Interaction View. The Interaction View covers the communicational dimension. It is expected to model all forms of human communication and human interaction within an IS. From this perspective, it addresses communication channels and interacting people and their actions including language-acts as seen by EO. Effectively, Language-acts as many other types of interaction acts are represented under this view as interactional patterns that can be reused in different contexts.

The State View. The state view uncovers and considers environmental conditions or states that enable a human agent to act. It is concerned with context, state and state dependencies related to human actions. Its key element is the *environmental state* (ES) that is a composition of observable elements such as physical things (known as *bodies*) and/or information elements (which are *information items* referred by its physical representation). The notion of ES is a NOMIS interpretation and adaptation of the *affordance* concept ([14] and, in OS, [13]).

The Physical View. The physical view looks to material aspects related to human actions. A perspective addressed by this view is the representation of business processes showing (human) action sequences and activities. In this view, also states and state transitions (driven by human actions) can be represented, which is a modelling representation inherited from TOA.

The physical context is another aspect of the physical view that can be specified, for example, per locations (space and time).

The Information View. The Information view covers the information dimension of human action. Most of human actions depend or rely on information in different ways. There are some key assumptions NOMIS makes in this respect: (1) information does not exist without material support: a *body* or a human actor and, (2) information is created by humans or things (*bodies*) and consumed only by humans. From a human action perspective, there is a focus on what information is required or consumed by the human performer, what information he/her has access and what information he/her produces. From a design perspective, it is useful to identify and model all information useful for a human action.

3   NOMIS Models

3.1   Models

Models are used to represent simplified views of reality, capturing its essential elements peranontology. Models define a language and, as any language, affects the way world is perceived. NOMIS Models are just a way of representing NOMIS vision of IS reality. Following a Semiotic triadic sign model [15] NOMIS vision is a concept, a form of seeing and understanding an IS, and NOMIS Models one of its possible representations as it is shown in Fig. 2.

Modelling, in general, may be expressed by using natural languages, analytical or mathematical formal languages, visual means such as diagrams and schemes, or even

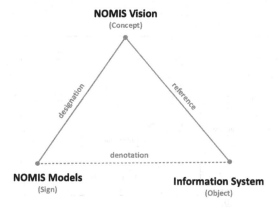

Fig. 2. The NOMIS Modelling Approach

simulations. NOMIS models can be expressed by diagrams showing its *essential elements* and their relationships, although they can be complemented by auxiliary tables and/or textual rules. This section will focus in NOMIS Model diagrams and its notation.

3.2 NOMIS Metamodel

The *essential elements* represented in NOMIS Models correspond to the key concepts in NOMIS Vision and they are:

- Human Actions – *observable* human actions
- Actors – human performers
- Bodies – physical things
- Information Items – information without a physical support
- Language Actions (or Coordination-acts) – speech actions
- Environmental States – context for actions

It is also possible to have composites of these elements: a group of human actions as activities, a group of actors representing a team or organisation, or a group of bodies or information items.

A complete Metamodel of NOMIS showing its *essential elements* was presented in [4] and is reproduced in Fig. 3. This metamodel conveys the NOMIS modelling language abstract syntax.

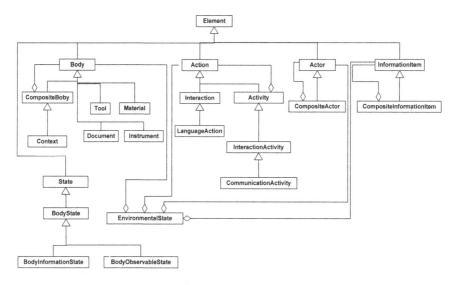

Fig. 3. NOMIS Metamodel

3.3 NOMIS Modelling Notation

An important purpose of models, as with any language, is to communicate. From this viewpoint, they can be used informally as a sketch to communicate system aspects or, otherwise, models can be used formally as blueprints for system development and in this last case, be subjected to creation rules following a formal specified syntax.

To facilitate communication, understanding and ease of writing, NOMIS modelling language concrete syntax or notation, provides different ways of writing model diagrams using NOMIS model elements and their relationships. This differentiation is inspired in the ways Semiotics recognises a representation refers to an object (see, e.g., [12]):

Symbolic – the representation does not resemble the object being represented and is fundamentally arbitrary or purely conventional. This is the case of textual languages

Iconic – the representation is perceived as resembling the object by being similar in possessing some of its qualities. For example, it could be a typical computer icon used for applications, a portrait or a scale-model

Indexical – the representation is not arbitrary, but is connected in some way to the object. Usually indicates something. An example from [12] is a clock indicating the time of day

Thus, NOMIS notation defines three ways or three concrete syntaxes for writing NOMIS Model elements, namely:

(1) A simple geometric form with a *symbolic annotation* for the element type. In this case, all elements are rectangles with a small letter representing the element type that is shown inside a circle positioned close to rectangle' upper-right corner.

(2) A *symbolic geometric form* related to its type per a convention. In this case, each element type will have a different form.

(3) An *iconic form* that represents its type. In this case a simple icon is suggested for each element type being represented.

The symbols used in (1) and the representation for each element used in (2) are shown in Table 1 for each element type. The form and presentation aspect of icons used in (3) will be left for a tool to define them.

Table 1. NOMIS elements notation

Element	Description	Symbolic annotation	Symbolic form
Actor	The human actor element	A	
Action	The human action element	AC	
Interaction	An interaction between two actors	IA	
Language Action	A language action involving actors	LA	
Information Item	An atomic information item	I	
Body	A simple body. Includes its specialised types namely document, material, instrument, tool or context	B Also **DOC, MAT, INST, TOOL, CTX**	May include a circled letter —B, D, M, I, T or C
Body State	A conceptual body state. Not used for showing a body, only its state	BS	
Composite element	A composite element may be any of the above that is composed by one or more elements of the same type.	C Initial letter	Added inside the element
Environmental State	Represent a composite of bodies, information items, actor and actions	ES	

NOMIS model elements are represented as nodes in diagrams. Nodes are connected by lines that represent relationships between those elements. There are different types of lines depending on the relationship. Lines may also be directed for clarifying the role each element plays in the relationship. The meaning of a line connecting two elements may depend on context such as the type of elements being connected. In Table 2 there is a list of the different line types used to relate nodes in NOMIS models and their description.

Table 2. Line types used to connect NOMIS model elements

Line format	Linking...	Description
——	A body and an action	Defines an involvement relationship.
	An action and an actor	Human performer of an action. When there is only one actor linked to a specific action
	A body and an information item	Information carried by a body
	An action and an information item	Information related to the action context
→	Two actions	Indicates a sequence of actions.
	From actor to action	The actor initiating the action
	From action to actor	The addressee of an action. Usually in the context of communicative actions
	Two actors	For specifying a communication link
	From actor to information item	Information created by an actor
	From information item to actor	Information consumed by an actor
	Two body states	A transaction between two states. It happens when a certain human action occurs.
	From body to action	A body which state will be changed by an action.
	From action to body	A body created or which state was changed by an action
	From body to information item	An information item created by a body
	From information item to body	An information item registered in a body
- - - ▶	Two model elements	An existential dependency between two elements
⊕——	Two model elements	Usually applies to model elements of the same type to refer a composite element. It can also be used by an environmental state to indicate its elements.
⟹	From action or activity to environmental state	The beginning process of an environmental state
	From environmental state to action or activity	The ending process of an environmental state

Besides nodes and lines, it is also possible to define areas grouping different elements. Information fields may be represented using these areas.

Finally, special adornments are defined to add specific element information. The following types of adornments are available:

- {} – Curly brackets – to show the state of a body or the role of a person. The state or role name appear inside the brackets below the body or person name. If different nested states apply they are shown separated by commas.
- <> - Angle brackets – a placeholder for a concrete NOMIS element. Instead of providing a concrete element, an abstract element is given that can be instantiated by elements of the same type. It should appear inside angle brackets. For example, '<action 1>'. Used in templates for actions.
- [] – Square brackets – to provide additional information for a relationship. For example, in the case of a decision where two or more sequences of future actions are possible, helps to clarify the decision taken for each outgoing line.
- () – Parentheses – for notes and commentaries. The text inside should not be considered as part of the model.

- « » – Guillemets – to specialise meaning of an element. For example, an existential dependency may include the word 'legal' to mean a *legal* dependency between elements.

4   Modelling Information Systems Using NOMIS: A Course System Case Study

This section presents a case study of a course IS and shows a few models using the NOMIS modelling notation described in the previous section. There is no intent to provide the complete case study model but just a few aspects not covered in [4] and an illustration of some other aspects of the NOMIS modelling approach.

4.1   Case Study: An E-Learning System

This case study addresses a typical class course usually taught in licentiate degrees engineering courses at the School of Technology of the Polytechnic Institute of Setúbal. These courses run for a semester, having about 15 weeks of face to face teaching with one or more classes per week. Classes may be theoretical, practical, laboratories or theoretical-practical. Their duration varies between 1 h and 2 h. Apart from laboratories all classes take place in common class rooms equipped with a video-projector and a whiteboard. Before starting a course, it is necessary to get information about enrolled students such as name, student number, contact information, etc. and to prepare a few documents, namely a course form with information regarding course contents, evaluation method, bibliography and some other data. When a course is running, teaching is usually done face to face in a class room. It is common in these classes to give students some teaching materials such as presentation slides handouts, tutorials, articles, bibliography, exercises, etc. and some additional information such as deadline for exercises, evaluation schedules, extra class times, etc. Outside classes, teachers have attending hours for receiving students. Sometimes is also necessary to contact students when a situation demands it: it may be something preventing a class to be taught or other out of the ordinary circumstances. In some courses, there is a project work involving 1 to 4 students where they must meet and collaborate outside classes. After classes are finished there are student evaluations, and resulting grades should be written in a form (obtained before) and delivered to the school secretariat. Also, it is necessary to fill a report per class type and per course concerning student attendance, grades, subjects effectively taught and other related information.

Computer support to teaching uses the school IS for official information such as course syllabus, student and teacher information, course schedules, etc. and Moodle for course related information such as course materials, communication between teachers and students, etc.

4.2   Applying NOMIS – First Steps

Although NOMIS Modelling approach does not propose a methodology a first step is to find its kernel elements in the problem domain: human actions and their performers. These elements are collected using a model artefact named Human Action Table (HAT). HAT registers human actions, their intervening human actors and related elements such as bodies (things), *information items* and locations. In Table 3 there is a simple example of a course HAT. At this point it is not necessary to have a complete description, and missing elements may help to uncover important details. Some human actions identified correspond to general activities, e.g. "to teach", in this case action detail or atomicity will depend on model's purpose, such as to communicate, to design or to implement the system.

Table 3.   Initial human action table of a typical course

	Human actions	Initiator	Addressee	Bodies	Information items	Local
1	To teach (face to face)	Teacher	Student	Slides, texts, pens		Class room
2	To attend class	Student				
3	To distribute document	Teacher	Student	Document		
4	To inform about something	Teacher	Student		Information	
5	To inform about something	Student	Teacher		Information	
6	To create exercise	Teacher		Exercise form	Exercise information	
7	To request exercise execution	Teacher	Student	Exercise form		
8	To do exercise	Student		Exercise form		
9	To submit exercise	Student	Teacher	Exercise form		
10	To evaluate exercise	Teacher		Exercise form		
11	To write course report	Teacher		Course form	Report information	
12	To produce course information	Teacher			Course Information	
13	To distribute course information	Teacher	Student		Course Information	
14	To attend students	Teacher	Student			

4.3 Interaction and Physical Views

This system does not have elaborated action sequences, being composed mostly by interactions between teacher and students identified in the HAT by the initiator and addressee human elements. Two of these interactions are related to exercises requested by teachers and, communication between students and teachers. EO models these kinds of interaction using *business patterns* ([16]) understood as the fundamental building block for modelling any organisation at the ontological level. NOMIS can express these type of interaction patterns using Human Interaction Diagram (HID) from the interaction view. In Fig. 4 there is a HID showing both interactions. As in EO, in NOMIS the request exercise is depicted as a pattern – in this case a *composite interaction activity*. This means a composite action (expressed by the plus sign inside the activity symbol). This activity can be further decomposed using an action Sequence Diagram (ASD) from the physical view as an activity pattern. Usually, ASD diagrams are used to show typical business processes as a kind of UML Activity Diagrams but in this case, it is used to show sequences of speech-acts as human actions (represented inside ovals). The emphasis here is the NOMIS ability to represent activity patterns as the one shown in Fig. 5 where < work > is a general action and can be replaced with different concrete actions such as exercise, examination or even projects.

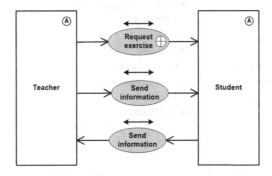

Fig. 4. HID showing interactions

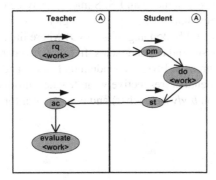

Fig. 5. An ASD showing the request work pattern

4.4   Information View

Although it is possible to show connections between human actions or *bodies* and information in specific NOMIS diagrams, e.g. (1) show all information required, auxiliary
or produced by a human action or (2) show connections between human information
interpreters and respective body information carriers, here the emphasis is on how
information is collected and represented. In this case, NOMIS uses an Information Items
Table (IIT) where information items and its supporting bodies are described. In
Table 4 some information items, required in thee-learning case study, are shown.

Table 4. Some course information items

	Information item	Information	
		Content	Related supporting bodies
1.	Enrolment Information	Student information	
	Description	• Student's name • Student number • Sex, date of birth • Contact	
2.	Teacher Information	Teacher information	
	Description	• Teacher's name • Category • Title • Contact	
3.	Course Information	Course information	
	Description	• Course name • Course • Semester	

4.5   State View

NOMIS course state view is an important system view. It shows fundamental environmental states (ES) providing an overall system perspective. Business processes are just
paths between ES or *paths* to achieve an ES. Some ES may be understood as *goals* as
they correspond to desired states such as "to complete a course". ES are shown in
NOMIS using Environmental State Diagrams (ESD) where links between the different
action states represent existential dependencies. In Fig. 6 it is depicted a course system
EDD where a running course (an ES) is dependent on teacher and student ES. These ES
on the other hand are dependent, respectively, on teacher information (an information
item) and person (a person *body* as teacher) and enrolment information and person (as
student).

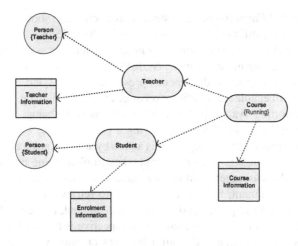

Fig. 6. Course system EDD

4.6 Norms and Information Fields

A last and important element to be modelled per NOMIS is *norms*. Many of these norms can be extracted from NOMIS diagrams such as some norms regarding action sequences, existential dependencies, and information required or auxiliary to actions among others. A small list of course system norms for illustrative purposes are:

- Classes Scheduling;
- Semester Calendar;
- Teacher attending hours;
- Teachers responsibility to create class summary, course evaluation rules, bibliography and theoretical contents;
- Teachers responsibility to produce course reports, and to send evaluation information to the school;
- General school evaluation rules

Some of these norms may just be used as information in the context of human actions or, for example, be incorporated in the model.

In the course system context, there are different norm systems or information fields (IF). These are the school, the department and the course. Each of them may use its proper terms and have some rules. For example, a student may not attend a course unless it is a registered student per the school norms but, sometimes due to a possible delayed registration process it is authorized within the course scope (IF) to attend it without being legally registered.

5 Implementing an Information System Per NOMIS

The previous section provided a short and simple analysis and modelling of a course system. In this section, our goal is to present a simple implementation of an e-learning system to support that (*human*) course system. This application should be one practical application of NOMIS, still many other forms of using NOMIS in practice are possible.

The implemented e-learning system is a computer system that will be used to support some of the human actions modelled using NOMIS. Its simple use will be as a repository for class materials such as texts, documents, presentation slides, etc. and as a communication tool that will enable information exchange among participants. A consequence of using this supporting system is that human actions will change, for example "to request an exercise", a physical action of giving a piece of paper to a student will be replaced by a menu entrance that supports this action by sending an electronic document to that student. This change is often neglected when implementing business processes as an example. In this case, there will be new human actions for the e-learning system such as to store a document, to send a document, to retrieve a document, to send a message, to retrieve a message, to send and store a document, to view a document, etc. An advantage of designing a system from this perspective is that each relevant human action can be individually analysed from a business oriented view and its computer support can be furnished appropriately. Also, effective user needs can be fulfilled accordingly. Besides furnishing support for specific human actions the system can also help by giving useful information related to actions such as how to execute them, norms affecting those actions, or available tools. A separate awareness system may be designed and implemented with this purpose.

5.1   NOMIS Platform Architecture

For implementing the e-learning system a basic Client-Server based architecture using the Internet was chosen (see Fig. 7). However, this architecture was further adapted to be aligned with NOMIS concepts. Accordingly, there are two separate modules: (1) to handle application specific aspects and (2) to handle NOMIS related features. The last one is a kernel middleware – NOMIS middleware – used to provide support for user actions, user information and user communication functionalities. NOMIS middleware includes a relational database to support business data and a logic layer responsible to handle requests from applications. The application module, on the other hand, handles most technical aspects, including presentation logic, interaction with NOMIS middleware, technical parts of application logic and may include its own database of technical data. Separation of technical and business aspects is an essential characteristic of this platform and its based applications. This separation is accomplished by assigning to NOMIS middleware the management of any element seen as part of the business domain.

This architecture is not specific of the e-learning application and can be reused by any other NOMIS application.

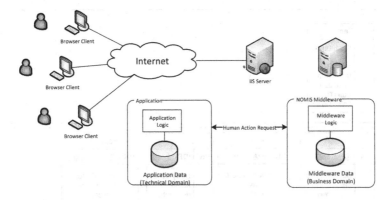

Fig. 7. The e-learning platform architecture

5.2   NOMIS Middleware

NOMIS middleware (NOMIS MW) is an independent layer responsible for connecting an application to general business information and human action supporting features. Basically, it consists of a database composed by a group of tables that store all important business related information and a logic layer responsible for managing access to it. NOMIS MW tables store NOMIS elements and relationships between them. There is a table per each element: Person, Action, Body, Activity and Role (a *person state*) and, for each valid relationship between elements: Action-Body, Person-Body, Body-Body, Role-Action, Role-Person, Activity-Role and Activity-Activity.

A distinctive feature of NOMIS MW tables is that all tables, except for relationship tables, contain a group of similar columns having the following structure:

ID	**GUID**	Name	Description	**StartTime**	FinishTime	.....

Bold column fields represent required data and cannot be empty.

This table structure is partially inspired by the Semantic Temporal Database (STDB) proposed by OS ([1]). In fact, it keeps its temporal dimension by having a start and finish time for each element, allowing it to change.

The GUID field stores a global unique identifier that is attached to each record and table. It is possible using this strategy to change completely the information about a person, for instance using a different information table, as the GUID will stay the same. Thus, the person information will be relative to its existing period.

Figure 8 shows the kernel tables of NOMIS MW DB that are divided in 3 groups: meta-elements, elements and relationships. The first group just contains the *Element* table. This table stores a list of all tables stored in the database managed by NOMIS MW. The *Element* table allows to identify and to find any table by its GUID (table GUID field) plus its name (tableName). This is because tables stored as business domain tables have a name that results from the concatenation of its regular name with its GUID. This allows duplicated table names.

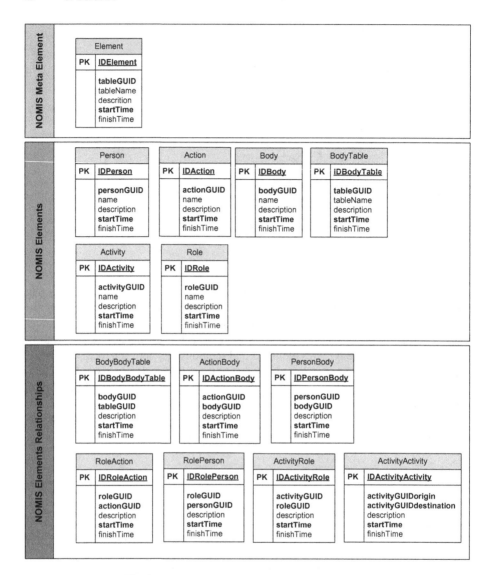

Fig. 8. NOMIS Middleware database kernel tables

The second group consists of tables for registering information regarding NOMIS basic elements that includes *persons, actions, bodies, activities and roles* and third group contains tables for storing relationships between NOMIS basic elements.

To show the flexibility of this schema, as an example, it is possible to have a person's name and birth date registered in the NOMIS MW DB. In this case the person will have an entry in the *Person* table that will serve to identify him/her, but the actual name and birth date will be registered separately in a *PersonInformation* table. The *PersonInformation* table name and its GUID will be registered as an element in the *Element* table, the *tableGUID* will also appear in the *BodyTable* as a separate record. The specific name and birth date will be a record in this *PersonInformation* table identified by a unique GUID. This GUID identifying that information will be registered in the *Body* table. From this approach, any GUID should refer a record or a table. In the case of a table it will appear in the *Element* table and may refer to any NOMIS kernel tables, or, otherwise to an application specific *body* table. The strategy behind this implementation choice is that it is possible to change any application element without having it constrained by the technical implementation. In the last example if it was necessary to change person information by having also information about his/her sex, this could be achieved by creating a new *PersonInformation* table with an extra field for the sex added information. The GUID referring to the person information just needs to stay the same, but the information record is now in a different table with new information. The flexibility introduced allows NOMIS MW to cope with business changes although it makes the system more complicated technically. Nevertheless, it is the author believes that most technical problems can be treated rigorously and scientifically, and a solution provided no matter how complicated they are if there are no business domain aspects embedded.

5.3   The E-Learning Prototype

A prototype using NOMIS Platform architecture was developed using the Microsoft.NET platform, a screen shot is shown in Fig. 9. Some notes regarding this implementation:

1. The school, each course and each class is defined as an activity giving a context for actions.
2. Information Items are supported and created as tables and records in the database, or otherwise as documents referred also by records in the database.
3. Three roles were created, namely administrator, professor and student.
4. Actions correspond to ASP.NET pages triggered by menu selections, buttons or hyperlinks.

NOMIS MW does not deal with visualisation and interaction aspects; those can be designed by a designer and implemented using application specific visualisation controls. From an application point of view, NOMIS MW can furnish all actions available for a certain activity, considering its user, associated role, any applicable norm and all contextual information stored on bodies. This separation helps keeping the design independent of application technical details.

All necessary information about available activities, action, and bodies is provided through NOMIS MW.

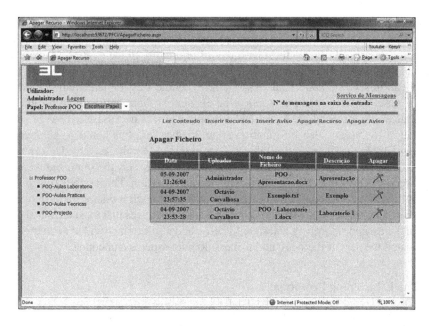

Fig. 9. Screen shot of the e-learning application prototype

6   Conclusions and Future Work

This paper presented an overview of NOMIS Vision and its modelling aspects including NOMIS elements metamodel and NOMIS modelling notation. A case study of a course system was used to show some practical examples of NOMIS notation application and also to deliver a real system according to NOMIS approach as one possible implementation. The e-learning prototype implemented took advantage of a NOMIS specific infrastructure that could be used for other NOMIS applications.

NOMIS modelling approach is fully described in [17].

Regarding future work there is much to do to validate and test NOMIS modelling approach. A new prototype is necessary to uncover additional modelling and practical aspects. One possibility is the use of Model-Driven Engineering to produce different applications using some ideas from the created prototype infrastructure. In this respect, NOMIS metamodel and the modelling notation can be used to create, respectively, the abstract and the concrete syntax of a Model-Driven approach.

References

1. Liu, K.: Semiotics in Information Systems Engineering. Cambridge University Press, Cambridge (2000)
2. Holt, A.: Organized Activity and Its Support by Computer. Kluwer Academic Publishers, Dordrecht (1997)
3. Dietz, J.: Enterprise Ontology, Theory and Methodology. Springer, Heidelberg (2006)

4. José, C.: A new way of modelling information systems and business processes - the NOMIS approach. In: Shishkov, B. (ed.) Business Modeling and Software Design. Lecture Notes in Business Information Processing, vol. 220, pp. 102–118. Springer, Heidelberg (2015). ISBN 978-3-319-20051-4

5. Cordeiro, J., Liu, K.: UML 2 profiles for ontology charts and diplans - issues on meta-modelling. In: Proceedings of the 2nd International Workshop on Enterprise Modelling and Information Systems Architectures, St. Goar, Germany (2007)

6. Cordeiro, J., Liu, K.: A UML profile for enterprise ontology. In: Proceedings of the 2nd International Workshop on Enterprise Systems and Technology, Enschede, The Netherlands (2008)

7. Buckingham, R.A., Hirschheim, R.A., Land, F.F., Tully, C.J.: Information systems curriculum: a basis for course design. In: Buckingham, R.A., Hirschheim, R.A., Land, F.F., Tully, C.J. (eds.) Information Systems Education: Recommendations and Implementation. Cambridge University Press, Cambridge (1987)

8. Hirschheim, R., Iivari, J., Klein, H.: A comparison of five alternative approaches to information systems development. Australas. J. Inf. Syst. 5(1), 3–29 (1997)

9. Leont'ev, A.: Activity, Consciousness, and Personality. Prentice-Hall, Englewood Clifs (1978)

10. Cordeiro, J., Filipe, J., Liu, K.: Towards a human oriented approach to information systems development. In: Proceedings of the 3rd International Workshop on Enterprise Systems and Technology, Sofia, Bulgaria (2009)

11. Falkenberg, E., Hesse, W., Lindgreen, P., Nilsson, B., Oei, J., Rolland, C., Stamper, R., Van Assche, F., Verrijn-Stuart, A., Voss, K.: FRISCO: A Framework of Information System Concepts, The IFIP WG 8.1 Task Group FRISCO, December 1996

12. Chandler, D.: Semiotics: The Basics. Routledge, London (2002)

13. Stamper, R.: Signs, norms, and information systems. In: Holmqvist, B., et al. (eds.) Signs of Work. Walter de Gruyter, Berlin (1996)

14. Gibson, J.: The Ecological Approach to Visual Perception. Houghton Mifflin, Boston (1979)

15. Peirce, C.S.: Collected writings. In: Hartshorne, C., Weiss, P., Burks, A. (eds.) Collected Papers of Charles Sanders Peirce, vol. 8. Harvard University Press, Cambridge (1931)

16. Dietz, J.: The deep structure of business processes. Commun. ACM 49(5), 59–64 (2006)

17. Cordeiro, J.: Normative Approach to Information systems Modelling. Ph. D thesis, The University of Reading, UK (2011)

Why Plan?

Coen Suurmond[✉]

RBK Group, Keulenstraat 18, 7418 ET Deventer, Netherlands
csuurmond@RBK.nl

Abstract. Finished product planning is a key business process for companies. It is about finding the balance between service levels and cost, and is therefore critical for the success of the company. In this paper the structure of the problem will be analysed and compared with literature about sales & operations planning as well as ERP solutions. In the analysis general process logic will be contrasted with idiosyncratic characteristics of the individual company. The use of different kinds of information will be discussed, in combination with the formal sign system of the computer and the social sign system of human communication.

Keywords: Business processes · Process logic · Organisational semiotics · Sales & Operations Planning

1 Introduction

Finished product planning is a key business process for companies. This planning decouples demand from production and it is a highly determining factor both for market volume and for profit margins. On the market side customer service level and lead time are key for market share while on the production side it is crucial to keep down variable costs. In this paper a specific product group (fresh meat) for a specific market (multi-store retail chains) will be used to analyse the business processes and information flows that are in play, and it will be examined how this problem is covered in literature and by ERP software.

In this paper the paired concepts of process logic/idiosyncrasy will play an important part. Process logic will mark the necessary general structure underlying the actual business processes of the individual company. This structure will always be present in every business in a particular market, because certain structures are inherent to and inevitable in operating with these products on those markets. Alongside this there are the idiosyncratic characteristics of the individual company. Companies after all do differ, even though they operate with the same products in the same market segment. The individuality of the company is the foundation of the existence of any company on the market. As John Kay pointed out, the distinctive capabilities of the company are what distinguishes the company from its competitors and that form the foundation for the success of the company. And, again as pointed out by John Kay: "A firm can achieve added value only on the basis of some distinctive capability – some feature of its relationships which other firms lack, and cannot readily reproduce" [1].

B. Shishkov (Ed.): BMSD 2016, LNBIP 275, pp. 46–69, 2017.
DOI: 10.1007/978-3-319-57222-2_3

The analysis of business processes in terms of process logic and idiosyncratic characteristics has two aims. Firstly, it is a method to map business processes in a way that helps external consultants (specialists in general patterns) and internal employees (specialists in specific details) to come to a mutual understanding and a common basis. Secondly, it is about the awareness of the intangible, the understanding that not everything can be reduced to schemas and fixed rules. Information systems should not be a goal onto themselves but rather serve to improve the market position of the company, which they must do by adequately supporting the business processes. The process logic provides insight into the general structures, while the idiosyncratic characteristics provide insight into the way in which the processes actually happen within the company (including the often blurred boundaries between processes). This approach should also help in getting a feel for the distinctive capabilities of the company, competitive strengths that must be preserved and possibly enhanced in developing a new business information system.

Besides the paired concepts of process logic/idiosyncratic characteristics the analysis of the nature of the information in business processes with relation to formal and social sign systems used forms a second pillar of this analysis. Computer systems are formal sign systems, highly capable in processing declarative information, but they have trouble with vague boundaries, "unclean" categorisation and weighing heterogeneous norms that cannot be fulfilled simultaneously against each other (delivery in full but slightly delayed or delivery on time but slightly less than ordered? Delivery should be at the right time in the right quantity with the right quality, which 'right' might be relaxed in which context?). Social sign systems are better suited to deal with meaning in context, modalities, and intentions (discussed in an earlier paper in 2015) [2]. In the creation of a business information system awareness of the nature of the information and the conscious choice for the right sign systems is critically important for the effectiveness and efficiency of the business processes. Of the coordination mechanisms identified by Mintzberg direct supervision and mutual coordination are much more based on social sign systems, while the application of formal sign systems presupposes standardisation [3]. The effectiveness and efficiency of business processes are of course dependent on the criteria regarding the correctness, timeliness and completeness of information as formulated by Starreveld [4], and on the criteria regarding the relevance and presentation of information as formulated by Grice [5].

The paper consists of the following sections. After a short introduction to the problem area, the business processes involved are analysed in the example case. Generic literature about sales and operations planning is discussed in the next section, followed by an analysis of the planning processes in relation to business. The penultimate section discusses requirements for planning systems, taken into account the nature of the information involved and taken into account both the nature and the generic process logic of the planning processes and the individual characteristics of the company. The last section gives some conclusions.

2 Planning for Pre-packaged Fresh Meat Products

This section is concerned with the analysis of finished product planning for the production unit for pre-packaged fresh meat in retail chains. A typical production unit produces some 100 to 200 different products of pre-packaged fresh meat on a daily basis. Incoming shop orders need to be made available ready-to-ship on the loading dock for transport, delivery reliability must be above 99.7%. The products have an internal shelf life of at most two days. Everything is produced from fresh ingredients each day. And, of course, waste and production costs must be kept to a minimum.

Many products have a fairly stable demand pattern. Demand is however highly irregular in case of promotions, product introductions (which do not have a demand history) and a number of articles that are weather-dependent. Products which have been part of a promotion in the past weeks and seasonal products also have demand irregularities.

Planning is generally done in a large spreadsheet in which the order history over the past weeks for each distribution timeslot is recorded along with the demand prognosis for promotions and in which the planner records the amounts per product per day that need to be produced. This last list is processed further within the production planning to create production orders as well as lists for the resource, man-hour and machine-hour needs. Each business within this sector has developed its own particular solutions over time, the common characteristic is the use of spreadsheet with order history as input and production lists as output. The expected demand for promotions is mostly determined in a separate process and then made available to the planner.

To sketch an example case: On a Thursday afternoon in early May the planner is planning for the next week. At the end of the next week there is a national holiday and many people plan on having a barbecue. Hence, demand for barbecue products like pork belly slices, sausages, steaks and burgers (typically small-sized) might be 3 to 5 times the average demand. Next week's promotion is the pork loin steak with a discount of 25%. Seven different products are sold with this particular steak in varying sizes of slices and with varying amounts of slices in one package. Demand for promoted regular products at this discount is normally 150 to 200% of average demand, with a shift towards the larger packages. However, when people go barbecuing, they will buy less regular meat products like pork loin steak. The marketing department of the retail chain has informed the production unit that the quality of its barbecue products will be highlighted in advertisements and further publicity.

2.1 Process Logic

Every company that produces for a market in which the lead time between order time and delivery time is less than the time necessary to produce the goods will work with a (semi) finished product stock. This stock must be sufficient to fulfil the orders within the delivery reliability requirements in this market. Further, the stock has to be as low as possible because of warehouse costs and to minimise waste. Finally, production will have requirements regarding the frequency and size of the production batches.

All of this leads to the following three processes that will always be found (but, more often than not, implicitly rather than explicitly):

1. Determining expected demand
2. Determining the target stock level
3. Determining the production output

The process logic of the planning process is represented in the following schema. It shows both the structure of the planning process, the transitional data between the planning steps and the calculations and interpretations at each planning step. As the choice of the terms 'calculation' and 'interpretation' must make clear, in each step different kinds of information (discussed in Sect. 2.3) and different kinds of sign systems are involved (discussed in Sect. 2.4) (Fig. 1).

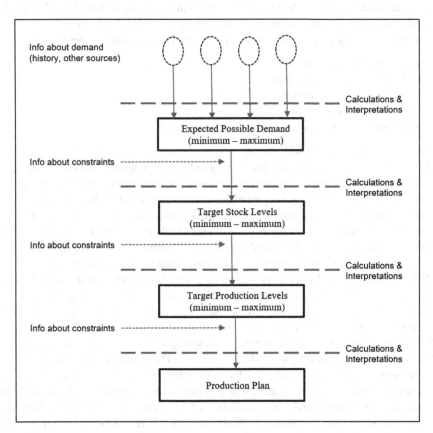

Fig. 1. Process logic of the planning processes

The dynamic structure of the planning process is determined by the timeslots for loading groups of orders to be delivered. Before the scheduled loading time the orders must be picked and made available at the loading docks. In each distribution timeslot a set of orders is picked, and in each production timeslot a set of products is produced.

Shops have a timeslot for ordering. Expected demand is specified per distribution time-slot, which would correspond with one or more ordering timeslots. The end times of ordering timeslots and distribution timeslots are fixed, the end time of production time-slots is more flexible (within bounds).

During the production day actual demand is gradually replacing expected demand, actual production output is replacing planned production output and available stock levels are fluctuating. This is monitored by tow control loops. The first checks expected and actual demand against available stock levels. Most normal variability should be absorbed here, and production will not be disturbed by minor deviations. The second control loop checks available stock levels against actual and planned production output, and will change the production plan as needed.

Given the daily delivery to the shops in combination with the internal shelf life of two days at most, the full product range will be produced and distributed in a 24 h cycle. For each day and each timeslot expected demand will be estimated, target stock levels will be set and production output levels will be set. The planning moments are:

1. After each ordering timeslot
2. Just before the production day
3. Just before the production week
4. A few weeks before the production week
5. About four to six weeks before the production week

After each ordering timeslot the planning is checked and adjusted where necessary (and possible), one day in advance production orders are generated and fresh raw mate-rials are ordered, the week before the production week production schedules are set and suppliers will be informed about expected demand, and the same applies for the planning moment a few weeks before the production week (same information, less certainty. In the first planning moment about four to six weeks in advance of production promotions are planned (because of the increased quantities it is important to have agreements in place with suppliers regarding price and expected demand of raw materials).

In the example the planner must plan with a very broad range of possible demand for the barbecue products, due to the high volatility of such products. Due to the adver-tisement campaign the availability of the barbecue products is of extra importance, shifting the balance between the costs of non-availability (loss of consumer confidence) and the costs of waste towards the former. This will have consequences for the planning of the target stock levels for the products involved. The actual weather will influence the last minute shopping (weather better than expected) or the consumption of the purchased barbecue products (weather worse than expected). Therefore, the planner will plan production capacity and raw materials such that the production of the barbecue products can be increased or decreased on short notice. There will be a trade-off between production capacity for barbecue products and production capacity for the promoted pork loin steak and other regular meat products (more demand of the former will impli-cate less demand of the latter). During the week, the planner will monitor continuously actual demand, available stocks and actual production output. As long as demand can be met by available stocks, he will not update his planning for the current production day. As part of his standard routine, he will update the planning for the next days on a daily basis, taking into account actual stocks, developments in demand, and production capacity.

2.2 Idiosyncrasies in Individual Companies

Companies differ from each other in the way they execute their key processes, and for the production of fresh food for retailers the finished product planning is such a key process. In this planning process external success on the market (delivery reliability, lead times) and internal success for the company (minimising production costs) come together. The way formal sign systems and informal sign systems are used to support this difficult and critical process is highly characteristic for each individual company. Depending on the distribution of knowledge and experience in one company the 'real' decisions and adjustments might be made by production management (using demand and stock information), and the planner is no more than a rather passive spreadsheet-driver and data cruncher. In another company, the planner plans and the shop floor executes. In a third company, production and management meet each day in order to prevent upcoming problems and smooth out existing problems. Each company can either flourish or be ailing. It all depends on the quality and the fit of the information to and from the planning process and on the quality of the persons who make the decisions.

Typically, this variety has both historical causes and business reasons. The business reasons are rooted in adaptations of the company to its situation and markets. The adaptations can both be designed as the execution of a formulated strategy or emerged from many small business decisions, in the latter case it the adaptation is the result of an evolutionary process.

In a company boundaries between the processes are often blurred, both organisationally and in the spreadsheets used for planning. Much of the knowledge and information is personal and non-coded [6]. Many problems are either 'spirited away' by some creative and experienced old hands, or solved in informal communication. Sometimes, this is a good thing, because the problem solving capabilities of the company are much greater than one would expect from studying organisation charts and documents about process flows. Sometimes, it is good but too vulnerable because of the dependencies on one or two key figures in the organisation. Sometimes, it is bad because problems are not really solved, only moved out of perception.

While process logic can clearly be defined, the real life execution of business processes is much harder to grasp. Every company has developed its own ways by "micro-adaptations" of its business processes, and the sum of these patterns define the idiosyncratic way the company is operating. It also defines the individuality of the company that distinguishes it from its competitors.

Situations as sketched in the example make clear that a clear-cut hierarchical decision model is not a good fit for its planning processes in this kind of industry. Planning, distribution and production have to collaborate intensively in order to make the initial planning decisions, and to adapt quickly to changing demand. Experience, gut feeling and anticipation play an important role. All levels in the production organisation know about the dependency of barbecue products on weather forecasts, and will anticipate on changes when the weather is changing. Typically, experience and gut feeling for demand fluctuations are not bound to a specific role or function in the hierarchy, but will be found in people with a length of service years close to the primary processes.

2.3   Nature of Information in Planning

In this paragraph the nature of the information used in finished product planning will be analysed, using the categorization of the three subprocesses as defined in the paragraph about process logic: (1) determining expected demand, (2) determining the target stock level, and (3) determining the production output. Subsequently, the role of different kinds of sign systems in representing different kinds of information will be analysed briefly. The section concludes with a discussion of the use of different sign systems in planning and its relation to the idiosyncratic characteristics of the company.

Information for Determining Expected Demand

In the process 'determining expected demand' (forecasting) the single information product appears to be a list with the expected shop orders grouped by timeslot and by saleable item, and the primary source of information is demand history. However, although extrapolation from history to expected demand may lead to a convenient list of hard data, it does not tell the whole story. Firstly, demand history is never the only source of information. In case of promotions and product introductions no relevant and reliable demand history is available (although, the history of promotions and product introduction might offer useful indications), and demand for some products might be dependent on future conditions (weather) or situations (events, bank holidays). Other information sources are needed, and the information from these sources must be interpreted in context. The interpretation of the weather forecast, especially in case of a possible sudden change of the weather, is an example. The assessment of the impact of publicity (kind and scale) in case of promotions and product introductions is another example. Secondly, expected future demand is never a single value, but rather a spread. If you were to discuss expected demand for a certain product with a group of experts, they would say that demand is expected somewhere in the range between X and Y.

Information for Stock Levels

Given the outcome of the process 'determining expected demand', the job of the stock planner is to set the target levels such that stock will be sufficient when demand is at the maximum level of the range, and stock will not be wasted when demand is at the minimum level. Depending on the volatility of demand and on the allowed storage life of products in stock, the planner can have an easy job (steady demand, longer internal storage life) or an impossible job (highly volatile demand, very short storage life). Impossible situations are not primarily the problem of the planner however, especially if this is a recurring issue. It is a problem of setting realistic norms for planning, probably for someone higher up in the organisational hierarchy.

It gets interesting in the border area when the planner has a difficult but doable job. In this area the planner must be creative and use all his available knowledge and information sources. The planner might collect further information from experienced demand experts in order to reduce the expectation spread, or organise extra production capacity in order to react quickly (quicker than normal production schedules would allow) in case of impending stock shortages. The planner will juggle with delivery risks and production reaction times in order to find his solution. Background information about what was possible or impossible in comparable situations in the past and informal discussions play a major role in this kind of decisions.

Information for Setting Production Levels

The third process must set production levels such that production efficiency is optimised. Lot size and production capacity are the primary determining factors. Both factors represent discontinuity. Often, products (or semi-finished products) are optimally produced in fixed amounts, due to the capacity of machinery. Optimal operation times for production lines vary in units of x hours (8 h is a typical value), due to work schedules (people work in shifts). The combination of lot size and optimal operation times will lead to a production mix that satisfies the minimum and maximum stock levels set in the preceding process. In standard situations this can all be calculated according to fixed patterns and decision rules. In some situations not all requirements can be met at the same time. In these cases additional information is needed, either in finding ways to squeeze a little more out of production, or in making sure that some products will be produced in the required quantity, or in assessing the weight of the different norms in the given situation and accepting the additional risk or additional cost.

Information in the Example Case

In critical planning situations as sketched in the example, information about possible demand will be drawn from a lot of different sources. Demand history is an important source, but must be combined with situational knowledge. Comparable "barbecue-weeks" in the past will be considered. People will discuss the circumstances at spring holidays in previous years: how was the weather, how early in the year was this holiday, and further relevant circumstances. In planning for promotions, the same mechanisms and the same kinds of information apply. Although the repetitive patterns in promotions are much more stable than in the barbecue challenges, each and every promotion will be discussed against the background of the typical circumstances for that individual promotion. The information from the planning process about target stock levels and target production levels will be mostly quantitative, but the planner will also want to inform his colleagues about the stability of the planning and the likeliness and kinds of changes.

2.4   Sign Systems

Considered from the viewpoint of the process logic as analysed above, the information about expected demand, stock level planning and production-level planning seems pretty straightforward and a perfect fit for the domain of formal sign systems. Essentially it is about three consecutive datasets with the same structure: date, timeslot, item code, quantity. In demand this dataset represents an expectation, in stock-level planning and in production-level planning the dataset represents a target.

Considered from the more detailed analysis of the information actually used in real planning situations, it will be clear that other kinds of information and other kinds of sign systems are involved. The inaccuracies of demand expectation, actual stocks and actual production output must be dealt with; the planner works with patterns based on experience and history; risks and possibilities are discussed between planning, sales and production; and accompanying instructions are given to the operators in the shop-floor processes. Information takes the form of background knowledge, consulting colleagues, oral communication, and written notes.

In the example given, the planner (and the other people involved in making and execution planning decisions) will use a mix of sign systems. Assessment of the possible demand for barbecue products will be partly based on formal sign systems such as demand history and possibly per-ordering by shops, and partly on social sign systems in consultations. The same applies to the communication of planning decisions. The core will obviously expressed in a formal sign system: production date + item-number + minimum/maximum quantities-to-be-produced. Additionally, the planner must inform the executing departments about the changes that might happen, and how likely changes are going to happen. In case of promotions, there are often some typical patterns in the planning, accompanied by routine communication about the expected demand development (e.g. "in the beginning strong demand, sinking in the course of the week") and about the points in the weeks when the suppliers of raw materials must be informed about changes.

3   Sales & Operations Planning

The subject of finished product planning is in literature and computer systems often covered under the name of Sales & Operations Planning. As the analysis in this section will show, this is a rather ill-defined blanket term under which a lot of different issues are gathered. However, for two reasons it is useful to discuss shortly how this concept is treated in literature and systems. Firstly, because the underlying notions are important and relevant. Secondly, because it determines how managers and consultants think and talk about the important operational issue of finished product planning in relation to customer satisfaction and production efficiency.

3.1   Definitions of Sales & Operations Planning

The subject of the case is the coordination between production and expected demand using finished product planning, an area termed Sales & Operations Planning in the literature and for which ERP systems provide support. It is then useful to look at what the literature says about this and to what extent literature can support the analysis of the case. First a definition from internet: "Sales and Operations Planning (S&OP) is an iterative business management process that determines the optimum level of manufacturing output. The process is built upon stakeholder agreement and an approved consensus plan" [7]. This definition fits the theme of this paper, although the term 'optimum' in the definition is an empty shell without criteria and it is a planning process rather than a management process. The definition proceeds to state that "The process is built upon stakeholder agreement and an approved consensus plan. To help stakeholders agree on a plan of action based on real-time data, S&OP software products include dashboards that display data related to equipment, labour, facilities, material and finance. The purpose of the dashboards is to provide the stakeholders with a single, shared view of the data". This is not true in the situation considered here. The planner has a delegated responsibility to solve the planning problem within the set norms and to signal when he is structurally unable to meet the norms. Occasional deviations are permitted (and delivery reliability prevails then over costs), structurally both norms need to be met. Determining tight but achievable norms is a mutual undertaking in which all stakeholders are involved and in which at least commitment, if not consensus, needs to be achieved. Operational planning is different in nature. This holds even more strongly if Sales & Operations Planning is not done on a monthly basis, but, as in the case, on a weekly and daily basis.

The definition in the APICS dictionary, which should be an authoritative source given the status of APICS "the premier professional organisational for supply chain management", according to its website, with over 43000 members and more than 300 international partners, provides even less of a guide. Because of the language used I will cite the long lemma in full:

(APICS Dictionary, 2008, p. 121f)
"Sales and operations planning – a process to develop tactical plans that provide management the ability to strategically direct its business to achieve competitive advantage on a continuous basis by integrating customer-focussed marketing plans for new and existing products with the management of the supply chain. The plan brings together all the plans for the business (sales, marketing, development, manufacturing, sourcing, and financial) into one integrated set of plans. It is performed at least once a month and is reviewed by management at an aggregate (product family) level. The process must reconcile all supply, demand, and new-product plans at both the detail and aggregate levels and tie to the business plan. It is the definitive statement of the company's plans for the near to intermediate term, covering a horizon sufficient to plan the resources and to support the annual business planning process. Executed properly, the sales and operations planning process links the strategic plans for the business with its execution and reviews performance measurements for continuous improvement. See: aggregate planning, production plan, production planning, sales plan, tactical planning." [8]

This is a definition (or description) of everything and therefore of nothing. Why should Sales & Operations Planning not be about the common daily operational practice of coordinating demand and availability and about no more than that? What does something like "a process to develop tactical plans that provide management the ability to strategically direct the business ..." add to our understanding of the problem?

3.2 Literature About Sales & Operations Planning

Donald Sheldon writes in his World Class Sales and Operations Planning (co-published with APICS) "The S&OP process can have a major impact on the management of inventory" [9]. He then devotes chapters to "Creating the Demand Plan" and to "Operations Planning for the S&OP Process". For Sheldon the S&OP process is the coordination between the various subplans ("Stated in its simplest terms, the S&OP process is a monthly planning cycle where plans for both customer expectations and internal operations are reviewed for accuracy, process accountability, lessons learned, and future risk management", where it should be essentially about the planning process itself. Of course there is an important role for higher level long term planning in companies to coordinate market developments, production capacities and resource needs. In this kind of higher level coordination operational norms must also be determined and adjusted, and possible measures should be agreed upon to 'land' changed norms with the relevant internal and external stakeholders. Donald Sheldon recognises the subordinate role of software: "All that is needed is a spreadsheet and good problem-solving tools and skills" [9]. The question remains, however, where the information for this problem solving will come from, and how to organise the different kinds of information flows (both formal via systems and informal via humans).

Robert Davis analyses what he calls the push-pull hybrid for supply chain management. "This hybrid model is based on the premise that you push produce and pull distribute" [10]. This analysis matches what was described above as the structure of the problem. His further analysis concentrates on what is happening in the supply chain as a whole. The chapter about inventory optimisation discusses the development of inventory policies that can be translated into algorithms and executed automatically. This approach does address the problem of how to develop ways of coping with the problem of inventory levels, but it does not address the problem of the individual planner who uses information and who makes decisions.

Shaun Snapp (S&OP in Software) describes the standard S&OP process as follows: (1) review and sign off the demand plan; (2) review and sign off the supply plan, and (3) review and sign off the financial plan. And he gives the time features as a planning horizon between 1 and 5 years, a monthly planning frequency, and a monthly planning bucket. This is not quite the horizon the companies discussed here are working with. Planning of inventory levels is not in his list of plans to sign off, Snapp discusses dynamic safety stock under the title 'How Misunderstanding Service Level Undermines Effective S&OP'. He writes: "Safety stock is often set in companies by simply allowing

Fig. 2. Structure of Sales & Operations Planning in literature

individuals to guesstimate what the safety stock value should be and then provides them with the rights to make the safety stock adjustments". This is followed by the remark that in his experience he never saw this working well, and "Stock levels should not be controlled by manually adjusting the safety stock. Instead, safety stock should be dynamically calculated and automated, and only changed as a result of changes in the variability of supply or demand" [11]. The last part is obviously true (from 'only changed as...'), but the first part presupposes that variability of demand is represented perfectly in the computer system, with all relevant information taken into account. This clearly cannot always be true. And, if manual adjustment of demand forecast is allowed, planners quickly learn the trick how to adjust demand in order to get the safety stock level they want (Fig. 2).

3.3 ERP Systems and Sales & Operations Planning

The ERP systems of course offer solutions for S&OP. Hamilton in his book about MS Dynamics AX, paragraph 10.1: "You can automatically calculate the safety stock requirement based on variations in historical usage and the desired customer service level" [12]. A bit further in the same chapter, in paragraph 10.7: "When using the min-max coverage code, you specify the item's minimum quantity and maximum quantity for each relevant site/warehouse. The minimum quantity represents the average daily usage multiplied by the item's lead time". So, you either have safety stock, taking variation of demand into account; or you have a min-max policy where average demand represents the minimum stock needed? Dickersbach gives in his book "Supply Chain Management with SAP APO™" the following structure of the demand planning process (somewhat shortened in my representation): (1) Forecast; (2) Check on plausibility of the forecast; (3) Production planning. Inventory planning is not mentioned at all [13] (Fig. 3).

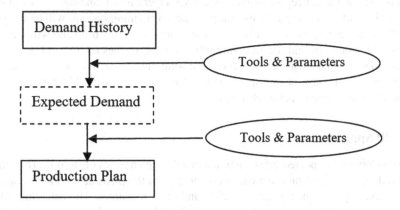

Fig. 3. Structure of Sales & Operations Planning in ERP systems

3.4 Comparison of Sales & Operations Planning in Literature and in ERP

Both the approach of Sales & Operations Planning in the literature (analysis and development of guidelines) and in ERP (solutions in practice) consider a number of different perspectives on the involved business processes of sales and production. Where they differ is in their choice of explicit and implicit aspects of the complex issues in Sales & Operations Planning. In the literature the interests of the different stakeholders are covered explicitly: in the creation of the Sales & Operations plans there is an pivotal mutual adjustment between the stakeholders. The goals and conditions formulated in the plans will then form the framework in which the daily and weekly operational decisions are made. The negotiation process between the various stakeholders is something that takes places in the longer term, quarterly, semi-annually or yearly. Operational issues are kept in the background, and not explicitly discussed.

In the ERP approach it is the operation issues that are made explicit. In the daily and weekly process interests in the areas of sales, delivery reliability, stock management and production efficiency need to be weighed against one another to arrive at concrete decisions. Of course, in this short term balancing of interests there is no daily or weekly negotiation process between stakeholders. In the practice of ERP solutions this balancing is translated into settings and parameters.

In summary: the literature analyses the S&OP in terms of the longer term setting of goals and conditions based on an explicit process of negotiation between stakeholders and operation issues remain undiscussed. The ERP approach in contrast is focused on the taking of operational decisions with an implicit balancing of stakes, hidden in settings and parameters.

4 Planning Systems

In the last section the concepts involved in Sales & Operations Planning were discussed, in this section different commonly used approaches to planning systems will be analysed. The ERP approach and the spreadsheet approach are commonly used and will therefore be discussed. The third and fourth commonly used approaches are the ad hoc solution for individual companies and the specific niche solutions for specific markets. The latter two approaches can have any structure and will not be discussed (although they might be more frequently used than is assumed).

4.1 ERP Approach

In ERP systems the expected sales are translated through a series of steps into quantities to be produced. Production orders are generated from the plans as well as the specification of the requirement for raw materials and other resources. The behaviour of the planning process in the system can be determined in advance by choosing system settings and parameters; in the operational planning process the planner can influence system behaviour by setting parameters and/or by the adjustment of intermediate results if needed. The first step in the planning process is to determine expected sales, the second step is the determining of the production plan based on a combination of expected sales, available stocks and production capacities.

The planning process in ERP systems is geared towards the generation of the optimal production plan. To arrive at this plan the system needs to be informed of current stocks and orders, of expected future orders and of available resources and their costs. Further, the system must have criteria to determine what constitutes an optimal plan (in general the minimisation of costs given certain conditions). Finally, the system must be informed regarding the flexibility of the resources as well as the options and costs in adding or removing certain resources.

The result is a production plan with production orders per (sub-)process in production and their specification of requirement of resources. In terms of scheduling the production plan can range in detail from just presenting the production orders and requirements in a fixed order to a detailed plan with starting and ending for each production order for each work centre / production line on the other. Also, planning and scheduling might be executed by different systems.

Essentially, this approach to planning has the following characteristics:

1. The goal is an optimal production plan
2. Inputs are current orders, demand history and available stocks
3. Settings determine the way in which demand history is translated into expected sales
4. Conditions and criteria determine what is considered an optimal production plan

For the planner this approach can lead to the following characteristics in practice (best case):

1. The system is transparent, it is clear to the planner how the system arrives at its results
2. The planner can see the chosen settings of the systems and how and where these settings affect the results
3. The planner can manually adjust starting conditions, intermediate results or end results to prevent the system from arriving at the wrong results (the basis for such adjustments must be that the planner knows that the system cannot have access to certain relevant information) and because of the transparency of the system the planner can also judge the side effects of his adjustments

However, this approach can also lead to the following characteristics for the user (worst case):

1. The system is a black box of which the inner workings are unknown to the planner
2. Settings, criteria and conditions are part of this black box
3. The planner thus cannot know the side effects of any manual adjustments
4. The integrated nature of ERP systems leads to a situation in which all product registration must refer to the system-generated production orders

Regardless of the best case or worst case situation, there are two principal objections to this approach of planning. Firstly sales and production are not kept sufficiently separate; and secondly each change in realised sales, realised production or available stocks leads to a recalculation of the production plan. On top of this comes the practical objection that as the system shows more characteristics of the worst-case-scenario sketched above, the planner will be more likely to tweak the system such that it produces acceptable results.

4.2 Spreadsheet Approach

It is by no means an exception for businesses to conduct the planning fully or in part through spreadsheets. An important feature of working with spreadsheets is the decentral nature of the solutions. Anyone with some skill and perseverance can achieve usable results and avoid in this way the often felt limitations of central systems for managing master data and operational data. When a categorisation of e.g. items or customers from the central system does not fully meet the planner's needs an additional column is added easily and quickly. In the added column the planner records an additional characteristic of the customer or item (or a deviating value of an existing characteristic!) and the planner can continue with a categorisation that is right for his needs.

In the output from spreadsheet solutions to other environments all kinds of provisions can be made depending on the situation to make the exchange of data work. It is also not uncommon to feed information to production departments directly from a spreadsheet. Because of the isolated character of the spreadsheet, its information can freely be interpreted, supplemented, or neglected. Where ERP systems are marked by 'tight couplings', spreadsheet solutions are marked by 'loose couplings'.

Much has been written already regarding the risks of working with spreadsheets in a business context. There is an organisation dedicated to the research of these risks (eusprig.org). Spreadsheets make it easy for the user to treat the data inconsistently, structures in spreadsheets are hidden, the dimensions make users scroll both horizontally and vertically and hinder a clear overview, etc, etc. These are risks that partly originate from the isolated nature with loose couplings, and partly from the allowance of spreadsheets for syntactically or semantically incorrect constructions. On the other hand, the loose couplings allow the incremental search for good solutions in each subarea separately (according to the principles described in the Reference Model for Open Distributed Systems (RM-ODP) [14]), which can lead to effective and efficient solutions. At the same time: (1) because of the ad-hoc nature of the realisation of couplings from spreadsheets (adapt until it works), (2) because of the individual nature of the solution (with little to no stimulation towards documenting), and (3) because of the evolving nature (over time errors are solved, adjustments are made to selections, conditions and formulas and the presentation is altered), these solutions can become very hard to comprehend and thus to maintain over time. Changes in personnel add significantly to this problem. The use of spreadsheets can then become the execution of a series of instructions until an output is obtained which can then be used in other business processes. When the output is deemed unacceptable, just try another iteration with tweaked inputs.

The loose couplings make it possible for the relationship between the data in the spreadsheet and the real data to become less restricting than with ERP systems. There is more room for human interpretation as well as more room for additional information outside of the systems. When a target quantity from a spreadsheet is not met, a short discussion might suffice to determine how much needs to be produced in addition. In ERP systems this can be a lot more difficult, for example because deviations are automatically signalled and corrected, or because production orders cannot be closed and reported back because the quantity has not been reached.

4.3 Comparison of ERP and Spreadsheet Approaches

The first major difference between the two approaches is the degree of integration. An ERP solution uses master data and operational data that are shared with other business processes that are represented in the solution. This holds both for the input side (demand history and available stocks) and for the output side (production orders and available stocks). A spreadsheet solution has a much lower degree of integration with other computer systems and all kinds of filters and functions can be applied on the input and output functions to fit the data. The system-enforced consistency in the ERP solution can equally be an advantage or a disadvantage in practice. In the ideal world as envisioned by IT people it is a major advantage since everyone is working with the same data. In our real world of business processes, however, it can be a major disadvantage as each change in the master data has unexpected (and often inexplicable) consequences in other business processes and because it is much harder to add relevant information to the operational data (or because this has unforeseen implications for other processes). Planning through individual spreadsheets enables the planner to remain in his own sphere to a much greater extent, with all of its advantages and disadvantages.

The second major difference is the freedom of the planner to create and optimise his own filters and functions in the spreadsheets. He is not bound by the models of central systems and is thus able to (re)act much faster. This is probably the most important reason (or cause?) for the frequent use of spreadsheets by planners. The other side of the coin is of course the personal nature of solutions through spreadsheets. Here, the organisation must find a balance between flexibility and stability, taking into account (1) that essentially planning is a complex process and that personal experience often plays a large part, and (2) that it is often not true that ERP systems are documented to such an extent that new employees can easily and quickly get up to speed with the ERP solution.

The shared characteristic between ERP solutions and spreadsheet solutions is the focus on generating the production plan. For a given production period with a given demand history and given stocks the system generates a list of quantities to be produced, possibly subdivided into subprocesses and order of subtasks. However: although the production control is shared (set of production orders for each workplace, with more or less detail regarding order, dependencies and required resources), the ensuing control of product registration is highly different. In ERP systems production planning is usually also the only basis for product registration (recording used and registered quantities must occur in the production orders generated by the integrated ERP system). In control through spreadsheets this is a much looser coupling (or the coupling is even entirely absent within the systems). From spreadsheets production orders can be created directly or indirectly upon which consumption of inputs and production of outputs are registered. The monitoring of used and produced quantities is often much looser than with production orders in ERP systems, and the use of different item numbers (substitutes on input, deviating qualities on output) is often much easier in loosely coupled systems. This greater 'looseness' can be experienced as an advantage or as a disadvantage depending on the situation (and often ad hoc based on the particular desired or undesired results). The essence is that in integrated ERP systems the couplings are usually tighter and in the use of Excel looser. What is desired or undesired, and what should be better allowed or disallowed in a given situation is an entirely different question!

5 Why Plan?

In the preceding two sections the concept of Sales & Operation Planning and the approaches to planning systems were discussed. While the literature analyses the problem in terms of balancing the interests of stakeholders, the ERP approach focuses on the generation of an optimised production plan. In the ERP approach the balancing of stakes is hidden in parameters and settings, and the planning process itself often seems to be reduced to a calculation model. This brings us to the fundamental questions: "why plan?", "what are the responsibilities of the planner?" and "what is the status of a plan?". To illustrate the relevance of this question, the next paragraph will present the questions a customer asked his software supplier about the behaviour of his planning system. The questions show a model-based world view, rather than a business-based world view. The subsequent paragraph discusses the relation of a resulting plan with reality: is a plan a representation of a future reality that should be proven to be true, or is a plan "just" an instrument for target setting and coordination? The final paragraph gives a recapitulation of the criteria to be used in designing a planning system.

5.1 "What Is the Issue Here?"

A picture of confusing, vague and contradicting terminology in combination with conceptual weaknesses arises from the works in the earlier sections of this chapter. Neither in the literature nor in the software clear structures of the problem area are defined. A concrete example of the translation of this messy approach into actual customer requirements is the following set of questions for candidate software suppliers by a company in the food industry:

- "How will stock adjustments automatically influence the production schedule?"
- "Sequence of production is determined by the scheduling process. Disruptions in other processes (up and down) lead to automatic rescheduling of production capacity; manual adjusting to schedule needs to be validated and recorded as an exception"
- "How will the production schedule be adapted in case of (1) late delivery of raw materials"; (2) delays in production runs; (3) changes in available stock caused by quality inspections; (4) rush orders; (5) break down of production lines;
- "Reject of the output of finished product at the end of the production line, how will the system adapt?"

These questions show a model-based and reductionist approach to the sales and operation planning process. The planning system is provided a forecast from the central ERP system (just one value, no information about spread), processes this to an optimal production plan, and any deviation or disruption results in adjustments to the production plan. A fully deterministic production process is assumed, as well as full and real time information about the actual situation on the shop floor.

This approach encounters three kinds of fundamental objections. Firstly the representation of production in the computer system does not fully coincide with production reality. Apart from a certain time-lag, production registration often depends on predefined classifications that not always match the reality of the shop floor. Secondly, production is not an exact science and net output will often differ from planned output. What is the criterion or threshold value for a difference to count as a relevant deviation? This is an awkward issue, especially as it easily leads to a lot of additional parameters to be managed. Thirdly, a continuous flow of changes in the production plan will have negative effects on effectiveness and efficiency.

5.2 Planning and Reality

What is the purpose of a plan and what is the purpose of planning as a business process? There are many different possible answers to these questions, of which we will now identify two kinds. The first kind of answer states that a plan must represent some future state of affairs. This implies that a plan has a pretension of truthfulness and that a plan should be confirmed by future developments. Deviations from the plan are a violation of what should have happened, a violation of the projected reality. Such deviations require correcting measures in the execution of the plan. And the deviations can lead to adjustments to the plan, to make plan and reality correspond once again.

The second kind of answer we might call action-oriented. A plan in this view is an instrument to coordinate future actions. This happens firstly by creating a common framework ("we expect demand between X and Y" or "quantity X will be produced tomorrow" or "the final stock must be at least X and at most Y tomorrow"). Secondly this happens by indicating activities and/or intermediate results together with their mutual dependencies and time windows. Planning is a way to organise and evaluate activities in advance with their relationships, to facilitate the execution of the processes.

In ERP systems the focus usually seems to be on the first approach, to which an important reduction in information is added. Uncertainties and bandwidths have no place in these systems, all information is made absolute and exact in the system. This reduction has two consequences. Firstly, the shop floor employees get less information than they need from the system. After all, the execution is not absolute and exact and shop floor employees have to know about tolerances in a given situation. Is a to be produced quantity indicative, a minimum, a maximum or something else? Thus, they must obtain this information regarding tolerances and bandwidths from other sources, and this might easily lead to unmanaged hidden practices. Secondly, in practice the realised quantity will often deviate from the planned quantity. These "deviations" are signalled in the systems and must be handled. When the shop floor is hampered by this, they will quickly learn to put the information into the system such that no issues are raised. In other words, registration and feedback are decoupled from reality and are used to satisfy the system. The combination of these consequences leads to an ERP system that is decoupled to a greater or lesser extent from the physical and organisational reality, but which is viewed by managers as the 'true' representation of reality.

5.3 Planning for Business

For the business the most important operational norms are about service levels and about cost levels. Self-evidently, the purpose of the planning processes should be to enable the primary processes to meet the operational business norms. Planning processes are by their nature to be considered as support processes. And, as in all supporting business processes, the criteria for its outputs are to be derived from the needs of the primary processes to be supported.

The two basic informational questions for fulfilling any task in a business context are: (1) "which information is needed to fulfil this task properly?" and (2) "which information is needed by subsequent tasks that must be produced from this task?". Obviously, for supporting processes the second question must come first. It asks the planning processes to provide the primary processes with all variable information to do their jobs. This includes information about what must be done and about what may be done. The difference between "must" and "may" is an indication of the space for discretionary decisions on the shop floor. This information about leeway for shop floor decisions essentially gives the shop floor a share of the responsibility for optimising service levels and cost levels. How the shop floor is using its discretionary space is yet another aspect of a business information system. For now, it is important to stress that the acknowledgement of the existence of discretionary space on the shop floor implies that coupling between planning, production orders and production must not be too tight. The first question asks the planning processes to take into consideration all relevant information to determine stock levels and production levels.

Generally, it is not the task of the planning process to state invariant information, this kind of information should be provided for by job training and organisational standards. Furthermore, besides specific organised training, handbooks, posters on the shop floor, et cetera, much of this kind of information belongs to the realm of "established practices". In a stable and well organised organisation, people in the primary processes know about the behaviour of processes and people, know something about interdependencies and know about tolerances and short cuts. It is the task of the planner to tell the people executing the primary processes when customary practices are not to be followed (this assumes the planner knows about customary practices, a condition that not always will be met!).

6   Information Systems for Planning in Business

To prosper in business, the business processes of a company must be both efficient and effective. The effectiveness is related to the quality, value and usefulness of the output of the company for its customers, the efficiency is related to costs and consumed resources. Effectiveness has to do with doing the right thing, efficiency has to do with doing things in the right way and doing things first time right. Both elements are caught in one of the OED meanings of "efficient": "Effective, producing the desired result with the minimum wasted effort". In the context of business processes, the first part represents effectiveness or doing the right thing, and the second part represents the efficiency as the maximisation of the output/input ratio or doing things in the right way.

The planning processes as supporting processes (1) must contribute to both the effectiveness and efficiency of the primary processes, and (2) must be executed in an effective and efficient way. Part of the first requirement is obeying the maxims of Grice in presenting information to the primary processes: (1) be informative, (2) be truthful, (3) be relevant, (4) be clear, brief and orderly [5]. Please note: the maxim "be truthful" for planning does most certainly not mean the planning must give a true description of a future state, but on the contrary that planning truthfully informs about what is known and what is unknown!

6.1 'Hard' Aspects of Planning and Planning Systems

The process logic of planning for a given market with a given kind of products should be reflected in the structure of the planning processes itself, as well as in the structure of the supporting planning system. A planning system should not be set up as just a tool box to produce the desired outputs (aside from the question whether desired outputs are correctly defined), as often seems to be the case in both ERP solutions and spreadsheet solutions. Edsger Dijkstra wrote in 1968: "My second remark is that our intellectual powers are rather geared to master static relations and that our powers to visualize processes evolving over time are relatively poor developed. For that reason we should do (as wise programmers aware of our limitations) our utmost best to shorten the conceptual gap between the static program and the dynamic process, to make the correspondence between the program (spread out of text space) and the process (spread out in time) as trivial as possible" [15]. In designing business processes, subprocesses and thereupon the systems supporting the business (sub)processes, these remarks of Dijkstra should be heeded. The invariant logical blocks of the business process should be determined, the information flows between the logical blocks should be identified, and the tasks and responsibilities for executing the processes in each logical block should be defined. This approach guarantees a stable process architecture, which can be adapted and evolve over time without loss of structure.

About the use of formal sign systems in business processes two lines of reasoning could be applied. Both lines start with the observation that standardisation is an instrument for improving efficiency of processes, and that standardisation of information implies using standardised coding for information transfer to and from processes. The first line of reasoning equates the use of standardised coding of information with the application of ICT systems, thus enhancing the efficiency of information processes both by standardisation and by the use of formal sign systems. The presumption in this line of reasoning is that the information produced by the formal sign system is at least equivalent to the information provided by non-formal sign systems, and possibly better because of the greater rigidity of formal sign systems. Formal sign systems enforce clear coding, consequently unambiguous meaning, and thus more efficiency in information processes.

The second, more critical, line of reasoning would analyse the conditions for successfully applying formal sign systems. Given a standardisation of coding information in a social sign system (conventions about the use and interpretation of terms and values), the step towards a formal sign systems implies the provision of definitions of terms and values that cover (1) the explanation of the meaning of the terms, (2) the explanations of the effects of the values in the information processing on other terms and values, (3) criteria for classification of real-world situations into the available values and (4) criteria for the interpretation of the available values into their meaning in the real world. Practically, these conditions will never be fully met and people will always find a way of utilising the formal sign system according to the business norms, the organisational norms and the personal norms. In other words, formal sign systems applied to the social world are dependent on all kinds of social practices and social conventions.

Formal sign systems never can exist just by themselves, they are always embedded in our social world. Developers of planning systems should be aware of this. The outcomes of the planning processes are executed in the real world, and the planning processes are dependent on inputs from the real world. Reductive rationalisation, idealisation and formalisation will not work for the social world of the company, its customers and its suppliers. However, where planners, managers and IT developers all tend to do their jobs by abstraction and modelling, there is a risk that in developing planning systems the rationality of the models take priority, and incompatible irregularities of the real world are either wished away, explained away or defined away.

6.2 'Soft' Aspects of Planning and Planning Systems

Idiosyncratic characteristics of a company set it apart from its competitors. Of course, this can be either positive or negative (in the latter case the company eventually might end up bankrupt). The idea of ERP suppliers to implement "best practices" at its customers is at odds with the idea that the market position of a company is determined by the way in which it distinguishes itself. Mathias Kirchmer has indicated that for a company the majority of its business processes can be considered a commodity (he mentions 80%) [16]. It is then prudent for a company to copy the commodity processes from companies that have given them careful thought. The focus should be on those processes that make a difference for the company. In general, the planning processes will belong to the 20%, firstly because these processes are highly integrated in other business processes, secondly because these processes must take the typical situation of the company into account, thirdly because they are a highly determining factor in service level and costs. The process logic represents the invariant aspects of the planning structures. The implementation of the process logic, however, can be highly individual. In one company the planners are knowledgeable about market and products and plan with narrow margins, in a second company the planners are just "number crunchers" and some old hands on the shop floor supported by contact with the sales department can quickly and easily adapt to changing situations. In a third company the planning might consist of a hard core of elementary calculations, supplemented by informal contacts between key persons in planning, sales, production and distribution.

Planning systems should be clearly structured in logical units, and the behaviour of each unit should be comprehensible for human planners. In that case, the planner can use his own judgement in interpreting the planning results, use alternative information sources (including 'soft' information from colleagues and customers), make specific arrangements with managers of primary processes ("do you think you could squeeze in another job?"), and adjust the planning information accordingly. In this way, the planner uses both formal sign systems and social sign systems to do his job.

6.3   Recapitulation

Prior to formulating guidelines for an information system supporting the planning processes the two main business criteria for such a system must be stated clearly. Firstly, the system must support the planning process in achieving the company's goals of service levels and costs. Secondly, the continuity of the system must be warranted. The first criterion requires that the system be judged by the results of the business process of planning as a whole, and requires that the development of the system is not to be reduced to the functionalities of software systems (be it a full-fledged ERP system or an in-house developed spreadsheet application). It is not the computer system that delivers a plan, the planner does. And in doing so, the planner must be able to take into account all relevant information, not just information that is represented in the computer systems. In the same vein, the planner must provide the shop floor processes with all relevant information for doing their jobs, not just with computer output.

The second criterion requires that both the operational use of the system and its support and adaptations over time are not dependent on the knowledge of a few key persons. Of course, people matter. Experienced planners see more, sense more, and act more easily than inexperienced planners. But experiences that matter should belong to the planning process itself and not to the knowledge of peculiarities and hidden structures of the systems used in the process.

The solution is to develop a system build on organisation structures which (a) reflect the organisational responsibilities, (b) which define all relevant information to be routinely provided by the planning to the shop floor, (c) which define all relevant information to be provided to the planning by the shop floor and by other departments, and (d) define the communication and interaction structures both in routine situations and in non-standard situations. This organisational structures will be supported by IT systems (1) which are based on representation of the structure of the process logic, (2) which allow for human intervention at the junctures of the sub-processes, (3) which are based on understandable calculation models, and (4) which are loosely coupled to production registration. Business criteria of efficiency and effectiveness must be applied to determine which information is better represented and processed by IT systems and its formal sign systems, and which information is better represented and processed by social sign systems.

An information system developed along these lines will probably apply solutions that are provided by suppliers external to the company (either commercial of-the-shelf software such as ERP modules, or custom-made by a software developer), and such elements and the knowledge behind it can be also be used by competitors. Or, the other way around, a company can profit from the knowledge and experience gained by the third party at other companies.

7   Conclusions

The problem area is about how to combine agreed service levels with minimising costs. The Sales & Operations Planning literature clearly indicates the comprehensive character of the problem, different viewpoints have to be taken into account. In structuring the problem field the literature is less helpful, firstly because of the confusing use of terminology, secondly because of the time horizon of months and years, and thirdly because of the lack of attention for the day-to-day work and challenges for the people involved in planning. Software, as could be expected, does not help either. It offers toolboxes of statistical instruments, dashboards, and algorithms without much notion of how to apply which instrument in which situation. The fact that a planner is responsible for his decisions, and that the planner has to combine information from many sources in order to deal with variance, inaccuracy and conflict of norms is not discussed in the literature.

Essentially, the problem area is about two main control loops decoupled by a third intermediate control loop. The first main loop is about service levels, available stock and expected demand. The second main loop is about production output and efficient production. The intermediate loop is about stock control, firstly for decoupling variance of demand from smooth and efficient production processes, and secondly for dealing with all kinds of disruptions, deviations and inaccuracies in both the business processes itself and in available information about the business processes.

The approach is about finding solutions that do justice to both the structure of the problem (process logic, formal sign systems) and to the intricacies of the particular company that must organise its information in such a way that its competitive power and distinctive capabilities are enhanced (how it has found its own ways of dealing with the challenges, idiosyncratic characteristics, social sign systems). Human judgement and human communication must be combined with computing power.

In terms of the coordination mechanisms of Mintzberg [3] we see a combination of standardisation (and formal sign systems) and mutual adjustment (with social sign systems). Standardisation and rigid definitions of data help to organise information flows and to automate the processes of determining demand, setting stock levels, and setting production levels in standard situations. Dealing with conflicting norms in non-standard situations, however, is about mutual adjustment and human responsibilities. Squeezing out that little bit extra is about human creativity and problem solving.

To conclude with Kay: distinctive capabilities are about the characteristics that distinguishes the individual company from its competitors, and that cannot be readily copied. The challenge is to find the right combination of formal and social sign systems that addresses the needs of actual planners in actual companies and that builds on the existing competitive power of the company. The high level talk of the literature nor the reductive approach of ERP software helps here much.

References

1. Kay, J.: Foundations of Corporate Success. Oxford University Press, Oxford (1998)
2. Suurmond, C.: Information systems and sign systems. In: Liu, K., Nakata, K., Li, W., Galarreta, D. (eds.) ICISO 2015. IFIP, vol. 449, pp. 20–29. Springer, Cham (2015). doi: 10.1007/978-3-319-16274-4_3
3. Mintzberg, H.: The Structuring of Organizations. Prentice Hall, Englewood Cliffs (1979)
4. Starreveld, R.W.: Leer van de administratieve organisatie. Samson, Alphen aan de Rijn (1963)
5. Grice, P.: Studies in the Ways of Words. Harvard University Press, Cambridge (1989)
6. Boisot, M.H.: Knowledge Assets. Oxford University Press, Oxford (1998)
7. The TechTarget Network. http://serachmanufacturingerp.techtarget.com/definition/Sales-and-operations-planning-SOP
8. APICS: APICS Dictionary. Apics, Chicago (2008)
9. Sheldon, D.H.: World Class Sales & Operations Planning. J. Ross Publishing, Ft Lauderdale (2006)
10. Davis, R.A.: Demand-Driven Inventory Optimization and Replenishment. Wiley, Hoboken (2016)
11. Snapp, S.: Sales & Operations Planning in Software. SCM Focus Press, Las Vegas (2016)
12. Hamilton, S.: Process Manufacturing Using Microsoft Dynamics AX. Scott Hamilton Press (2016)
13. Dickersbach, J.T.: Supply Chain Management with SAP APO™. Springer, Heidelberg (2009)
14. RM ODP, Information Technology – Open Distributed Processing – Reference Model: Overview. ISO/TEC 10746-1. ISO/TEC, Genève (1998)
15. Dijkstra, E.W.: A case against the GO TO Statement. EWD215 (1968). https://www.cs.utexas.edu/users/EWD/ewd02xx/EWD215.PDF
16. Kirchmer, M.: Value-driven Design and Implementation of Business Processes. In: Shishkov, B. (ed.) Proceedings of the Fourth International Symposium on Business Modeling and Software Design, pp. 297–302. SCITEPRESS (2014)

Assessing Business Processes by Checking Transaction Documents for Inconsistency Risks and a Tool for Risk Assessment

Takafumi Komoto[1(✉)], Kokichi Futatsugi[1], and Nobukazu Yoshioka[2]

[1] Japan Advanced Institute Science and Technology, Nomi, Japan
{komoto,futatsugi}@jaist.ac.jp
[2] GRACE Center, National Institute of Informatics, Tokyo, Japan
nobukazu@nii.ac.jp

Abstract. Business processes can be assessed by checking transaction documents for inconsistency risks and can be classified into two categories. Inconsistency refers to a mismatch between items (product name, quantity, unit price, amount price, etc.) among transaction documents. For any process in the first category, the consistency of any pair of transaction documents in the process is checked, and there is no risk of inconsistency. For any process in the second category, the consistency of some pairs of transaction documents in the process cannot be checked, and there is a risk of inconsistency. This paper proposes a method and a tool for the assessment of risk inconsistencies. The assessment can be used to design and evaluate business processes for a company's internal control over financial reporting. A business process diagram and inconsistency risk detection algorithm for classifying business processes is provided. A BPA-tool (Business Process Assessment tool) is also presented.

Keywords: Internal control · Transaction documents · Reliability · Inconsistency risks · Checked documents matrix · BPA-tool

1 Introduction

From the viewpoint of internal control, management has a responsibility to establish business processes that do not cause deficiencies over financial reporting. When deficiencies over financial reporting are pointed out by auditors, companies lose the reliability of their investors [1–3].

Certified Public Accountants (CPAs) examine the consistency among accounting transaction documents (slips, vouchers, etc.) related to transactions when performing an accounting audit. They check whether there is a mismatch between them and confirm the reliability of transactions [5].

If such checks and confirmations performed by CPAs to posted transactions are incorporated into the business process, more reliable transactions may be realized.

© Springer International Publishing AG 2017
B. Shishkov (Ed.): BMSD 2016, LNBIP 275, pp. 70–82, 2017.
DOI: 10.1007/978-3-319-57222-2_4

Company workers check between received slips and archived slips on the same transaction for consistencies in product name, quantity, unit price, and amount price in business processes. In other words, checking and confirming the consistency of transactions are already performed on-site.

However, these checks are independently performed at each department of a company during the business process. Therefore, any inconsistencies among whole documents in transactions cannot be detected solely by checks performed in one department when such transactions pass through multiple departments.

For example, there are transaction documents "a", "b", and "c" in a transaction. When division "A" checks transaction documents "a" and "b", and division "B" checks transaction documents "b" and "c", inconsistencies in whole documents for the transaction are detected considering a transitive relation between "a" and "c" through "b". Conversely, when division "A" checks documents "a" and "b", and "B" only has document "c" any inconsistencies between them cannot be detected because there is no relation between "a", "b", and "c".

The detection of inconsistencies between transaction documents depends on what divisions check in transaction documents, i.e., the business process.

This paper proposes a method for assessment of risk inconsistencies. The assessment can be used to design and evaluate business processes for a company's internal control over financial reporting. A business process diagram and an inconsistency risk detection algorithm for classifying business processes are provided.

The paper is organized as follows. The next section describes business process modeling using our business process diagram while Sect. 3 introduces an inconsistency risk detection algorithm for classifying business processes. Section 4 presents a case study. Section 5 also presents a risk assessment tool. Section 6 discusses related work. Section 7 concludes this paper.

2 Business Process Diagram

A business process diagram is a diagram used to describe business processes of a company by listing business events and archived transaction documents and checked documents set. At first we will explain the elements and notations of the "business process diagram" using a simple example.

2.1 An Order-to-Delivery Process Diagram

This simple diagram (Fig. 1) describes an "order-to-delivery process" in which a company orders goods from a vendor, and the vendor delivers the goods to the company. In this process, the company orders goods from the vendor with a purchase order document. When the vendor receives the purchase order document, it prepares the goods for shipping and delivers them with an invoice. The company receives the goods with the invoice and checks between the purchase order and the goods to ensure consistency with the invoice. The diagram in Fig. 1 describes the "order-to-delivery process."

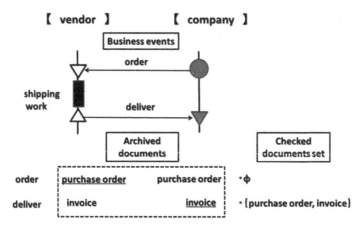

Fig. 1. Order-to-delivery process diagram

In this diagram, 【vendor】 and 【company】 show entities. An "order" and a "deliver" are events in the transaction process. The events are indicated by arrows pointing from a sending entity toward a receiving entity of a transaction document. The events are run sequentially from top to bottom along a timeline of the entities.

The sides of an arrow are visualized by the following symbols to distinguish between a transmission and a reception.

"●": start of the process, "▽": end of an event
"△": start of an event, "▼": end of the process

On a side of the timeline between "▽" (end of an event) and "△" (start of a following event), work at the acceptance event can be described. (The work can be omitted.)

In general, each transaction document is issued in accordance with a business event in the transaction. A "purchase order" and an "invoice" issued in this business process are described sequentially in the dashed frame indicating the archived transaction documents under the timeline of each entity. A line is drawn under a received document to distinguish it from a sent document. Business events, an "order" and a "deliver", can be described in the side of the dashed frame to link to the transaction documents, a "purchase order" and an "invoice".

In general, workers of a company also check between a received transaction document and archived transaction documents on the same transaction for consistencies in product name, quantity, unit price, and amount price in business processes. In the "order-to-delivery process diagram", the state of transaction documents, whether checked or not by a division receiving a transaction document, is described.

At first, when 【vendor】 receives a purchase order, it does not keep any documents. Therefore, a checked documents set φ(empty set) is described. Next, when 【company】 receives an invoice, it keeps the purchase order. As 【company】 checks between the invoice and the purchase order, a checked documents set {purchase order, invoice} is described.

2.2   Elements and Notation of Business Process Diagram

As shown using the simple example, the business process diagram consists of the following elements.

- "Division": entity that performs the work in the process.
- "Timeline": time flowing from top to bottom.
- "Event": things needed to send and receive a transaction document from one division to another division in a predetermined order.
- "Transaction document": documented work instructions and/or operating report in the business process.
- "Archived documents": transaction documents that the divisions sent and received.
- "Checked documents set": set of documents that the department is keeping (including a received document).

"Division", "Events", "Transaction document", "Archived documents", and "Checked documents set" are symbolized and defined as follows.

- Division a, b ∈ Div (Div: the entire division)
- Event e_n (a, b) ∈ E (E: the entire event): the n-th event to send and receive a document from division "a" to division "b".
- Event order n ∈ N (N: natural number)
- Transaction document d_n ∈ Doc (Doc: all documents): the document to send and receive in the event e_n (a, b)
- Archived documents S_n (a): documents that division "a" sent and received until the event e_n
- Checked documents set V_n: set of the documents S_n (a) that division "a" received the document d_n in the event e_n.

The elements and notation of the business process diagram notation are shown in Fig. 2.

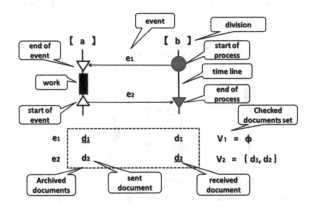

Fig. 2. Business process diagram

2.3   Preconditions for Business Process Diagram

There are some preconditions for the business process diagram to represent practical standard business processes.

In a business process, when a person in charge in the division receives a transaction document, he/she works in accordance with business rules and issues a transaction document for reporting his/her task or indicating a task of the next division. When he/she receives a transaction document from another division, and archive documents of the transaction are kept in this division, he/she can prevent an operational error by comparing the common items (product name, quantity, unit price, amount price, etc.) between the received document and archived documents.

Business process diagrams are used to detect inconsistency risks by examining mistakes or frauds. Accordingly, in the business process diagram it is assumed that transaction documents are not changed during storage and delivery. In other words, a sent document and a received document concerning the same event are regarded as the same.

It is also assumed that the event order of the business process is fixed. In general, business events in the company, in accordance with the principle of the separation of duty, are performed without being indicated by a transaction document. Therefore, in the business process diagram, the division not receiving a transaction document cannot send a transaction document except at the start of the event.

For example, in the purchase order process, the accounting division cannot pay for goods without receiving disbursement approval by the procurement division. In other words, each business event is carried out in the usual fixed order.

2.4   Example of Business Process Diagram at Risk for Inconsistency

Figure 3, which has a slightly modified business process diagram compared with Fig. 1, 【company】 division of Fig. 1 is divided into 【purchase】 division and 【warehouse】 division. The business event of receiving a report from 【warehouse】 division to 【purchase】 division is added.

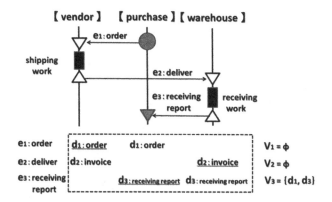

Fig. 3. Business process diagram at risk for inconsistency

Looking at the checked documents set V_i, received report d_3 and order d_1 is compared. However, invoice d_2 is not compared. Therefore, inconsistencies cannot be detected even if there is an error in the invoice. The business process diagram in Fig. 3 is at risk for inconsistency of transaction documents.

3   Inconsistency Risk Detection Algorithm

When a business process diagram is given, we provide an inconsistency risk detection algorithm that determines whether the business process has inconsistency risks among transaction documents.

The inconsistency risk detection algorithm is based on the equivalence relation of transaction documents. Transitive closure for the checked document matrix of the business process diagram is calculated using the Floyd-Warshall algorithm [6].

When the elements of the transitive closure matrix are all 1, no risk of inconsistency is decided. When the elements of the transitive closure matrix are 0, a risk of inconsistency is decided.

3.1   Documents Check and Equivalence Relation

"Documents check" compares common items of a received document to archived documents in the receiving division. Common items of transaction documents in the business process are product name and quantity, unit price, amount price, etc.

We determined that "documents check" serves as an equivalence relation as the result of the following analysis of "documents check".

Document d_1 is naturally compared with itself (reflexivity law). When document d_1 is compared with document d_2, document d_2 is compared with document d_1 (symmetric law). In addition, if document d_1 and document d_2 are compared, and document d_2 and document d_3 are compared, then document d_1 and d_3 have also been compared (transitive law).

Comparing reflexivity law and symmetry law is a convincing operation. For transitivity law, it has also been determined that a convincing operation can be assumed.

It should be noted that our discussion is based on the assumption of the sameness between the sent document and the received document, and the transitive law of "documents check".

3.2   Inconsistency Risk Detection Algorithm

The state of the comparison with the entire set of transaction documents of business process diagram $Doc = \{d_1, \cdots, d_n\}$ is represented by a matrix (Checked Documents Matrix).

Checked documents matrix $T(i, j)$ is set as 1 if document d_i and document d_j are compared. $T(i, j)$ is set as 0 if they are not compared.

Since the checked documents have an equivalence relation, the diagonal elements (i, i) are consistently 1 by reflexivity law, and (i, j) component and (j, i) component are equal by symmetric law.

We will explain the Checked Documents Matrix T using the following example. The entire set of documents of the matrix are Doc = $\{d_1, d_2, d_3\}$.

$$
\begin{array}{cc}
\text{Checked Documents} \\
\text{Matrix } T^0
\end{array}
\qquad
\begin{array}{c}
 \\
d_1 \\
d_2 \\
d_3
\end{array}
\begin{array}{ccc}
d_1 & d_2 & d_3 \\
\left(\begin{array}{ccc}
1 & 1 & 1 \\
1 & 1 & 0 \\
1 & 0 & 1
\end{array}\right)
\end{array}
$$

Checked Documents Matrix T^0 describes how document d_1 is compared with d_2 and d_3, but document d_2 is not compared with d_3.

However, document d_2 and d_1 are compared, and document d_1 and d_3 are compared in T^0, so document d_2 and d_3 are also compared by transitive law.

At first glance, document d_2 and d_3 seemed not to be compared in T^0. But matrix T^1 applying the transitivity law represents the true state of checked documents.

$$
\begin{array}{cc}
\text{Checked Documents} \\
\text{Matrix } T^1 \text{ of applying} \\
\text{transitive law}
\end{array}
\qquad
\begin{array}{c}
 \\
d_1 \\
d_2 \\
d_3
\end{array}
\begin{array}{ccc}
d_1 & d_2 & d_3 \\
\left(\begin{array}{ccc}
1 & 1 & 1 \\
1 & 1 & 1 \\
1 & 1 & 1
\end{array}\right)
\end{array}
$$

As described above, continuing to apply the transitivity law for initial checked documents matrix T^0, by calculating T^1, $T^2 \cdot \cdot \cdot$, transitive closure T subsequently cannot be applied by the transitivity law any more. Transitive closure T represents the true state of checked documents.

Then, starting from the initial checked documents matrix T^0, by applying the transitivity law, if the elements (i, j) of checked documents matrix T (transitive closure) are all 1, all the documents have been checked. Therefore, there is no risk of inconsistency in the business process. Conversely, if the elements (i, j) of transitive closure T include zero, no documents are checked with each other. Therefore, there is a risk of inconsistency in the business process.

The inconsistency risk detection algorithm of the business process diagram is as follows.

<Inconsistency Risk Detection Algorithm>

(1) Set the initial checked documents matrix T^0.
   - All elements of T0 are set to 0, and for Checked Documents Set V_i of the business process diagram, when V_i contains document d_i and d_j, (i, j) of T^0 is set to 1 for all i.
   - Diagonal elements of T^0 are set to 1. When the element (i, j) is 1, the symmetry element (j, i) is set to 1.
(2) Calculate the transitive closure of checked documents matrix T^0.
   - Calculate the T^n by applying the Floyd-Warshall algorithm [6].

【Floyd-Warshall Algorithm [6] 】
The (i, j) element of the matrix T^k is t^k_{ij}.
for k = 1 to n
$T^k = a (t^k ij)$ is a new matrix
for i = 1 to n
for j = 1 to n
$t^k_{ij} = t^{k-1}_{ij} \vee (t^{k-1}_{ik} \wedge t^{k-1}_{kj})$
return T^n.

(3) When the elements of the transitive closure T^n are all 1, there is no risk of inconsistency in the business process. When the elements of T^n are not all 1, there is some risk of inconsistency in the business process.

4 Case Study by Standard Purchase Order Process

The assessment of the standard purchase order process is performed in this case study. First, we make the business process diagram of the standard purchase order process (Fig. 4) and extract the checked documents matrix from the checked documents sets

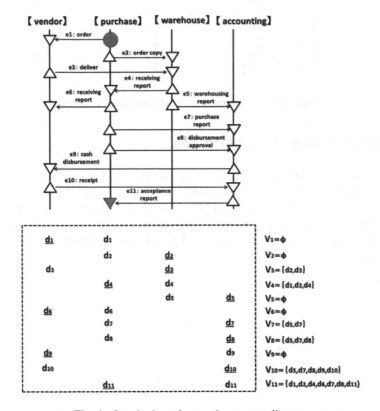

Fig. 4. Standard purchase order process diagram

V_i (for all i). Next, the inconsistency risk detection algorithm is applied for checked documents matrix T0, and the inconsistency risk of the process is judged.

4.1 Purchase Order Process Diagram and Inconsistency Risk Judgment

In the standard purchase order process, the purchase division orders goods from the vendor and notifies the warehouse division of the order. The vendor delivers the goods to the warehouse, and the warehouse receives them and sends the receiving report to the purchase division. The purchase division requests the accounting division for the payment in accordance with the invoice. The accounting division completes the disbursement and informs the purchase division about it to prevent duplicate payments [3, 4].

This standard purchase order process diagram is shown in Fig. 4.

The inconsistency risk detection algorithm is applied to the checked documents matrix T^0, as shown in Fig. 5. Since the elements of transitive closure matrix T^{11} are all 1, no risk of inconsistency in the standard purchase order process is determined.

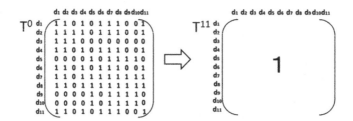

Fig. 5. Transitive closure matrix T^{11} of checked documents matrix T^0

5   Business Process Assessment Tool

The assessment of the business process is supported by the BPA-tool (Business Process Assessment tool). The BPA-tool is used MS-Excel (Microsoft Excel) and VBA (Visual Basic for Application). You need to get Microsoft Excel to use the BPA-tool.

The BPA-tool consists of two sheets of MS-Excel and three macros of VBA. Two sheets are Business Process sheet (Figs. 6 and 7) and Checked Document Matrix sheet. (Figs. 8 and 9)

No.	Division/Check	vendor	purchase	warehouse	accounting	Checked Documents Set
	Check	0	1	1	1	
1	order	▽	●			
2	oder copy		△	▽		
3	deliver	△		▽		
4	receiving		▽	△		
5	warehousing			△	▽	
6	receiving	▽	△			
7	purchase		△		▽	
8	disbursement		△		▽	
9	cash	▽			△	
10	receipt	△			▽	
11	acceptance		▼		△	

Fig. 6. Business process flow in the business process sheet

No.	Division/Check	vendor	purchase	warehouse	accounting	Checked Documents Set
	Check	0	1	1	1	
1	order	▽	●			
2	oder copy		△	▽		2
3	deliver	△		▽		3 2
4	receiving		▽	△		4 2 1
5	warehousing			△	▽	5
6	receiving	▽	△			
7	purchase		△		▽	7 5
8	disbursement		△		▽	8 7 5
9	cash	▽			△	
10	receipt	△			▽	10 9 8 7 5
11	acceptance		▼		△	11 8 7 6 4 2 1

Fig. 7. Checked documents set in the business process sheet

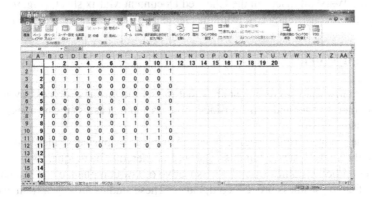

Fig. 8. Initial checked document matrix T^0 in checked document matrix sheet

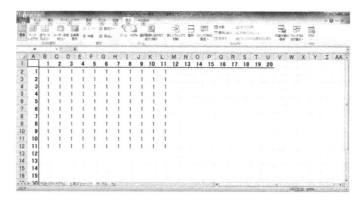

Fig. 9. Ttansitive closure matrix T^n of T^0 in checked document matrix sheet

Three macros are Voucher macro, Matrix macro, Warshall macro. Voucher macro is to calculate the checked documents set V_n from the Business Process Flow in Business Process sheet. Matrix macro is to set the initial checked documents matrix T^0 from the checked documents set V_n. Warshall macro is to calculate the transitive closure T^n of the T^0.

5.1   The Assessment by Using the BPA-Tool

The assessment of the purchase order process by using the BPA-tool is shown as follows.

(1) Create the purchase order process flow by hand in the Business Process sheet. (Fig. 6)
(2) Execute Voucher macro in the Business Process sheet. (Fig. 7)
(3) Execute Matrix macro in the Checked Document Matrix sheet. (Fig. 8)
(4) Execute Warshall macro in the Checked Document Matrix sheet. (Fig. 9)
(5) Judge the inconsistency risk from the elements of the transitive closure T^n.

6   Related Work

We are currently unaware of any studies that model the business process by focusing on the documents generated in the business process and that assess the business process for inconsistency risks.

From the perspective of specific practical analysis of business rules and business processes, the study described in this paper is considered to be unique.

Business process studies from the perspective of law compliance and standards are part of the field of business process compliance. These studies provide a framework for internal control in accordance with the Committee of Sponsoring Organizations of the Treadway Commission (COSO) and in accordance with health care privacy as established by the U.S. Health Insurance Portability and Accountability Act of 1996 (HIPPA) by analyzing the entire laws and standards [7, 8]. However, this paper does not provide a specific method that conforms to the standards established by COSO and HIPPA.

We are aware of a Resources, Events, and Agents (REA) study that analyzes and models financial accounting systems. In that study, all aspects of financial accounting are analyzed, but specific proposals for accounting audits are not provided [9].

7 Conclusion

Comparison of received transaction documents with archived transaction documents by a person in charge of each division in a company is naturally performed to prevent any errors in the operation of each division. However, we cannot conclude that such a simple check in each division is enough to ensure consistency for the entire set of transaction documents in the business process, despite consistency in transaction documents belonging to individual divisions.

As indicated above, if the business process is properly designed, the consistency for the entire set of transaction documents is ensured. This operation approximately corresponds to auditing done by CPAs to confirm the existence of transactions.

This paper proposes a method of assessing business processes by checking transaction documents for inconsistency risks. This method consists of a "Business Process Diagram" and an "Inconsistency Risk Detection Algorithm".

Using the "Business Process Diagram" and the "Inconsistency Risk Detection Algorithm", business processes can be classified in two categories. For any process in the first category, the consistency of any pair of transaction documents in the process is checked, and there is no risk of inconsistency. For any process in the second category, the consistency of some pairs of transaction documents in the process cannot be checked, and there is a risk of inconsistency.

When a business process is properly designed to meet the needs of the business process in the first category, inconsistency risks can be reduced.

We confirmed in the case study that the standard purchase order process established in the practices, due to the accumulation of experience over many years, is a business process in the first category.

This study aims to establish a high-quality method for inconsistency risk evaluation that can be incorporated into business rules and business processes by analyzing documents that are created on the basis of business rules and business processes. In this study, we modeled the business processes of transactions and assessed them for consistency risks. We will pursue logical verification by using CafeOBJ to refine our "Inconsistency Risk Detection Algorithm".

We will research a method to investigate mistakes and fraud in business processes in the future.

Acknowledgements. We thank Prof. Syuji Iida and Dr. Yasuhito Arimoto, Prof. Takao Okubo, Prof. Naoharu Kaiya, Mr. Motoharu Hirukawa, Ms. Junko Torimitsu for their valuable comments and feedback for our approach.

References

1. Shimizu, K., Nakamura, M.: Internal Control for IT Professionals. Zeimukeiri Kyoukai, Tokyo (2007). (in Japanese)
2. Maruyama, M., Kamei, S., Miki, T.: Readings from Internal Control Environment. Shoeisha, Tokyo (2008). (in Japanese)
3. Sasano, M.: Introduction and Practice of Internal Control. Chuokeizaisha, Tokyo (2006). (in Japanese)
4. Kaneko, A.: Business Seminar Company Accounting Introduction, 3rd edn. Nihon Keizai Shimbun Inc, Tokyo (2001). (in Japanese)
5. Yamaura, H.: Financial Auditing Theory, 2nd edn. Chuokeizaisha, Tokyo (2002). (in Japanese)
6. Cormen, T., Leiserson, C., Rivest, R., Stein, C.: Introduction to Algorithms, vol. 2, 3rd edn. MIT Press, Cambridge (2009)
7. Breaux, T.D., Vail, M.W., Anton, A.I.: Towards regulatory compliance: extracting rights and obligations to align requirements with regulations. In: RE 2006, pp. 46–55 (2006)
8. Siena, A., Perini, A., Susi, A., Mylopoulos, J.: Towards a framework for law-compliant software requirements. In: ICSE Companion 2009, pp. 251–254 (2009)
9. McCarthy, E.W.: The REA accounting model: a generalized framework for accounting systems in a shared data environment. Acc. Rev. **3**, 554–578 (1982)

Sensitive Business Processes Representation: A Multi-dimensional Comparative Analysis of Business Process Modeling Formalisms

Mariam Ben Hassen[(⊠)], Mohamed Turki, and Faïez Gargouri

ISIMS, MIRACL Laboratory, University of Sfax,
P.O. Box 242, 3021 Sfax, Tunisia
mariem.benhassen@isims.usf.tn,
mohamed.turki@isetsf.rnu.tn,
faiez.gargouri@isims.rnu.tn

Abstract. This paper presents a multi-perspective evaluation framework for assessing the expressiveness of current widely used business process modeling formalisms, in order to select the most suitable for representing sensitive business processes (SBPs) to improve the identification of crucial knowledge that is mobilized by these processes. Aiming at SBPs, a specific framework that helped previously to build a business process meta-model for knowledge identification is applied in a systematic manner in order to evaluate a number of currently available BPM formalisms under six perspectives, namely functional, organizational, behavioral, informational, intentional and knowledge perspectives. Furthermore, the result of the evaluation led us to justify the choice of the better one positioned nowadays, the standard BPMN 2.0. Besides, we have illustrated the practical applicability of this notation on a medical process in the context of the organization of protection of the motor disabled people of Sfax-Tunisia.

Keywords: Knowledge management · Sensitive business process · Business process modeling · Business process Meta-model

1 Introduction

The necessity to formalize and manage knowledge produced and used in organizations has rapidly increased in the last few years. In order to improve competitive advantage, such organizations have been increasingly conscious of the necessity to formalize and capitalize knowledge produced and mobilized by their business processes (BPs). According to this view, business process modeling (BPM) has become crucial concern for successful organizations to improve the identification, acquisition, storage, dissemination, sharing, creation and (re) use of their individual and organizational knowledge.

Considering the large amount of knowledge to be preserved and enhanced, modern organizations must first identify and model the SBPs which are likely to mobilize crucial knowledge on which it is necessary to capitalize. In fact, the more organization's BPs are sensitive, the more they can mobilize crucial knowledge. Few existing research on Knowledge Management (KM)-BPM focusing on the identification,

© Springer International Publishing AG 2017
B. Shishkov (Ed.): BMSD 2016, LNBIP 275, pp. 83–118, 2017.
DOI: 10.1007/978-3-319-57222-2_5

analysis and modeling of SBPs in order to localize and identify the crucial knowledge. We quote: the Global Analysis METHodology (GAMETH) proposed by Grundstein [1], the identifying crucial knowledge methodology [2] and the Sensitive Organization's Process Identification Methodology [3]. However, these methods do not explicitly and conveniently address the critical operation of «SBPs modeling». A SBP typically lacks a description and a representation that allow to explicit the rich semantics embedded into a SBP. So, the specification of a precise conceptualization, with a subjacent representation notation, that explicitly and adequately integrate the knowledge dimension within their actions and other relevant SBP aspects, is still an open issue. In fact, a SBP has its own characteristics that distinguish them from classical BPs. In fact, a SBP commonly mobilizes a high number of critical activities with very specific knowledge «crucial knowledge» (tacit and explicit). It presents a diversity of knowledge sources and possesses a high degree of dynamism in the objectives' change and high complexity.

Some conventional graphical BPM formalisms, include, amongst others, Event Driven Process Chain (EPC) [4], Business Process Modeling Notation (BPMN 2.0) [5], Unified Modeling Language (UML 2.0) activity diagram [6], Specification Language (PSL) [7], Process Business Process Modeling Ontology (BPMO) [8] and Role Activity Diagram (RAD) [9], have been adapted to allow the representation of the intrinsic elements of knowledge within BPs. But, these languages/notations do not include all the required features to describe a SBP. Moreover, some authors have attempted to develop process-oriented knowledge modeling approaches, where basic phenomenon is knowledge, including the Business Process Knowledge Method (BPKM) [10], DECOR [11], CommonKADS [12], Knowledge Transfer Agent (KTA) Modeling Method [13], PROMOTE [14], the work of Donadel [15], DCR Graphs [16], Knowledge Modeling Description Language (KMDL 2.2) [17, 18], GPO-WM [19], Oliveira's methodology [20], and the Notation for Knowledge-Intensive Processes (NKIP) [21], etc. However, none of these proposals, as shown in [22], adequately addresses all the relevant SBP elements.

In order to address existing limitations and improve the SBP representation, we proposed, in previous work [22, 23], the Business Process Meta-Model for Knowledge Identification (BPM4KI) BPM4KI comprises concepts from several perspectives that are crucial for a complete understanding, characterization and representation of a SBP, namely the functional perspective, the organizational perspective, the behavioral perspective, the informational perspective, the intentional perspective and the knowledge perspective. The generic meta-model we have developed is semantically rich and well founded on COOP, a core ontology of organization's processes proposed by Turki et al. [24] which is useful to characterize the concepts useful for the analysis and identification of SBPs. Furthermore, BPM4KI serves as a comprehensive evaluation framework of the expressiveness and adequacy of current widely-used BPM formalisms, to check their suitability to cover all the relevant elements of a SBP. Precisely, the (objective) evaluation facilitates selecting and justifying the most appropriate BPM formalism for the representation of SBP taking its semantic dimensions into account.

The overall goal of the present work is to carry out an evaluation of which BPM4KI elements are potentially supported by the above-mentioned language meta-models. Besides, it presents a practical example using the best evaluated formalism. Furthermore, it points alternatives for representing elements that not adequately addressed yet.

The remainder of the paper is structured as follows. Section 2 presents the core concepts that describe SBPs and related work about their modeling. Section 3 presents the main characteristics of current formalisms for BPM. Section 4 presents our proposed evaluation framework for assessing the expressiveness of the different BPM formalisms to select the most suitable for representing SBPs. Section 5 presents a particular case study in the domain of health care. Section 6 concludes the paper and underlines some future research topics.

2 Sensitive Business Processes

2.1 Main Characteristics of SBPs

According to Ben Hassen et al. [23], a SBP represents the core process of organization which constitutes the heart of the organization's activities. It is commonly mobilizes very specific knowledge «crucial knowledge» (i.e. the most valuable/important knowledge on which it is necessary to capitalize). It includes a high number of critical activities which mobilizes and produces different types of knowledge: (i) imperfect individual and collective knowledge (tacit and/or explicit) (i.e. missing, poorly mastered, incomplete, uncertain, etc.) which are necessary for solving critical determining problems; (ii) a great amount of heterogeneous knowledge recorded on diverse knowledge sources (dispersed and sometimes lacking accessibility); (iii) expertise and/or rare knowledge held by a very small number of experts; flexible knowledge owned by experts; (iv) very important tacit organizational knowledge (like competences, abilities and practical experiences).

Moreover, it contains activities that valorize the acquisition, storage, dissemination, sharing, and creation and (re) use of individual and organizational (tacit and explicit) knowledge, in the sense that it mobilizes a large diversity of knowledge sources consigning a great amount of very important heterogeneous knowledge. Its execution involves a large number of business domains/competencies (in terms of internal and external organization unit/agents operating in the BP), having distinct experience and expertise levels. Furthermore, it include a high number of organizational collaborative activities that mobilize, exchange, share and generate new individual and collective knowledge that is created by dynamic conversion of existing ones in the process in order to achieve organizational objectives. So, it depends on knowledge flows and transfer of data, information and knowledge objects between communicating process participants. Other typical characteristics of SBPs presented in Ben Hassen et al. [23] include: (i) A SBP is unstructured or semi-structured. Yet, a flexible process typically contains a very dynamic and unpredictable control-flow, comprising complex activities (individual and/or collective) that may frequently change over time or at design-and run-time. The process agents (e.g. experts) is often not able to predetermine the overall process structure in terms of the activities to be executed and their ordering, the data and knowledge sources to be exploited and the roles and resources required for process progression and completion. (ii) It is driven by constraints and rules. Indeed, process participants may be influenced by or may have to comply with constraints and rules that drive organizational actions performance and decision making. (iii) It possesses a high degree of dynamism in the objectives' change associated to it, essentially, in decision making context. The change of organizational objective leads to a new organizational distal intention (which is necessary to control the SBP) and influences experts' decision making. (iv) Its contribution to reach strategic objectives of the organization is very important. Also, their realization duration and cost are important.

According to above mentioned, representing and organizing the knowledge involved in SBPs is very complex, especially when applying traditional approaches. However, it is difficult to find out an approach/formalism that addresses all or at least most of these characteristics in the representation of a SBP model. Nevertheless, the Object Management Group [5] states that, in addition to underlining the concepts inherent to a domain, a notation enhances the clarity of the models and allows the ability of communicating the concepts uniformly. The selection of a suitable BPM formalism for representing SBP models is still an open issue, allowing the knowledge mobilized and generated by the BP instances to be located, identified, modeled, stored and reused. In this context, several BPM approaches and notations are found in literature as likely to represent SBP.

2.2 Analysis of Contemporary Approaches and Formalisms for SBP Representation

Although there is abundance of BPM formalisms and despite their diversity, only a few were applicable for SBP modeling. Some traditional workflows/BPM formalisms that are widely-followed in current research and practice scenarios (such as BPMN, EPC, UML AD), have been adapted to allow the representation of the intrinsic elements of knowledge within BPs. However, they do not fulfill all requirements that have to be considered for modeling SBPs. Table 1 presents a summary of the strengths and weakness of the conventional BPM formalisms with respect to characteristics/issues relevant to the SBP modeling. These formalisms were mainly analyzed from the following two points of view (1) possibilities to represent data, information and knowledge, and (2) possibilities to represent process logics. Both views are important for representation of static and dynamic aspects of SBP.

In addition, the literature shows a set of approaches and notations dedicated for the representation of processes with high knowledge intensity (KIP) [17], originate from the knowledge modeling context. In these processes, the principal success factor is adequate modeling of knowledge conversions. It is noteworthy that SBP shares many common characteristics with KIP approaches. In fact, KIPs are processes whose conduct and execution are heavily dependent on knowledge workers performing various interconnected knowledge intensive decision making tasks. KIPs are genuinely

Table 1. Analysis of Conventional BPM formalisms for SBP Modeling

Conventional workflow/BPM formalisms	Strengths
– Event-driven Process Chains (EPC) [4] – Business Process Modeling Notation (BPMN 2.0) [5] – UML 2.0 Activity Diagrams (UML AD) [6] – Process Specification Language (PSL) [7] – Process Business Process Modeling Ontology (BPMO) [8] – Role Activity Diagram (RAD) [9] – Petri net [25]	• Largely used in current research and practice scenarios in organizations • Suitable for process perspective representation (that display a defined, well structured, highly stable and (low) complex sequence of activities) • Support data and information inclusion into BP models • Identify (implicitly) certain issues related to knowledge flows, such as the information sources that are required, generated, or modified by an activity
	Weakness
	• Focus on the representation of "deterministic" BP, composed by a well- structured control flow among its activities, low uncertainty and complexity (that is the existence of few and pre-defined exceptions) • Not suited to deal with the flexibility, frequent exceptions, and common changes in SBP activities • Shortcomings concerning the inclusion and modeling of knowledge dimension (knowledge types, individual and collective dimension of knowledge/actions, knowledge conversion types, etc.) • Limited capabilities to explicitly and strictly separate data from information during BPM (information and data flow are modeled using the same modeling constructs) • The owner of data, information, and knowledge is not indicated • Less appropriate for BPM that involve the cooperation of multiple agents

knowledge, information and data centric and require substantial flexibility at design- and run-time. These approaches that focus on KM within the BP level have not been widely adopted by organizations and are still very incipient. Also, they have limited capabilities, in the sense that they do not conveniently include process perspective, as well as they do not provide an opportunity to clearly distinguish between data, information and knowledge.

The CommonKADS [12] approach focuses on knowledge representation. Various stages of modeling attempt to establish a structured approach so that knowledge can be managed with the support of technical and engineering tools. Three basic points characterize these demands: the details of the skills involved in process execution, the representation of the processes through artifacts and semantic analysis, and the opportunities for improvement regarding the process and use of knowledge.

The BPKM- Business Process Knowledge Method [10] provides a methodological guidance for the implementation of BP-oriented KM. It presents a meta-model for integrating BPM aspects with KM. This meta-model transcribes the four perspectives of a workflow: task, organizational, logical and data. It was extended to include KM tasks that support BPs represented by the elements: knowledge management task, knowledge object and knowledge archive.

Two other approaches of knowledge representation are the DECOR approach [11] and the Knowledge Transfer Agent (KTA) Modeling Method [13]. The first describes how to create knowledge transferring models. The method consists of modeling and analyzing in three distinct levels of detail. The DECOR Project delivers context-sensitive organizational knowledge and has its focus in representing processes knowledge across diagrams embedded in organizational memory. It aims to structure the BP, the dynamic context, contextual information and the representations of memories embedded in the production process.

In the method proposed by Donadel [15] aims to support the management of knowledge resources related to BPs. The organizational value chain is mapped and the knowledge aspects that may influence the organizational processes are represented. The aforesaid knowledge oriented approaches do not explicitly differentiate between tacit and explicit which is relevant in SBPs due to, for instance, the high degree of tacit knowledge developed and exchanged among agents through inter-organizational collaboration. And most of them do not provide special attention to the graphical notation for BP representation. Furthermore, knowledge is modeled using another specific knowledge modeling notations (e.g., KMDL, GPO-WM, Oliveira) and only few of them include process perspective (e.g., PROMOTE, RAD)).

The Knowledge Modeling Description Language (KMDL) [17, 18] formalizes KIPs with a focus on certain knowledge-specific characteristics in order to identify process improvements in these processes. It represents both tacit and explicit knowledge of the process. Thus, the different possibilities of knowledge conversion can be modeled and the flow of knowledge between actors is depicted. However, this notation does not distinguish between data and information, and does not address the representation of artefacts and dynamic aspects of BP and modeling agents. Besides, it is hard to understand and to apply for the purpose of facilitating the involvement of modeling participants.

The method for integration of KM into BPs (GPO-WM) [19] describes and evaluates the current state of handling core knowledge domains, to gather improvement ideas for systematic knowledge handling and to integrate selected KM methods and tools into existing BPs. The notation does not allow the modeling of knowledge conversions. The abovementioned proposals focus on storing and sharing knowledge. Thus, they lack the ability to model in an adequate manner the decisions, actions and measures, which are causing a sequence of processes. Most of these methods are convenient only for knowledge management experts and require additional training for non-experts.

The method for integrated modeling of BPs and knowledge flow based on a Role Activity diagram (RAD) [9] provides integration of BPs and knowledge flow and helps

KM build on existing process management efforts. This method does not differentiate between tacit and explicit knowledge and does not present different types of knowledge conversion that are relevant in SBP. Also, it does not present and separate data and information from knowledge.

Supulniece et al. [26] argued an extension of BP models with the knowledge dimension in order to take advantage of some opportunities such as identifying, planning and managing required knowledge for the role that participates in a particular activity; evaluate the amount of lost knowledge if a person would leave the organization; improve understanding about the knowledge usefulness, validity and relevance for particular activities; enable competence requirements management and proactive training. They extended BPMN incorporating concepts defined by KMDL [17], where three different objects: knowledge objects, information objects and data objects were used. However, the proposed approach does not present knowledge flow between process participants; it lacks information about the knowledge structure; it does not integrate and separate the different knowledge types (like experience, basic knowledge, general knowledge) and it does not explicitly represent the tacit knowledge that is owned by a particular person.

Recently, Netto et al. [21] proposed KIPN, a notation for building KIPs graphical model that promotes the cognitively-effective understanding of this process. KIPN covers all characteristics defined by the knowledge-intensive processes ontology (KIPO) [27]. It comprises a set of diagrams to represent the main dimensions within a KIP: the KIP, socialization, decision and good diagrams. In KIPN, activities are detailed through socializations. The agents interact and collaborate, contributing to the creation and acquisition of knowledge. Agents' contribution is represented by innovation, intention, belief, desire, feeling, experience and mental image elements, that are difficult to be predicted and then modeled. The notation is able represent tacit knowledge through informal exchange and mental image elements, but it still does not capture explicitly the knowledge conversion. Moreover, NKIP is very incipient, hard to understand, not yet used and applicable for KIP modeling in current research and practice scenarios and not adopted by any available modeling tools.

Despite it mobilizes crucial knowledge within an organization and their key role for organizational KM, existing BPM approaches/notations have shortcomings concerning their ability to explicitly incorporate the knowledge dimension within BPs models as well as relevant issues at the intersection of KM and BPM. None of those proposals conveniently includes or addresses all or at least most of the SBPs important characteristics presented previously (critical activities (individual and/or collective), intensive acquisition, sharing, storage and (re)use of knowledge in challenging activities, large number of agents (external and internal) who have various business domains and different knowledge levels, high degree of tacit knowledge mobilized and exchanged among many experts, diversity of information and knowledge sources involved, high degree of collaboration (intra/inter-organizational) among agents/experts, dynamic conversion of knowledge, flexibility and dynamic aspects, deliberate actions, the influence of (distal) intentions in achieving objective and decision making, etc.). This leads to ambiguity and misunderstanding of the developed SBPs models.

2.3 SBPs Specification: A Business Process Meta-Model for Knowledge Identification Based on Core Ontology

Based on the limitations of the approaches and formalisms described in the previous section, we have proposed, in previous research [22], a semantically rich conceptualization for describing a SBP organized in a meta-model, the Business Process Meta-model for Knowledge Identification (BPM4KI), which integrates all aforementioned perspectives. This meta-model intends to develop a rich and expressive graphical representation of SBPs in order to improve the localization and identification of crucial knowledge. BPM4KI is a well-founded meta-model whose concepts and relationships are semantically enriched by the core ontology organization's processes (COOP) [24]. BPM4KI covers all relevant aspects of BPM and KM within a SBP, and is composed by six perspectives:

- **Functional Perspective**, represents the BP elements which are being performed. The main concept that reflects this dimension is *Action*. It includes: *Individual Action, Collective Action, Action of Organization, Inter Organizational Action, Organizational Action, Organizational Individual Action, Task, Organizational Unit Action, Organizational Sub Process, Organizational Critical Activity, Organizational Intensive Activity* and *Organizational Collaborative Activity*.
- **Organizational Perspective**, represents the different participants (the organizational resources) invoked in the execution of process elements as well as their affiliation. It display the process flows between different organizations and participants involved. The basic element of this perspective is *Agentive Entity* and includes: *Collective, Organization, Informal Group, Organization Unit, Human, Expert, Internal Actor* and *External Actor*.
- **Behavioural perspective**, represents the concepts required to demonstrate the flows of activities and information, coordination between different participants as well as concepts that effect, trigger or control flows of activities (such as, pre-conditions, post-conditions, triggers, constraints, business rules, etc.). The basic and generic concepts of this perspective are *Control Flow, Flow Node, Control Node, Connecting Object, Association, Message Flow, Contingency, Conditional Control Flow* and *Non Conditional Control Flow*.
- **Informational perspective**, describes the informational entities (such as data, artefacts, products and objects) which are generated, consumed, or exchanged within a process or an activity. It also includes both their structure and the relationships among them. The following concepts are related to this dimension: *Resource, Material Resource* (like informational and software resources), *Physical Knowledge Support, Event, Contingency, Input Object* (like data and information), *Output Object* (as data, information, services and results) and *Collaboration Protocol*.
- **Intentional perspective**, provides an overview perspective of the process and captures important BP context information. It describes major BP characteristics and addresses the intentional information (such as objective, strategies, quality characteristics, metrics, measurement units, the deliverables, the process type and the customer), in order to ensure the BP flexibility. It comprises: *Intention,*

Objective, Distal Intention, Collective Intention, Collective Distal Intention, Organizational Distal Intention, Objective, Individual Objective, Collective Objective, Organizational Objective, Strategic Objective, Operational Objective, Deliberate Action, Culminated Process, Output Object (deliverables), *Control Object* (e.g., performance measures, constraints, business rules, etc.), *Client, Sensitive Business Process, Knowledge Intensive Process, Inter Organizational Process, Internal Process, External Process, Partial External Process, Inter Fonctional Process, Core Process, Management Process, Strategic Process, Operational Process,* etc. (which are some process types).

- **Knowledge perspective**, provides an overview perspective of the organizational and individual knowledge mobilized and created by an BP/organization as well as the knowledge flow proceeding within and between BPs/organizations. It addresses all relevant aspects related to KM (collection, organization, storage, transfer, sharing, creation and reuse among process participants). This vantage presents: *Knowledge* (as an *Immaterial Resource*), *Tacit Knowledge, Individual Tacit Knowledge, Collective Tacit Knowledge, Organizational Tacit Knowledge Explicit Knowledge, Individual Explicit Knowledge, Collective Explicit Knowledge, Organizational Explicit Knowledge, Expert, Physical Knowledge Support* and *Knowledge Flow*.

It should be noted that some concepts are shared by different perspectives. For instance, *Collaborative Organizational Activity* and *Critical Organizational Activity* belong to all perspectives. Also, the concept *Physical Knowledge Support* belongs to the knowledge and informational perspectives.

Because of space limitation, we presents in Table 2 the definition of some core BPM4KI concepts from several perspectives described above.

Once modeled, the SBPs can be graphically represented, using an appropriate BPM formalism, in order to localize the knowledge that is mobilized and created by these processes. In fact, as a meta-model, BPM4KI defines the concepts and relationships in a SBP; nevertheless, it does not provide a specific graphical notation for them. However, Moody [32] argues that visual notations are effective because they provide powerful resources for the human visual system and are transmitted in a more concise and precise manner than ordinary text based language. The representation of a domain has as its main goal the understanding of its underlying concepts, and of how these concepts are interrelated. Although BPM4KI does not address the problem of representing this kind of process graphically, it opens a way to explore the potential of traditional BPM formalisms as well as the usage of the specific process-oriented knowledge modeling/KIP approaches for it.

In the following, we discuss the usage of BPM4KI concepts as a basis to model SBPs graphically.

Table 2. Core BPM4KI concepts definitions.

BPM perspectives	Concepts	Definition
Functional perspective *What BP elements are being performed?*	Individual Action	An Action that performed (carried out) by a single individual/person [28].
	Collective Action	A group of several individual actions combining their effects [28]. It may concern also actions that can be carried out collectively by the individuals making up the collective. It is controlled by a Collective Intention and has for proper part at least two Individual Actions contributing to it [28].
	Organizational Unit Action	An Action performed by an Organization Unit and which contribute to an Action of Organization (it is therefore an Organizational Action).
	Critical Organizational Activity	An Organizational Action that mobilizes and produces different types of knowledge (which may be crucial): (i) imperfect individual and collective knowledge (tacit and/or explicit) (i.e. missing, poorly mastered, incomplete, uncertain, etc.) which are necessary for solving critical determining problems; (ii) a great amount of heterogeneous knowledge recorded on diverse knowledge sources (dispersed and sometimes lacking accessibility); (iii) expertise and/or rare knowledge held by a very small number of experts; (v) flexible knowledge owned by experts; (iv) very important tacit organizational knowledge (like competences, abilities and practical experiences). The critical activity may threaten the SBP due to dysfunctions and constraints (internal or external) which affect it and generate determining problems [1].
	Collaborative Organizational Activity	A collective action carried out collectively by the individuals making up the Collective (whose the agent is at least two humans, organizational units or organizations) (internal or external to an organization), while respecting a collaboration protocol. In order to achieve a collective objective intentionally defined, this organizational activity mobilizes, exchanges, shares information and knowledge and generates/acquires new collective knowledge) through a number of interactions (among process agents/experts). It may correspond to any of the knowledge conversion types (such as

(*continued*)

Table 2. (*continued*)

BPM perspectives	Concepts	Definition
		internalization, externalization, combination and socialization). It require complex, rapid decisions among multiple possible strategies.
Organizational perspective *Where and by whom (which agents) BP elements are performed?*	Agentive Entity	An Intentional Agent, an entity which has a capacity to carry out (and therefore to repeat) Actions (in particular deliberate actions). An Agentive Entity can be an Human, an Informal Group, or an Organization, internal or external to an Organization. It can be specified in the form of a Collective, Internal Actor or External Actor.
	Collective	A group of humans unified by a joint intention to form a group capable of acting [28]. (Any Collective Action has for agent a Collective). It can be specified in the form of an Informal Group or an Organization (and their Organization Units).
	Organizational Unit	Any recognized association of people in the context of the enterprise. In a hierarchical structure, it may be the corporation, a division, a department, a group, a team, etc. [29]. Formally, an Organizational Unit is an Organization which is a unit of an Organization and which is managed by (and dependent on) an encompassing organization. It can be internal or external to an organization.
	Expert	An Experiencer (which is an Agentive Entity) who bears a Capacity To Perform a type of Action (e.g. a critical organizational activity) with high levels of experience, expertise, performance, creativity and innovation [30].
Behavioural perspective *When and how BP elements are performed? How the several execution of a BP vary?*	Control Flow	Flow that control the logical sequence of elements (i.e., Organizational Actions) to be executed in Business Process
	Connecting Object	The flow objects can be connected to each other or other information by four types of Connecting Objects: Sequence Flows, Message Flows, Associations and Data Associations [5].
	Sequence Flow	A Sequence Flow is used to show the order of Flow Elements in a Business Process. Each Sequence Flow has only one source and only one target. The source and target must be from the set of the following Flow Elements: Events (Start, Intermediate, and End), Activities (Task and Sub-Process; for Processes) and Gateways [5].

(*continued*)

Table 2. (*continued*)

BPM perspectives	Concepts	Definition
	Control Node	Gateways are used to control how the Process flows through Sequence Flows interact as they converge and diverge within a Process. (The Gateway controls the flow of both diverging and converging Sequence Flows). That is, a single Gateway could have multiple input and multiple output flows. Gateways can define all the types of Business Process Sequence Flow behavior: Decisions/branching (exclusive, inclusive, parallel and complex), merging, forking, and joining [5].
Informational perspective *What informational entities are generated/exchanged?*	Resource	An entity which has a capacity to enable actions (mobilizable for action) [28].
	Material Resource	Anything of material value or usefulness that is owned by a person or company [28]. It has actual physical existence (such as documentary, informational, material and software resources, etc.).
	Input Object	The Input Objects indicate what the Business Process or Organizational Activity intervene on. They are the elements that cause their realization (such as materials, data object or information object).
	Output Object	The Output indicates what the process or activity produce during or as a result of execution (like data output, information output, services, results or products). Information object and data object form the basis for knowledge distribution, transfer and generation.
	Contingency	An external and unpredictable event that influences the BP execution. It is responsible for determining the execution of unforeseen activities [27].
	Collaboration Protocol	A set of arrangements which govern the exchanges between the actors to achieve a collaborative organizational activity and reach a common objective [31]
Intentional perspective *What are the BP characteristics* *Why/How are decision taken in a BP*	Intention	A complex process whose content includes a representation of action, thus allowing an agent to be directed to that action (the deliberative state of agent) [24, 28].

(*continued*)

Table 2. (*continued*)

BPM perspectives	Concepts	Definition
	Distal Intention	An intention which plans the action (before its initiation) and then rationally controls to guide it and determine its success. This is a process whose content has an objective and a plan. A Distal Intention has for content an Objective. Formally, every Action of Collective is controlled by a Collective Distal Intention.
	Objective, Individual Objective, Collective Objective	An Objective is an Intentional description of the results to be achieved by the completion of the process. Depending on whether the content of a Collective Distal Intention or an Individual Distal Intention, an Objective can be either an Individual Objective or a Collective Objective (valid for an organization).
	Culminated Process	A Business Process is more precisely a Culminated Process which, when successfully carried out, culminates in a Result which is useful for a Client [24]. Therefore, it provide a result which have a value. (The result represents the deliverables which are either services or products).
	Sensitive Business Process	Represents the core process of organization which constitutes the heart of the organization's activities. It is commonly mobilizes a high number of critical activities with very specific knowledge «crucial knowledge» (tacit and explicit). It presents a diversity of knowledge sources and possesses a high degree of dynamism in the objectives' change and high complexity.
	External Process	A Business Process all parts of which have for agent (performed by) Agentive Entities which are neither affiliated to nor a unit of the Organization.
	Client	An Agentive Entity which uses the service of another Agentive Entity (the provider) (the client represents the agent benefiting from the result of the process). It can be either internal or external to the Organization.

(*continued*)

Table 2. (*continued*)

BPM perspectives	Concepts	Definition
Knowledge perspective *Which, how and where knowledge and* *knowledge sources are involved among the* *different activities?*	Knowledge	A fluid mix of framed experiences, values, contextual information, and expert insights that provides a framework for evaluating and incorporating new experiences and information. The knowledge is derived and is applied in people's minds. (Note that knowledge is useful for interpreting information while information is useful for transferring knowledge).
	Individual knowledge	Combination of individual's own knowledge, experience and skills. This knowledge is borne by an Individual (a Human) and includes, besides the intellectual capacity, the vision that every individual holds of the organization to which he/she is affiliated, as well as the explicit knowledge in the form of personal notes.
	Collective knowledge	Knowledge which is borne by a Collective. It's a knowledge sharable by several Agentive Entities. Their coverage can be global, or partial which bound to a structure.
	Organizational knowledge	Collective knowledge which is borne by an organization. A sum of individuals' knowledge which integrates a firm's experiences and firm-specific knowledge, and already existing in organizational systems, organizational routines, documents, decision-making procedures, practices, products, rules, and culture.
	Tacit Knowledge	Is personal and context specific knowledge, rooted in action, procedures, commitment, values and emotions. It consists of individual skills, experience, mental models, beliefs and perspectives which is difficult to be formalize, articulate, communicated, explained and shared by the persons who possess it. Explicitable or non-explicitable, it is acquired by sharing experiences, by observation and imitation and it is often transmitted by implicit collective apprenticeship or by a master–apprentice relationship. They are located in people's minds.
	Individual Tacit Knowledge	A (highly) personal implicit knowledge held by a one Expert, which resides in individual skills, mental models, talents, innate or acquired experiences and competencies, abilities, trades secrets, professional knack,

(*continued*)

Table 2. (*continued*)

BPM perspectives	Concepts	Definition
		insight, wisdom, shared behaviors (traditions, communities of practice, collusion), etc. It is often transferable in action, through apprenticeship/companionship. Their sharing degree is very low.
	Collective Tacit Knowledge	Knowledge held by (and shared by) at least two experts (which constitute a Collective), sharing a specific expertise domain, and mobilized through a collective action. It rooted in routines and embedded in their practices and decision choices. It is most often transmitted orally in an implicit manner, which may be shared and exchanged through direct interaction and communication with others, practice, observation, meetings, constructive discussions, collective thinking, learning, etc.). The sharing degree is low (it is restricted to collaboration experts communities working on a given problem).
	Explicit Knowledge	is formal, codified, articulated in writing/numbers, and can be relatively easily verbalized, communicated, transmitted (in a formal language) and stored (unrelated to people). In organizations, it often becomes embedded and represented, not only in documents or knowledge repositories (data and knowledge bases), but also in organizational routines, processes, practices, norms, etc.
	Physical Knowledge Support	A Material Resource (informational resource), having "source of knowledge information" interpreted and mobilized by the agents during the execution of their activities (these supports transmit not only information, but also significance). Available Knowledge (either Explicit Knowledge or External Knowledge) is borne by one or more Physical Knowledge Supports (e.g. documents, computer system, etc.) enabling their capitalization, formalization, storage, and sharing among stakeholders of the organization.
	Knowledge Flow	Represents the dynamics of Knowledge, i.e., all of organization, exchange, conversion, transfer, sharing, development and usage of Knowledge among the different sources of knowledge, agentive entities and among BP activities.

3 An Overview of the BPM Formalisms for SBP Representation

In this section, we describe the BPM formalisms which have been chosen for evaluation. Some are process oriented (UML AD, eEPC and BPMN 2.0) and some are knowledge oriented (PROMOTE, KMDL 2.2 and Oliveira). They represent the most frequently studied BPM formalisms in scientific/professional literature and practice scenarios.

Table 3. Incurrence context, goal domain and extent of concepts of BPM formalisms.

Incurrence context/Origin	BPM formalism	Goal domain/Primary purpose	Extent of concepts/Perceptual objects
(Software-) System modeling	UML-AD	Modeling and description of BPs and dynamic behavior (flows) in software systems	Activity, activity nodes, action, object node, control nodes, initial node, activity final node, flow final node, decision node, merge node, fork node, join node, activity partition/swimlane
BP modeling, analyzing, and redesigning	eEPC	Documentation and representation of BPs (with the goal to be easily understood and used by business people)	Functions, events, connectors/logical operators (AND, XOR and OR), information objects (enquiry data, delivery position), service objects (deliverables), application system and organization units, organizational roles
	BPMN 2.0	Document, model and implement BPs (BPMN can be used for many purposes, from high-level descriptive modeling to detailed modeling intended for process execution)	Flow objects (activities, events, gateways), data (data objects, data inputs, data outputs, data store, messages), connecting objects (sequence flows, message flows, data associations, data input associations, data output associations), swimlanes (pools, lanes), artifacts (associations, group, text

(continued)

Table 3. (*continued*)

Incurrence context/Origin	BPM formalism	Goal domain/Primary purpose	Extent of concepts/Perceptual objects
			annotations), resources, participants, collaborations, choreographies, conversations
(Process-oriented) Knowledge modeling	PROMPOTE	Model, analyze, assess and optimize knowledge intensive business processes	Business processes, roles, tasks, documents, knowledge flows
	KMDL 2.2		Business processes, roles, persons, tasks, information systems, artifacts, task requirements, knowledge conversions, information objects, knowledge objects, knowledge descriptor
	Oliveira		Business processes, agents, tasks, business rules, communicative interaction, requirements, knowledge conversions, information objects, knowledge objects, knowledge flows

3.1 UML 2.0 Activity Diagram

The UML is a graphical notation used in object-oriented software development for creating visual models. The Activity Diagram [6], one of UML behavioral diagrams, is particularly suitable for software systems processes' representation (which describes the sequence of activities and control flows). In UML 2.0, AD can represent the interaction overview of e-business. UML AD is a semi-formal language with the following basic graphical notations [6]: initial node and activity final node, activity, flow/edge, fork and join, decision and merge, partition/swimlane. Partition/swimlane is normally used to indicate who/what is performing the activities, which can specify the organizational perspective. The rest notations can represent the operational/functional and control perspectives. No particular notations are provided for the phenomena associated with data in UML AD. However, it allows to use texts linked to the flows and activities to indicate condition, object or message passed in the process. UML Activity Diagram is often asked to be combined with other UML diagrams to model multiple process perspectives. For example, UML Use Case Diagram can capture loose collections of related activities at the high level, which might provide a view of the structural perspective of processes.

3.2 Extended Event Driven Process Chain

EPC [32] is a semi-formal graphical BP language for modeling, analyzing, and redesigning BPs. EPC describes processes on the level of their business logic, and intends to be easily understood and used by business people [33]. A claimed major strength of EPC notation is its simplicity and ease of understanding [34]. EPC process models are event-driven, i.e. state-based, which means that the main focus for a process model is the representation of processes' states and their transition, rather than the interaction and communication among organizations. Processes modeled with EPC depict only the internals of an organization [34]. The EPC is based on the concepts of stochastic networks and Petri nets [25]. The core EPC elements are formed by few constructs (function, event, OR-connector, XOR-connector, AND connector, and control flow), which are understood as enough for specification and documentation of process models. EPC emphases more on the operational/functional and control perspectives than data transaction perspective.

The basic version of EPC was supplemented by other constructs (organizational unit, position, data, system, process link, and relation), resulting in the extended EPC (eEPC) [35], intended to supplement process models with organizational structure and data flow. The eEPC includes organizational units to represent roles or persons, information or resource object that can be seen as input or output to functions, and process path to describe hierarchies of EPC processes.

3.3 Business Process Modeling Notation

BPMN 2.0 [5] is a new standard of modeling BPs and Web service processes. BPMN is a semi-formal modeling language providing notations understandable by all business stakeholders. BPMN is one of the most recent BPMLs, so it is grounded on the experience of earlier process modeling languages, which ontologically makes it one of the most complete BPMLs [36, 37]. BPMN can be used within many methodologies and for many purposes, from high-level descriptive modeling to detailed modeling intended for process execution. The Object Management Group (OMG) made the BPMN 2.0 version [5] more technical and more IT oriented, so besides the graphical notation, BPMN encompasses a level of detail regarding modeling constructs, which enables BPEL code generation. So, by supporting the details of graphical object's properties, BPMN offers a standardized bridge for the gap between the BP design and process implementation. BPMN has a semantically rich graphical notation. Besides the regular constructs for activities' control flow behavior, BPMN offers a visual representation for abnormal flows, such as fault handling, escalation handling, and compensation handling. BPMN also supports data flow and interaction behavior. BPMN is considered amenable for being used in processes' elicitation within companies, as well as representation of processes' interactions among organizations [34].

3.4 PROMOTE

PROMOTE (Process-oriented methods and tools for knowledge management) [14] integrates strategic planning with the evaluation of KM and BP management and defines KM requirements on the basis of business needs [39]. The intended scope of the approach covers the analysis, the modeling, and the execution of knowledge-intensive processes. It extends the more general method of BP management systems including strategic decision, reengineering and resource allocation, and workflow and performance evaluation [39]. The additional KM related steps are creating awareness for enterprise knowledge, discover knowledge processes, create operational knowledge processes and organizational memory, and evaluate enterprise knowledge. The second element, discovering knowledge processes, deals with capturing knowledge-intensive business processes, hi the underlying reengineering stage of the BPMS method, process knowledge is getting documented. It consists of the sequence of activities and its related employees, organizational units, necessary data, application systems, and resources. The PROMOTE method now extends this process knowledge to additionally capture functional knowledge, consisting of the identification of knowledge-intensive activities, the description of relevant knowledge flows and the identification of knowledge flows between persons and processes. Although this approach introduces a systematic orientation for the necessary elements to be captured in knowledge-intensive business processes, a detailed description of how to elicit these additional items in a KM project and a discussion of the actual pitfalls in the practical implementation would be beneficial.

3.5 Knowledge Modeling and Description Language

KMDL is a semi-formal modeling notation for the detection, visualization, analysis and evaluation of BPs and knowledge flows [17]. The KMDL can be used to formalize knowledge intensive processes (KIPs) with a focus on certain knowledge-specific characteristics. This notation represents both tacit and explicit knowledge of the process, also the different types of knowledge conversion (the creation, use and necessity of knowledge along common BPs). Thereby, it identifies existing and utilized information as well as knowledge of individual participants and knowledge of the entire company. It helps to identify improvements in these processes, but it is unable to visualize the decisions, actions and measures which is causing the sequence of the process in an adequate manner. The current KMDL 2.2 [18] provides three perspectives onto the sequence of actions: (a) *process view* shows the BP as an execution of single tasks. presents only the sequence of activities and actors (IS, person, or group), similarly to high-level process representation in other business process modeling notations; (b) *activity view* models particular activity in detail if this is a knowledge intensive activity. It is possible to demonstrate the knowledge conversions and identify requirements for successful activity fulfillment; (c) *communication-based view* shows general communication channels, like conversation model in BPMN notation.

3.6   Oliveira's Methodology

The Oliveira's methodology [20] is an extension of Eriksson et al. [40] for BPM that is composed of diagrams representing a hierarchy of models. It uses constructs adapted from KMDL to model BPs, considering KM aspects.

The development context and primary purpose of the above mentioned formalisms is to provide the first comparative overview of their illustration spectrum of perceptual objects (see Table 2).

4   A Multi-perspective Evaluation Framework for Selecting SBP Modeling Formalism

Based on the potential of BPM4KI to portray the essential features of SBP, this section presents a comparative analysis of different BPM formalisms to represent SBPs. Precisely, in this research work, BPM4KI acts as a multidimensional evaluation framework for assessing the suitability of six selected BPM formalisms to cover all or at least most relevant elements of a SBP. We consider guiding and justifying the choice of the most suitable formalism for SBPs representation to characterize and improve the knowledge localization.

Before we present our evaluation framework for SBP representation, we will briefly refer to some related work about BPM languages (i.e. comparison and analysis) available in the field of meta-modeling and ontology. Many frameworks [40–43] have been proposed for evaluating the suitability of some BPM languages for specific purpose, according to generic meta-models. Most of them only focus on some aspects of BPM languages. Besides, the BWW (Bunge-Wand-Weber) ontological framework [44] has been widely used for assessing the ontological completeness and clarity of BPM languages, include [45–48]. Furthermore, several works addressing the integration of KM into BPs, incorporating the knowledge into BP models. França et al. [27] proposed KIPO, a formal meta-model/ontology that highlights the key concepts and relationships characterizing KIPs and used it as a reference for evaluating the adequacy of some existing BPM languages to represent each concept. However, this meta-model is not well adapted to represent SBPs. Sultanow et al. [49] created a systematic comparison of thirteen selected methods based on a multidimensional framework to summarize the differences, also the most suitable situation for using each method. However, this framework do not consistently support SBP model requirements and concepts. Therefore, considering existing research in the KM-BPM domain, the knowledge dimension (i.e. the knowledge required to perform activities, the knowledge created as a result of BP activities, the sources of knowledge and their localization, the explicit knowledge, the tacit knowledge, individual and collective dimension of knowledge/activities, the knowledge flows between sources and activities, the different opportunities of knowledge conversion, etc.) needed for BPM is not explicitly represented, integrated and implemented in BP meta-models.

Hence, a comprehensive evaluation framework of the representational capabilities of current BPM formalisms for SBPs is missing. For discussion purposes, in this section, we take the constructs from BPM4KI as a relevant set of elements that are required to precisely represent a SBP, and evaluated some existing formalisms, which are based on different fields, to verify their suitability to cover and represent each concept. The multi-dimensional evaluation provides not only a useful framework to summarize the advantages and limitations of each formalism, but also select the most suitable positioned nowadays for SBP modeling, in order to localize the knowledge mobilized and created by these processes, which may be crucial. The evaluated representation languages were UML AD, BPMN 2.0, eEPC (which are adopted by many available modeling tools in current organizations), PROMOTE, KMDL 2.2 and Oliveira's methodology. It should be noted that the evaluation of the six BPM formalisms provides a good starting point that can be easily extended with both further BPM formalisms and supporting tools.

4.1   Evaluation Method

The evaluation is carried out from each of the six perspectives making up the BPM4KI meta-model (which aspects of a SBP are covered). It was performed by three experts, who were responsible for observing how well the BPM4KI concepts could be represented in each language. The experts individually evaluated the correlation between formalism elements and meta-model concepts, considering its definitions and relationships.

An overview of the evaluation results can be found in the Tables 3, 4, 5, 6, 7, and 8. The rows represent the element of the meta-model. The columns represent the different BPM formalisms. The evaluation shows one assessment criterion with two possible symbols addressing one element of a BPM formalism. The assessment criterion consists of two positions, separated by a slash. The first symbol (position) illustrates if a certain BPM formalism offers a specific graphical notation element to explicitly symbolize a certain element of the generic BPM4KI meta-model. The second position shows, if the BPM formalism provides a concept that somehow allows describing this meta-model element with a workaround. The symbol "+" characterizes a success, otherwise it is denoted with a "−". So, our evaluation scale ranges from comprehensively fulfilled (depicted by +/+), partially fulfilled (−/+) to not fulfilled (−/−).

4.2   Result of Evaluation

The results of the comparative analysis conducted in this section underline that none of the studied formalisms fulfills all SBP modeling requirements. Generally, the functional and the behavioural perspectives are very well represented in all BPM formalisms, while the organizational and informational perspectives are only partly supported. But a lack of the models is that the knowledge and intentional perspectives are not explicitly supported. In fact, *Collective Distal Intention*, *Collective Objective*, *Individual Tacit Knowledge*, *Collective Tacit Knowledge*, *Individual Explicit Knowledge*, *Collective Explicit Knowledge* are not addressed at all, in any of the formalisms.

From the functional perspective (Table 4) the formalisms are compared according to the visibility of BP hierarchies, that is, for organizational action/activity, organizational unit action (including organizational sub process) and organizational individual action/ task. With regard to the formalism testing, the comparison with functional perspective is simple: all BPM formalisms are able to illustrate organizational activities as well as dividable organizational sub-processes. It should be observed that the

Table 4. Evaluation of BPM formalisms in terms of coverage of the functional perspective.

BPM4KI concepts	BPM formalisms					
	UML AD	eEPC	BPMN 2.0	PROMOTE	Oliveira	KMDL 2.2
Individual Action	+/+	+/+	+/+	+/+	+/+	+/+
Collective Action	−/+	−/+	+/+	−/+	−/+	−/+
Action of Organization	−/+	−/+	+/+	−/+	−/+	−/+
Inter Organizational Action	−/−	−/−	−/+	−/−	−/−	−/−
Organizational Action/Activity	−/+	−/+	+/+	−/+	−/+	−/+
Organizational Individual Action	+/+	+/+	+/+	+/+	+/+	+/+
Task	+/+	−/+	+/+	+/+	+/+	+/+
Organizational Unit Action	+/+	−/+	+/+	−/+	−/−	−/−
Organizational Sub Process	+/+	−/+	+/+	−/+	−/−	−/−
Organizational Critical Activity	−/+	−/+	−/+	−/+	−/+	−/+
Organizational Intensive Activity	−/+	−/+	−/+	−/−	−/+	+/+
Organizational Collaborative Activity	−/+	−/+	−/+	−/+	−/−	−/−
Functional Perspective Coverage	16/24	13/24	20/24	13/24	11/24	12/24

Coverage Legend: assigned symbols in each concept/dimension converted to values: Notation/Concept available/possible to represent (+/+, 2); Notation/Concept not available/possible to represent (−/+, 1); Notation/Concept not available/not possible to represent (−/−, 0)

description of one model element can vary from that of the other formalism. For example, the elements of BP hierarchies can be labeled as either function, sub-function or elemental function in eEPC [35]. However, the defined concepts-actions specification defined by the selected list of formalisms do not explicitly take into account the individual/collective dimension of the actions. However, taking into consideration such a dimension is very important in our research context, given that we are interested in the localization of knowledge mobilized to realize the BP. This knowledge taken in the action may be either individual or collective/organizational (tacit or explicit).

Table 5. BPM formalisms comparison out of the organizational perspective

BPM4KI concepts	BPM formalisms					
	UML AD	eEPC	BPMN 2.0	PROMOTE	Oliveira	KMDL 2.2
Agentive Entity	−/+	−/+	−/+	−/+	−/+	−/+
Collective	−/+	−/+	+/+	−/+	−/+	−/+
Organization	−/+	−/+	+/+	−/+	−/+	−/+
Organizational Unit	−/+	+/+	−/+	+/+	−/+	−/+
Informal Group	−/+	−/+	−/+	−/+	−/+	−/+
Expert	−/+	−/+	−/+	−/+	−/+	−/+
Internal Actor	+/+	+/+	+/+	−/+	−/+	−/+
External Actor	+/+	−/−	+/+	−/−	−/−	−/−
Organizational Perspective Coverage	10/16	9/16	12/16	8/16	7/16	7/16

As Table 5 demonstrates, the BPM formalisms partially provide the organizational perspective. No of them represents collective, organization, informal group and expert in an explicit concepts and only UML AD and BPM 2.0 show whether a role belongs to the organization or it is external. A lot of BPM formalisms utilize one concept to represent all types of entities agentives (e.g. UML AD, BPMN and KMDL) and do not distinguish between the different types. This differentiation could be very helpful for BPM formalisms with a focus on knowledge localization in BP. Indeed, only PROMOTE, Oliveira and KMDL, separate persons from their roles. This separation is very important also from the view of KM because knowledge is tied to individuals. PROMOTE has a model element for the organization units, with which the working environment or even the entire organization is able to be described hierarchically or systematically. In KMDL, organization unites can be presented with element labels like «team» or «uncertain person». All formalisms make it possible to group model elements together. With PROMOTE, for example, it is possible to group under participants and resources via so-called Swim lanes; similarly, with KMDL, it is possible to group under process steps with the related element «process step».

Also, the behavioural perspective is very well represented (Table 6). Moreover, the control flow as well as the control nodes are supported. However, no formalism is able to present exclusive event based decision and parallel event based decision, except

Table 6. BPM formalisms comparison out of the behavioural perspective.

BPM4KI concepts	BPM formalisms					
	UML AD	eEPC	BPMN 2.0	PROMOTE	Oliveira	KMDL 2.2
Control Flow	−/+	+/+	+/+	−/+	−/+	−/+
Connecting Object	−/+	−/+	+/+	−/−	−/−	−/−
Association	+/+	−/+	+/+	−/−	−/−	−/−
Sequence Flow	+/+	+/+	+/+	+/+	+/+	+/+
Message Flow	−/−	−/−	+/+	−/−	−/−	−/−
Control Node, Exclusive Decision, Inclusion Decision, Parallel Decision, Complex Decision, Exclusive Event Based Decision, Parallel Event Based Decision	+/+	+/+	+/+	−/+	−/+	−/+
Behavioural Perspective Coverage	8/12	8/12	12/12	4/12	4/12	4/12

Table 7. BPM formalisms out of the informational perspective.

BPM4KI concepts	BPM formalisms					
	UML AD	eEPC	BPMN 2.0	PROMOTE	Oliveira	KMDL 2.2
Input Object, Data Input Object, Information Input Object	−/+	−/+	+/+	−/+	−/+	−/+
Output Object, Information Output Object, Data Output Object	−/+	−/+	+/+	−/+	−/+	−/+
Resource	−/+	−/+	+/+	−/−	−/+	−/−
Material Resource, Informational Resource	−/+	−/+	−/+	−/+	−/+	−/+
Event	+/+	+/+	+/+	−/−	−/−	−/+
Contingency	−/−	−/−	−/+	−/−	−/−	−/−
Collaboration Protocol	−/−	−/−	+/+	−/−	−/−	−/+
Informational Perspective Coverage	6/14	6/14	12/14	3/14	4/14	5/14

BPMN 2.0. Besides, the knowledge modeling notations (KMDL, PROMOTE, and Oliveira) have shortcomings concerning their ability to explicitly support the process perspective representation, i.e. they do not address process logic to full extent and thus there is no possibility to represent data flows. However, the three control flow elements AND, OR and XOR exist in all of these formalisms. Then, from the process perspective, BPMN 2.0 and ARIS eEPC are more expressive for modeling this perspective as a whole. While BPMN offers extended notation for control flow organization, encompasses a high level of detail, numerous constructs (for modeling process logic, decision points, control flows, processes and event types, etc.) offering a very complex expressive model of BPs. In constrat, eEPC has less expressiveness than BPMN, and its constructs are considerable fewer and not so well specified as in BPMN. Furthermore, EPC process models are not intended for being detailed in order to be executed. It is a notation to model the domain aspects of BPs. The focus of the notation is mainly on domain concepts and processes representation rather than the formal specification or technical realization.

The informational perspective (Table 7) is better developed in BPMN 2.0. This notation stresses the process view representation, offering a number of symbols for modeling various processes and event types. For these tasks, BPMN is one of the most suitable modeling notations. However, data and information flow representation is considered secondary. Moreover, all other modeling formalisms under discussion do not separate accurately data from information, allowing the use of the same constructs and symbols for both concepts. Or, this distinction is useful and essential for our modeling context. Data and information form the basis for knowledge generation, distribution and utilization in the context of collaboration between BP agents.

As Table 8 shows, one of the main lacks of the BPM formalisms is that the intentional perspective is not explicitly supported at all. Not any formalism is able to represent the distal intention and objectives concepts. Furthermore, it is possible to present a Business Process, but it cannot be distinguished between the different typologies such as Sensitive Business Process, Core, Support and Management Process, etc. If the BPM formalism allows to show a process agentive entities, then it is also possible to present a Client (which can be either internal or external to the organization). If the BPM formalisms have an element to present some kind of a resource, then the notations are able to present a deliverable.

From the knowledge perspective (Table 9), ARIS eEPC incompletely supports this dimension. In fact, knowledge is represented by two object types, knowledge category and documented knowledge, and can be model by two model types, knowledge structure diagram and knowledge map. In the first diagram, knowledge categories can be organized into subgroups based on their content. While the second depicts the distribution of various knowledge categories within an organization. However, the source of knowledge cannot be related to the knowledge and therefore a statement about the interaction between tacit knowledge and explicit knowledge is not possible.

Table 8. BPM formalisms comparison out of the intentional perspective

BPM4KI concepts	BPM formalisms					
	UML AD	eEPC	BPMN 2.0	PROMOTE	Oliveira	KMDL 2.2
Intention	−/−	−/+	−/−	−/−	−/−	−/−
Distal Intention	−/−	−/+	−/−	−/−	−/−	−/−
Collective Distal Intention	−/−	−/−	−/−	−/−	−/−	−/−
Organizational Distal Intention	−/−	−/−	−/−	−/−	−/−	−/−
Objective, Individual Objective, Collective Objective	−/−	−/−	−/−	−/−	−/−	−/−
Deliberate Action	−/−	−/+	−/+	−/+	−/+	−/+
Organizational Objective, Strategic Objective, Operational Objective	−/−	−/−	−/−	−/−	−/−	−/−
Culminated Process	−/+	+/+	−/+	−/−	−/+	−/+
Business Process	−/+	−/+	+/+	−/+	−/+	−/+
Output Object/Deliverables	−/+	+/+	−/−	−/−	−/−	−/+
Control Object/Performance Measure	−/−	−/−	−/−	−/−	−/−	−/−
Client, Internal Client, External Client	−/+	−/+	−/+	−/−	−/+	−/+
Sensitive Business Process	−/−	−/+	−/+	−/+	−/+	−/+
First Level Processes, Organizational Sub Processes	+/+	−/+	+/+	−/+	−/+	−/+
Internal Process, External Process	−/+	−/+	+/+	−/−	−/−	−/−
Core Process, Support Process, Management process	−/−	−/−	−/−	−/−	−/−	−/−
Operational Process, Strategic Process	−/−	−/−	−/−	−/−	−/−	−/−
Intentional Perspective Coverage	7/34	12/34	10/34	4/34	6/34	7/34

The knowledge perspective is better developed for the more incipient knowledge modeling notations, i.e. KMDL 2.2, Oliveira and PROMOTE, which allow modeling knowledge flow perfectly. However, none of those proposals adequately and fully support the knowledge dimension (e.g., the differentiation between tacit and explicit knowledge, the different types of knowledge conversion which are relevant in SBPs due to, for instance, the high degree of tacit knowledge developed and exchanged among agents through inter-organizational collaboration, etc.). At the same time they have limited capabilities: (i) they have poor capabilities of process control flow modeling (decisions, actions, control flows, etc.), also they lack the ability to model in an adequate manner the process perspectives as a whole (the structural, behavioral, organizational and informational dimensions), (ii) Information and data concepts are not distinguished from knowledge concept.

Table 9. Evaluation of BPM formalisms in terms of coverage of the knowledge perspective

BPM4KI concepts	BPM formalisms					
	UML AD	eEPC	BPMN 2.0	PROMOTE	Oliveira	KMDL 2.2
Knowledge, Immaterial Resource	−/−	+/+	−/−	+/+	+/+	+/+
Tacit Knowledge	−/−	−/+	−/−	−/+	+/+	+/+
Individual Tacit Knowledge	−/−	−/−	−/−	−/−	−/+	−/+
Collective Tacit Knowledge	−/−	−/−	−/−	−/−	−/+	−/+
Organizational Tacit Knowledge	−/−	−/−	−/−	−/−	−/+	−/+
Explicit Knowledge	−/−	−/+	−/+	−/+	−/+	−/+
Individual Explicit Knowledge	−/−	−/−	−/−	−/−	−/−	−/−
Collective Explicit Knowledge	−/−	−/−	−/−	−/−	−/−	−/−
Organizational Explicit Knowledge	−/−	−/−	−/−	−/−	−/−	−/−
Physical Knowledge Support	−/+	+/+	−/+	−/+	−/+	−/+
Knowledge Flow	−/−	−/+	−/+	−/+	+/+	+/+
Knowledge Perspective Coverage	1/22	7/22	3/22	6/22	11/22	11/22

4.3 Summary of Evaluation

We have compared the BPM formalisms from six different perspectives, emphasizing the advantages and limitations of each notation. We have summed up our findings with respect to each of the perspectives we evaluated. In Table 10 BPM formalisms used in different perspectives are analyzed with different colors, where they have reached the maximum evaluation points or have missed only one point. The considered formalisms were very similar in the number of concepts represented (such as BPMN 2.0 and ARIS eEPC).

It becomes easy to recognize that high visibility from functional, organizational, behavior-oriented as well as informational perspectives characterize the BPMN2.0, eEPC, and UML AD formalisms. From the knowledge perspective, only KMDL 2.2 and Oliveira are highly visible, but they are inferior to the others in their evaluation from the informational perspective. However, the BP oriented knowledge modeling notations have not been widely adopted by organizations and are still very incipient. Therefore, they are hard to understand and apply for the purpose of facilitating the involvement of modeling participants, and convenient only for KM experts and require additional training for non-experts. Finally, a statement about the «best» BPM formalism can hardly be met; rather, we claim that only an observation about the optimal application of a given BPM formalism from a specific perspective is appropriate.

Finally, this evaluation results concluded that current BPM formalisms are not adequate for the representation of SBPs, since important SBP characteristics details could not be observed (either because relevant concepts were not addressed by existing formalisms or because these concepts were represented in a very high abstraction level). This may lead to ambiguous and unclear SBP models. BPMN 2.0 address the highest representation coverage of the set of BPM4KI concepts, incorporating requirements for SBP modeling better than other formalisms.

Table 10. Accumulation of BPM formalism evaluation per perspective

	Functional Perspective	Organizational Perspective	Behavioral Perspective	Informational Perspective	Intentional Perspective	Knowledge Perspective
UML-AD	16/24	10/16	8/12	6/14	7/34	1/22
eEPC	13/24	9/16	8/12	6/14	12/34	7/22
BPMN 2.0	20/24	12/16	12/12	12/14	10/34	3/22
PROMOTE	13/24	8/16	4/12	3/14	4/34	6/22
Oliveira	11/24	7/16	4/12	4/14	6/34	11/22
KMDL 2.2	1/24	7/16	4/12	5/14	7/34	11/22

Based in the previous assessment, we have chosen BPMN in this paper, as the most suitable BPM notations for representing SBPs to address our research problem, which consists in improving the localization and identification of the crucial knowledge that is mobilized by these processes. In brief, the best characteristics of BPMN are:

• BPMN is currently the BP notation most used among BPM practitioners (with a preference rate above 70%) [51].

• Very simple, easy to use and readily understandable and accessible by all business stakeholders.

• Expressiveness and richness of concepts offering a complex expressive BP model.

• BPMN is a BPM standard backed up by OMG, so the language definition is based upon a meta-model built with UML, the notation which is the de facto standard for modeling software engineering artifacts.

• BPMN is one of the most recent BPM languages, so it is grounded on the experience of earlier BPM formalisms, which ontologically makes it one of the most complete BPM formalisms [46].

• BPMN is the notation with more BPM tools support available (more than 80 diagrammatic tools).

• BPMN is extensible (with standard extension mechanisms).

• BPMN offers a standardized bridge for the gap between the BP design and process implementation [5].

Nevertheless, despite its strength representation, BPMN 2.0 does not yet provide support for SBP modeling. Some of its concepts should be adapted and extended to be convenient for a rich and expressive representation of SBPs. In fact, this notation does not explicitly support the key concepts of BPM4KI (as *Critical Organizational Activity, Individual Tacit Knowledge, Collective Tacit Knowledge, Expert, Knowledge Explicit Knowledge, Distal Intention, Collective Objective*, etc.). So, to overcoming the shortcomings of BPMN 2.0, this extension must take into consideration, on the one hand, the knowledge dimension, and on the other hand, integrate the new concepts of BPM4KI to represent issues relevant at the intersection of KM and BPM with a sufficient level of details.

5   Case Study: A SBP Model Representation

5.1   Case Study Description

In this section, we describe a case study carried out to demonstrate the feasibility, suitability, and practical utility of the evaluated approach to represent and analyze SBP. Precisely, this section illustrates a SBP model using BPMN 2.0, on top of the ARIS express tool [52] to evaluate its potential in providing an adequate and expressive representation of a SBP, to improve the knowledge localization and identification. The chosen process for this example reflects a medical care process in the Association of Protection of the Motor-disabled of Sfax-Tunisia (ASHMS). This organization is characterized by highly dynamic, unpredictable, complex and highly intensive knowledge actions. Particularly, we are interested in the early care of the disabled children with cerebral palsy (CP) [23]. In fact, the amount of medical knowledge mobilized and produced during this medical care process is very important, hetero-geneous and recorded on various scattered sources. One part of this knowledge is embodied in the mind of health professionals. Another part, is preserved in the orga-nizational memory as reports, medical records, data bases, therapeutic protocols and clinical practice guidelines). The created knowledge stems from the interaction of a large number of multidisciplinary healthcare professionals with heterogeneous skills, expertise and specialties (such as neonatology, neuro-pediatrics, physical therapy, orthopedics, psychiatry, physiotherapy, speech therapy, and occupational therapy) and located on geographically remote sites (University hospital of Sfax Hedi Chaker, University hospital of Sfax, Habib Bourguiba, faculty of medicine of Sfax, research laboratories, etc.). Therefore, the raised problem concerns on the one hand, the insufficiency and the difficulty to localize and understand the medical knowledge that is necessary for decision-making, and on the other hand, the loss of knowledge held by these experts during their scattering or their departure at the end of the treatment. The ASHMS risks losing the acquired know-how for good and transferring this knowledge to new novices if ever no capitalization action is considered. Thus, it should identify the so called «crucial knowledge» to reduce the costs of capitalization operation. Our main objective consists in improving the localization, identification and sharing of different types and modalities of crucial medical knowledge necessary for performing the medical care process of children with CP.

Indeed, this SBP is composed of several sub-processes which consists of a succession of many actions in the form of medical and paramedical examinations and evaluations in different specialties (like neonatology, neuro-pediatrics, physical medicine, orthopedics, psychiatry, physiotherapy and occupational therapy). The different BPs (such as process related to neonatology care, process related to neuro-pediatric care, process related to physiotherapy, etc.) require certain medical information as well as certain medical knowledge (results of para-clinical exams, hospitalization reports, patient-specific knowledge recorded in the medical case file, practice guidelines, etc.).

5.2   The SBP Modeling

In this study, we take into consideration the results of experimentation of the Sensitive Organization's Process Identification Methodology (SOPIM) proposed by Turki et al. [3] for the early care of children with CP. As a reminder, the proposed multi-criteria decision making methodology was conducted and validated in the ASHMS organization and aims at evaluating and identifying SBPs for knowledge localization. We have opted for the SBP «Process of neonatology consultation of a child with CP» to illustrate and evaluate the potential of BPMN 2.0 with regard to its applicability and capability of making relevant knowledge embedded in a SBP explicit. Indeed, this SBP is highly dynamic, very complex, in the sense that it involves a large number of organizational units, agents and experts (internal and external who are not affiliated to the organization) from various business/skills often residing in different physical locations), neonatology disciplines and critical organizational activities (individual and collective). It is very dependent on explicit knowledge sources and on tacit knowledge. In addition, it involves an intense collaboration and interaction between participants to achieve organizational objectives, make decision to deal with an unexpected situation and create value. Some of its activities are highly dependent on the experts experience, expertise and creativity.

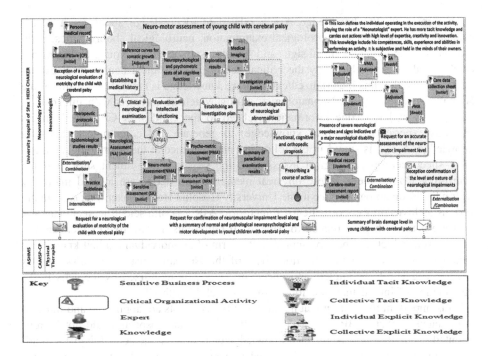

Fig. 1. Fragment of SBP model in BPMN related to the neonatology consultation of a child with CP

Figure 1 outlines a SBP model extract of the neonatology consultation process using BPMN 2.0, enriched with the knowledge dimension (modeled according to BPM4KI). As stated above, this notation does not, however, provide primitives to explicitly represent all relevant aspects related to knowledge dimension in BP models. To remedy for the shortcomings, we tried to extend this notation and started by integrating some specific graphical icons in the form of some BPMN modeling elements relating to several new BPM4KI concepts (see Fig. 1). The BPMN SBP model is evaluated and validated through some interviews made with 2 stakeholders: the neonatologist and the neuro-pediatrician. During our experimentation, we have identified different types of medical knowledge mobilized and created by each critical activity related to the SBP of neonatology care. We have distinguished missing or poorly mastered knowledge (individual or collective) necessary to resolve critical problems, expertise, unexplainable tacit knowledge and mastered knowledge necessary and relevant to the proper functioning and development of the activity or produced by the activity. We have also identified the different sources of knowledge, their localization, actors who hold the knowledge, the places where they are usable or used, their nature (like experience, basic knowledge, general knowledge), their degree of formalization (tacit/explicit dimension), their organizational coverage (individual/collective dimension), as well as their quality (perfect or imperfect).

For instance, the knowledge A_2K_{p1} related to «Knowledge about result of the evaluation of the clinical neurological examination, neurological abnormalities, cerebral palsy category, and clinical signs and symptoms associated of young children with cerebral palsy» is produced by the critical activity A_2 «Clinical neurological examination». Note that this materialized/externalized knowledge is created as a result of the activity execution by the Neonatologist, during which he interacts with information (i.e. source of knowledge information) related to the child with CP (based on his previous experiences and tacit knowledge) to generate and communicate his own knowledge. A_2K_{p1} is stored in the following physical media: the neurological assessment sheet, neuropsychological assessment, the sensitive assessment sheet and the neuro-motor assessment. These physical media of knowledge are located internally within the Neonatology service in the University Hospital Hedi Chaker, precisely in the various archives drawers or patients' directories. A_2K_{p1} is of a scientific, technical and measure nature which is related to patients. It represents a collective explicit knowledge, part of which can be represented in the form of an individual explicit knowledge recorded on the care data collection sheet of the Neonatologist. This knowledge is imperfect (general, incomplete and uncertain). A_2K_{p1} is mobilized by the activity A_3 «Evaluation of intellectual functioning of young child with CP».

It is important to mention that not all BPM4KI concepts are applicable and must be instantiated in every SBP scenario. Precisely, relevant tacit aspects could not be represented explicitly, such as: the tacit knowledge embedded in the neonatologist's mind, the knowledge conversion and the knowledge flows exchanged between communicating process participants and among activities, and the distal intentions which are responsible for making neonatologist to perform any action and achieve an organizational objective.

Therefore, extending BP models with the knowledge dimension would provide the following benefits:

- Possibility to relate different forms of knowledge, information and data to the BP model.
- Possibility to identify data, information and knowledge inputs and outputs in organizational activities.
- Illustrating and separating the data, information and knowledge sources that are required to perform BP activities and knowledge that are generated, created and/or modified as a results of activities.
- Enhance the localization and identification of knowledge (where knowledge can be obtained and clearly stated) as well as experts who hold the (internal) knowledge.
- Integration and distinction of different knowledge types.
- Specifying the different opportunities of knowledge conversion between knowledge types (the dynamic sharing, dissemination, generation and use of existing knowledge).
- Possibility to represent knowledge flows between sources, and among activities which are about knowledge creation and organization, knowledge distribution and knowledge reuse among BP participants.
- Giving an opportunity to improve understanding about the knowledge usefulness, validity, and relevance for particular activities (i.e. critical activities) in a SBP.

- Possibility to evaluate the amount of lost knowledge if a person-owner of knowledge-leaves the organization (i.e., to identify which tacit knowledge in which cases should be transformed into explicit knowledge).
- A deeply characterizing of the identified knowledge to determine which ones are more crucial to be exploited (i.e. illustrating the nature and degree of formalization of knowledge, the organizational value of knowledge, the organizational coverage of knowledge, their quality, etc.).

6 Conclusion and Perspectives

This paper presents a multi-perspective evaluation framework for assessing and selecting SBP modeling formalisms, taking the conceptualization defined by BPM4KI [22] as a baseline. Several BPM notations are reviewed, some are process oriented and some are knowledge oriented. Therefore, the evaluation allowed to justify and choose the better one positioned nowadays, the BPMN 2.0 standard, to improve the localization, identification and characterization of crucial knowledge. Furthermore, we evaluated the practical applicability of BPMN 2.0 through a SBP model of a real neonatology care process.

There are several open issues in this paper that we plan to address in the future to deepen the so-called problematic of knowledge identification mobilized by SBPs. Further work is underway to deepen the characterization of concepts relating to the notion of Sensitive Business Process and propose semantically rich and consensual definitions of concepts and dimensions necessary for the characterization and modeling of SBPs. So, we consider relying on «core» domain ontologies [53, 54] (which are based on top of the DOLCE foundational ontology [55]). In the medium term, we plan to offer a rigorous scientific approach to help implement an extension of BPMN 2.0 which integrate the core BPM4KI concepts. Indeed, the well known notation for modeling BPs often lack in visualizing and analyzing knowledge flows within these processes. To overcome these deficiencies, the proposed extension must enable the modeling, analysis and evaluation of SBPs by combining the perspectives of BPs and knowledge flows. Although such a hybrid approach could be challenging, the expected improvement in modeling processes that involve sensitive and/or crucial knowledge could be significant particular in as critical as the health care domains.

References

1. Grundstein, M.: From capitalizing on company knowledge to knowledge management. In: Morey, D., Maybury, M. (eds.) Knowledge Management, Classic and Contemporary Works, Chap. 12, pp. 261–287. The MIT Press, Cambridge (2000)
2. Saad, I., Grundstein, M., Sabroux, C.: Une méthode d'aide à l'identification des connaissances cruciales pour l'entreprise. Revue SIM **14**(3) (2009)

3. Turki, M., Saad, I., Gargouri, F., Kassel, G.: A business process evaluation methodology for knowledge management based on multi-criteria decision making approach. In: Saad, I., Sabroux, C.R., Gargouri, F. (eds.) Information Systems for Knowledge Management. Wiley-ISTE, Chichester (2014)
4. Korherr, B., List, B.: A UML 2 profile for event driven process chains. In: Tjoa, A.Min, Xu, L., Chaudhry, Sohail S. (eds.) CONFENIS 2006. IFIP AICT, vol. 205, pp. 161–172. Springer, Boston (2006). doi:10.1007/0-387-34456-X_16
5. OMG. Business Process Modeling and Notation (BPMN). Version 2.0 (2011a). http://www.bpmn.org/
6. OMG. Unified modeling language (UML), version 2.0 (2011b). http://www.uml.org/
7. Schlenoff, C., Gruninger, M., Tissot, F., Valois, J.: The process specification language (PSL) overview and version 1.0 specification (2000)
8. Cabral, L., Norton, B., Domingue, J.: The business process modelling ontology. In: 4th International Workshop on Semantic Business Process Management, Crete (2009)
9. Weidong, Z., Weihui, D.: Integrated modeling of business processes and knowledge flow based on RAD. In: IEEE International Symposium on Knowledge Acquisition and Modeling, China, pp. 49–53 (2008)
10. Papavassiliou, G., Mentzas, G.: Knowledge modelling in weakly-structured business processes. J. Know. Manag. 7(2), 18–33 (2003)
11. Abecker, A.: DECORConsortium: DECOR—Delivery of Context-Sensitive Organizational Knowledge. E-Work and E-Commerce. IOS Press, Amsterdam (2001)
12. Schreiber, G., Akkermans, H., Anjewierden, A., Hoog, R., Shadbolt, N., De Velde, W.V., Wielinga, B.: Knowledge Engineering and Management: The Common KADS Methodology. MIT Press, Cambridge (2002)
13. Strohmaier, M., Yu, E., Horkoff, J., Aranda, J., Easterbook, S.: Analyzing knowledge transfer effectiveness- an agent-oriented modeling approach. In: Proceedings of the 40th Hawaii International Conference on System Sciences, USA (2007)
14. Woitsch, R., Karagiannis, D.: Process oriented knowledge management: a service based approach. J. Univ. Comput. Sci. 11(4), 565–588 (2005)
15. Donadel, A.C.: A method for representing knowledge-intensive processes. M.Sc. dissertation. Programa de Pós-Graduação em Engenharia e Gestão do Conhecimento. Universidade Federal de Santa Catarina, Brazil (2007)
16. Hildebrandt, T.T., Mukkamala, R.R.: Declarative event-based workflow as distributed dynamic condition response graphs. In: Programming Languages Approaches to Concurrency and Communication-Centric Software, Cyprus, pp. 59–73 (2010)
17. Gronau, N., Korf, R., Müller, C.: KMDL-capturing, analyzing and improving knowledge-intensive business processes. J. Univ. Comput. Sci. 11, 452–472 (2005)
18. Arbeitsbericht (umfangreiche Beschreibung) – KMDL® v2.2 (2009). http://www.kmdl.de
19. Heisig, P.: The GPO-WM® method for the integration of knowledge management into business processes. In: International Conference on Knowledge Management, Graz, Austria, pp. 331–337 (2006)
20. Oliveira, F.F.: Ontology Collaboration and its Applications. MSc Dissertation. Programa de Pós-Graduação em Informática, Universidade Federal do Espírito Santo, Vitória, Brazil (2009)
21. Netto, J.M., Franca, J.B.S., Baião, F.A., Santoro, F.M.: A notation for knowledge-intensive processes. In: IEEE 17th International Conference on Computer Supported Cooperative Work in Design, vol. 1, pp. 1–6 (2013)

22. Hassen, M., Turki, M., Gargouri, F.: Sensitive business process modeling for knowledge management. In: Chen, Q., Hameurlain, A., Toumani, F., Wagner, R., Decker, H. (eds.) DEXA 2015. LNCS, vol. 9262, pp. 36–46. Springer, Cham (2015). doi:10.1007/978-3-319-22852-5_4

23. Ben Hassen, M., Turki, M., Gargouri, F.: A business process meta-model for knowledge identification based on a core ontology. In: Shishkov, B. (ed.) BMSD 2015. LNBIP, vol. 257, pp. 37–61. Springer, Cham (2016). Revised Selected Papers. doi:10.1007/978-3-319-40512-4_3

24. Turki, M., Kassel, G., Saad, I., Gargouri, F.: A core ontology of business processes based on DOLCE. J. Data Semant. **5**(3), 165–177 (2016)

25. Zhaoli, Z., Zongkai, Y., Qingtang, L.: Modeling knowledge flow using petri net. In: International Symposium on Knowledge Acquisition and Modeling, Wuhan, China, pp. 142–146 (2008)

26. Supulniece, I., Businska, L., Kirikova, M.: Towards extending BPMN with the knowledge dimension. In: Bider, I., Halpin, T., Krogstie, J., Nurcan, S., Proper, E., Schmidt, R., Ukor, R. (eds.) BPMDS/EMMSAD 2010. LNBIP, vol. 50, pp. 69–81. Springer, Heidelberg (2010). doi:10.1007/978-3-642-13051-9_7

27. Santos França, J.B., Netto, J.M., Barradas, R.G., Santoro, F., Baião, F.A.: Towards knowledge-intensive processes representation. In: Rosa, M., Soffer, P. (eds.) BPM 2012. LNBIP, vol. 132, pp. 126–136. Springer, Heidelberg (2013). doi:10.1007/978-3-642-36285-9_14

28. Kassel, G., Turki, M., Saad, I., Gargouri, F.: From collective actions to actions of organizations: an ontological analysis. In Symposium Understanding and Modelling Collective Phenomena (UMoCop), University of Birmingham, Birmingham, England (2012)

29. OMG. Organization Structure Metamodel (OSM). OMG Document bmi/2006-11-02 (2006)

30. http://www.laria.u-picardie.fr/IC/site/IMG/pdf/Agentive_entity-v1.1-OS.pdf

31. Morley, C., Berthier, D., Maurice-Demourioux, M.: Un modèle de processus métier pour les nouvelles formes d'organisation des activités. Actes du 11ème colloque de l'AIM (Association Information & Management) Systèmes d'Information et Collaboration: Etat de l'Art et Perspectives, Luxembourg, pp. 7–9 (2006)

32. Moody, D.L.: The physics of notations: Towards a scientific basis for constructing visual notations in software engineering. IEEE Trans. Softw. Eng. **35**(5), 756–779 (2009)

33. Scheer, A.-W., Nüttgens, M.: ARIS Architecture and Reference Models for Business Process Management. In: Aalst, W., Desel, J., Oberweis, A. (eds.) Business Process Management. LNCS, vol. 1806, pp. 376–389. Springer, Heidelberg (2000). doi:10.1007/3-540-45594-9_24

34. Korherr, B.: Business Process Modelling: Languages, Goals, and Variabilities.VDM Publishing (2008)

35. Tscheschner, W.: Transformation from EPC to BPMN. Technical report, Oryx Research (2010)

36. ARIS Expert Paper. Business Process Design as the Basis for Compliance Management, Enterprise Architecture and Business Rules (2007)

37. Recker, J.C., Indulska, M., Rosemann, M., Green, P.: Do process modelling techniques get better? a comparative ontological analysis of BPMN. In: Campbell, B., Underwood, J., Bunker, D. (eds.) Proceedings of the 16th Australasian Conference on Information Systems, Sidney, Australia (2005)

38. Recker, J.C., Indulska, M., Rosemann, M., Green, P.: How good is BPMN really? Insights from theory and practice. In: Proceedings of the European Conference on Information Systems, IT University of Gotteborg, vol. 14, pp. 1–12 (2006)

39. Karagiannis, D., Telesko, R.: The EU-project PROMOTE: a process-oriented approach for knowledge management. In: Reimer, U. (ed.) Proceedings of the Third International Conference on Practical Aspects of Knowledge Management (2000)

40. Eriksson, H.E., Penker, M.: Business Modeling with UML: Business Patterns at Work. John Wiley & Sons, New York (2000)

41. Söderström, E., Andersson, B., Johannesson, P., Perjons, E., Wangler, B.: Towards a framework for comparing process modelling languages. In: Pidduck, A.B., Ozsu, M.Tamer, Mylopoulos, J., Woo, Carson C. (eds.) CAiSE 2002. LNCS, vol. 2348, pp. 600–611. Springer, Heidelberg (2002). doi:10.1007/3-540-47961-9_41

42. Lin, F.R., Yang, M.C., Pai, Y.H.: A generic structure for business process modeling. J. Bus Proc. Manag. **8**(1) (2002). Emerald

43. Mendling, J., Neumann, G., Nüttgens, M.: A comparison of XML interchange formats for business process modelling. In: Proceedings of the EMISA 2004 Workshop. Information Systems in E-Business and E-Government. Lecture Notes in Informatics (LNI), vol. 56 (2004)

44. List, B., Korherr, B.: An evaluation of conceptual business process modelling languages. In: ACM Symposium on Applied Computing (2006)

45. Wand, Y., Weber, R.: An ontological model of an information system. IEEE Trans. Softw. Eng. **16**(11), 1282–1292 (1990)

46. Rosemann, M., Recker, J., Indulska, M., Green, P.: A study of the evolution of the representational capabilities of process modeling grammars. In: Dubois, E., Pohl, K. (eds.) CAiSE 2006. LNCS, vol. 4001, pp. 447–461. Springer, Heidelberg (2006). doi:10.1007/11767138_30

47. Recker, J., Rosemann, M., Indulska, M., Green, P.: Business process modeling: a comparative analysis. J. Assoc. Inf. **10**, 333–363 (2009)

48. Penicina, L.: Choosing a BPMN 2.0 compatible upper ontology. In: The Fifth International Conference on Information, Process, and Knowledge Management, eKNOW, pp. 89–96 (2013)

49. Prezel, V., Gavsević, D., Milanović, M.: Representational analysis of business process and business rule languages. In: Proceedings of the 11th IEEE International Conference on Enterprise Distributed Object Computing Conference. Annapolis, Maryland, USA, pp. 241–258 (2010)

50. Sultanow, E., Zhou, X., Gronau, N., Cox, S.: Modeling of processes, systems and knowledge: a multi-dimensional comparison of 13 chosen methods. Int. Rev. Comput. Softw. **7**(6), 3309–3319 (2012)

51. Harmon P., Wolf, C.: Business Process Modeling Survey, December 2011. BPTrends

52. The IDS-Scheer website (2013). http://www.ids-scheer.com/

53. Gangemi, A., Borgo, S. (eds.) Proceedings of the 14th International Conference on Knowledge Engineering and Knowledge Management (EKAW 2004), Workshop on Core Ontologies in Ontology Engineering, Northamptonshire (UK) (2004)

54. Kassel, G.: Integration of the DOLCE top-level ontology into the OntoSpec methodology (2005)

55. Masolo, C., Vieu, L., Bottazzi, E., Catenacci, C., Ferrario, R., Gangemi, A., Guarino, N.: Social roles and their descriptions. In: Dubois, D., Welty, C., Williams M.-A. (eds.) Proceedings of the Ninth International Conference on the Principles of Knowledge Representation and Reasoning, pp. 267–277 (2004)

Classification and Definition of an Enterprise Architecture Analyses Language

Julia Rauscher[(✉)], Melanie Langermeier, and Bernhard Bauer

University Augsburg, Augsburg, Germany
`rauscher@ds-lab.org`

Abstract. Enterprise Architecture Management (EAM) deals with the assessment and development of business processes and IT components. Through the analysis of as-is and to-be states the information flow in organizations is optimized. Thus EAM analyses are an essential part in the EAM cycle. To cover the needs of an architect the analyses pursue different goals and utilize different techniques. In this work we examine the different EA analysis approaches according to their characteristics and requirements. For that purpose we design a generic analysis language which can be used for their description. In order to manage the numerous approaches from literature we develop a categorization. The categories are created based on the goals, constructs and kind of results. We propose a two-dimensional classification into functional and technical categories. The goal is to provide a common description for EA analyses for an easy access to their goals and execution requirements.

Keywords: Enterprise Architecture Management · Analysis · EA analysis · Categorization · Characteristics · Requirements · Domain Specific Language · Meta language

1 Introduction

Analyses are one of the most important artifacts integrated in Enterprise Architecture Management (EAM) and are indispensable in the EAM cycle. The EA process contains five phases (Niemann 2006): Document, Analyze, Plan, Act and Check. Thus, analysis is an essential part in order to create and implement future plans. It supports decision making through an evaluation of the current architecture as well as potential future scenarios (Sasa and Krisper 2011). The result of analysis and planning actions is finally the creation of a target architecture. Those actions enable planning, acting, controlling and documenting through all layers.

The creation of an Enterprise Architecture (EA) model is time and cost consuming. Therefore, support for decision making and planning generates value and increases the acceptance of the EA initiative in an organization (Lankhorst 2013). Thus, analysis support is essential in order to generate value from an EA model. The execution of an analysis decomposes the analyzed object in its components.

© Springer International Publishing AG 2017
B. Shishkov (Ed.): BMSD 2016, LNBIP 275, pp. 119–139, 2017.
DOI: 10.1007/978-3-319-57222-2_6

Those single elements are examined and evaluated as well as the relationships and interactions between them. Applying existing analyses on established models is expensive, since the corresponding meta models typically require some adaptions (Langermeier et al. 2014). This makes reuse of existing solutions and research findings hard.

In current literature a great variety of analysis possibilities are described. In previous work we provided an overview of the different analysis approaches (Rauscher 2013). These approaches are mainly isolated, integrated ones are rare. The well-known EA frameworks deal only secondary with EA analysis, a common understanding of the term is not established yet (Buckl et al. 2009b; Närman et al. 2012). Nevertheless due to the importance of EA analyses, methods are required to specify them consistently (Buckl et al. 2009b; Johnson et al. 2007b).

The analyses rely on different technologies, like ontologies (Sunkle et al. 2013), probability networks (Närman et al. 2008) or expert interviews (Kazienko et al. 2011), have different preconditions and provide different kinds of results. E.g. preconditions can be required properties for model elements or specific data structures. Typical results are quantitative ones like an overall metric for the architecture, measures for specific architecture elements, but also a determined set of elements. Several analysis approaches focus on the dependencies between the elements of an architecture. For example, they are used to determine the impact of changes (e.g. de Boer et al. 2005). Other analyses focus on specific attributes of elements. For instance an availability analysis predicts the availability value for an element, dependent on several other factors modeled in the EA (Närman et al. 2012). Accordingly metrics based on attribute values can be calculated. They can be used as key performance indicator for the evaluation of the architecture and for decision making (Matthes et al. 2011). In those calculations also the relationships between the elements as well as the attributes of dependent elements can be considered. The analysis of timing aspects is very important for EAM. Therewith the evolution of the architecture can be monitored (Matthes et al. 2011). Every analysis supports a different goal and thus, for a sound evaluation of the architecture different kinds of analyses are required.

In this paper we want to analyze existing EA analyses from literature to determine their characteristics and their requirements for execution. Additionally we want to provide a uniform description technique to specify the different requirements, goals and outputs of the analyses. Due to the high number of analyses in literature we first categorize them and determine the requirements per category. The main goal of the categorization is to create a possibility to conduct analyses organized and controlled. Additionally the categorization enables the creation of new analyses and the selection of the best suited analysis depending on the goal and requested technique. Therefore we study the single analysis approaches regarding their requirements for execution and their provided results. This provides a sound overview of analysis approaches in the context of EA and of the issues they address. Based on the results we categorize them once according to their functional dimension, and once according to their technical dimension. The characteristics of the resulting categories are formalized while establishing a Domain Specific

Language (DSL). Such a language allows us to make the requirements of an analysis visible in a structural way. The calculated outcome as well as the preconditions in order to execute the analysis is easily accessible.

The remaining paper is structured as followed. First we introduce foundations of EA analysis (Sect. 2). Following we present in Sect. 3 our approach for determining the analysis categories. The categories themselves are also presented shortly with their main characteristics. The DSL to describe the analyses is introduced in Sect. 4. Its application is shown exemplary for one category. Finally we discuss the categorization and the DSL (Sect. 5).

2   Enterprise Architecture Analysis

Architectures are used to describe the elements of a system and the relationships between them. The term also comprises the process of creation and maintenance, the architecture work (Lankhorst 2013). EA focuses on elements like business processes, applications and the technical infrastructure of an organization. Often used layers are the strategic layer to represent the organization's strategy with its goals, the business layer describing the business processes and products, the information layer with the information objects, and the application layer as well as the infrastructure layer describing the soft- and hardware components (Lankhorst 2013; Winter and Fischer 2006). Despite the examination of different layers the focus of an EA are the dependencies between layers, i.e. how business and IT relate to each other. Layers are dependent according to the Align-Enable-Principle. The lower layers are the foundation for the upper ones, and the upper ones adjust the lower ones (Winter and Fischer 2006; Krcmar 2015).

The main reasons for analyses are receiving an overview of the architecture, its components and connections, and examining the as-is state (Langermeier et al. 2014). Furthermore weak points can be revealed, new advantages be discovered and various design alternatives be evaluated (Zia et al. 2011). Results of analysis activities are the development of a to-be architecture as well as an improved decision making. The focus of every analysis depends on the analysis type. Additional the questions of what is feasible and what is desirable are crucial (Johnson et al. 2007a). The process of analysis can be segmented in different phases and activities (Wan and Carlsson 2012). We used the parts "system thinking", "modeling", "measuring", "satisfying", "comparing with requirements" and "comparing alternatives" in this work to identify the characteristics of analysis categories.

As basis for our work we conducted a detailed literature research (Rauscher 2013; Rauscher 2015). We exclusively chose analyses, which purely analyze EA and are not transferred from other topics. Hereof a pure EA analysis has the focus on collecting data and discovering the current state of an enterprise architecture in a quantitative or functional way to create a summary, alter the state or control different aspects. The goal of this selection was to create an overview of current EAM analyses and to receive approaches utilizable for a categorization (e.g. Della Bordella et al. 2011; Johnson et al. 2007a; Razavi et al. 2011). We identified 105 EAM analyses which are roughly grouped into 40 EA analysis types

Fig. 1. Categorization approach

in previous work (Rauscher 2013). An analysis type describes analyses, which have the same rough scope and are built independently from the realization method. The goals of the contained analyses can differ significantly. Examples of types are 'Quality Analysis' (e.g. Närman et al. 2008), 'Requirements Analysis' (e.g. Aier et al. 2009) and 'Analysis of Costs' (e.g. Niemann 2006). The different types of analyses, which have been discovered in the literature research, can be treated as a first categorization. However this categorization only makes raw statements about the rough purpose of the contained analyses. Although analyses of the same analysis type have the same field of interest their individual goals and implementations can differ. Thus the classification in those types is not detailed enough to derive characteristics. Quality analyses, for example, can be conducted in various ways and can target different goals. For instance, this can be the quality of a whole system or maturity quality of a single artifact.

3   Categorization

The huge amount of different approaches clarifies importance of EA analyses and coherence of a successful architecture. To ease analysis activities and to get an understanding about current work we categorized them according to their characteristics. We define characteristics of an EA analyses as all necessary steps and components of an analysis to accomplish its goal. The characteristics are a main part of the categorization because they are guaranteeing the accuracy of the conducted analysis and the achievement of the goal. Figure 1 gives an overview of the categorization approach which is described in detail in Sect. 3.1. The resulting categories are presented in Sects. 3.3 and 3.4.

3.1   Categorization Approach

Preliminary work for the categorization includes the definition of a general understanding of an analysis to determine a general purpose construct. We could identify three main constructs of an EA analysis, which can be used as foundation for the categorization and determination of characteristics. These are data intake, processing and outcome. Other parts vary per analyses. Based on these parts we determine the meaning and boundaries of a category: Analyses can be merged to a category if they coincide at least in one of the three parts. As optimal condition all parts are equal, but this is usually not given. Therefore we classify different analyses to the same category if they have at least the same target or same processing technique.

After defining our basis we conduct literature research of current EA analysis (procedure see Sect. 2). We determined the construct for each of the identified EA analysis approaches. Thereby we ensured that only papers with a high elaboration level are used. Because of missing details it is not possible to analyze rough approaches and to identify their construct and characteristics. For elaborated analyses with less detailed parts, we made necessary assumptions. In the case that an EA analysis approach is realized using another non-EA related analysis approach, this non-EA analysis is included too. This proceeding ensures the construction of a data basis with categorize-able analyses according to the general construct of intake, processing and outcome.

Based on the experiences made while identifying the construct of the EA analysis we were able to refine our categorization approach. Considering different existing kinds of categorization (Lankhorst 2013; Buckl et al. 2009b) we conducted our approach with two main fields of categories: functional and technical. This decision brought the most advantages in comparison with other approaches because of the division in "How" (technical aspects) and "Why" (functional purpose). The additional distinction in architecture levels is not included in our approach because a plain allocation wouldn't be possible. Most analysis can be conducted in many levels or can only be performed by involving several levels. Through the new and detailed knowledge from the first evaluation of EA analysis constructs we introduce characteristics to ensure accuracy. We used the analysis' properties and steps as characteristics in order to retrieve detailed information about the category of each analysis approach.

After this step the final categorization of the analyses was received based on our main idea of distinction between functional and technical. The business functions of every analysis are determined based on the concepts *purpose dependent division* ("Fundamental", "Main" and "Decision-oriented") and *activity dependent division* ("System thinking", "Modeling", "Measuring", "Satisfying", "Comparing with requirements" and "Comparing alternatives") (Wan and Carlsson 2012). We used these concepts to analyze the identified analysis approaches according to their goals and activities. Thereby the functional categories have been determined by using a prepared template of aspects. This template consists of the analysis activities, the intermediate objectives and the main goal. After analyzing all approaches we identified 10 categories from classifying the various analyses goals. Attention should be paid to the fact of multiple classifications. For example, a security analysis is able to analyze dependencies and requirements and therefore can be assigned to both functional categories.

After we completed the functional classification, we conducted the technical categories. This procedure was more detailed and complex because of the large variety of existing methods in EA analysis. Only analyses with the same method and same steps of goal attainment can form a technical category. This constraint is necessary to enable discovery of shared characteristics. The already mentioned template was altered for creating technical categories. The new focus lies on the constructs, methods, techniques (including single steps) and artifacts. First, rough technical categories have been determined based on the dimensions "quantitative", "analytic", "simulation" and "functional" (Lankhorst 2013). After this preliminary stage detailed categories were created. Each identified analysis approach passed through this procedure. In contrast to functional categories every analysis was assigned to one specific technical category. As final result we concluded with 17 technical categories.

We decided to choose a two-dimensional classification and not a more detailed fragmentation, because of the high amount of differences within the approaches. Every analysis has special characteristics when sharing the same technique. Therefore it was not possible to identify categories or classifications on a lower level of abstraction. However a high abstraction level involves the danger of missing necessary details. To involve all aspects of every analysis we observed every analysis in its functional and technical view.

Altogether 105 analysis approaches fulfilled our criteria and have been incorporated. Only nine of them couldn't be classified. These ones were too specific and individual for the mapping to a category. For each analysis we identified exactly one technical category and at least one functional category. To create an overview of all possible combinations of categories three matrices were created. Two matrices represent the combination of the analysis approaches and the categories. The functional matrix has more possible combinations because analyses can achieve more targets simultaneously. However the technical matrix has only one combination per analysis. For example, Närman et al. (2008) is assigned to the functional categories **System Analyses**, **Attribute Analyses** and **Quality Analyses** and to the technical one **Bayesian Networks**. To provide an overview of the functional and technical combinations both matrices have been joint, which resulted in a shared matrix (see Fig. 2). Thus, we get an overview of the realization techniques of a functional category and also the other way round for which analysis goals a technique is used. The numerical values in the table represent the amount of analyses in current literature, which match to both categories, the functional and the technical one. However the sum of the values is more then 96 because of the fact that some analyses have multiple functional categories.

Functional \ Technical	Bayesian Networks	Business ENtities	PRM	Social Network	AHP	Time Evaluation	Tree	KPI	Comparison	Views	Lifecycle	Ontology	EID	Weak Points	Matrices	Design	Structural	Other
System	1		2											5				
Attribute		7		3		1			2					4	2			
Dependencies	1		2				2		2		1	1			6			
Quality	2	2	8		2	6	1	2						4	6			2
Design				4					4			1			2	1	1	
Effects									3	2		1	4	5				
Requirements									2	1								
Financial							3								2	2		
Data													1					
Business Objects		1		3	2	1			2	1		1		2				
Other									1						2			1

Fig. 2. Dependency matrix of the functional and technical categories

3.2   Identification of Characteristics

As only properties and steps can show the components responsible for classification, we introduce characteristics to ensure accuracy. We define a characteristic as requirement, since an analysis can only be conducted target-aimed with all indispensable artifacts. Requirements support the achievement of goals and are used to identify hidden characteristics (Van Lamsweerde 2001). Whereas properties can differ significantly, on some spots we had to choose the most elaborated or create a higher abstraction level. There are two types of characteristics: category specific ones and general characteristics. The second type includes a meta model and scenarios, determined at the beginning of an analysis. Another universal characteristic is the main goal. These three characteristics have to be conducted for all analyses. Together they provide a high level of abstraction.

For the specific characteristics we distinguished five different kinds. The conducted kinds of characteristics are important for the identification of properties from technical analyses. Whereas functional categories have rough properties, technical categories have similar structure. We identified the following kind of characteristics: *Input*, *Conditions*, *Construct*, *Measurement*, and *Output*. The basis of an analysis is always represented in terms of *Input* data. In every case an architecture or scenarios, in form of an model, are needed to conduct the following steps and final measurements. Before the main part of an analysis can be performed, sometimes *Conditions* are needed. For example the possibility of succeeding must be given. Most of the *Conditions* are analysis independent and therefore can be seen as generally valid. The main part and procedure of an analysis is the *Construct*, containing all details of the procedure. It's required to conduct all details successfully to be able to finish the analysis. Examples are detailed steps, mathematical algorithms, relationship types and weighting of artifacts. To prove and measure the results and its calculation, every analysis needs some kind of *Measurement*. This characteristic is responsible to witness the achievement of goals. Mainly a *Measurement* is conducted using scales, KPIs and metrics to control functional and non-functional goals (Davis 1989). This characteristic can vary dependent on the analysis and its goals. As last characteristic kind the *Output* was identified. It includes the way of presentation and type of outcome such as percentage, graphics or matrices. This category is crucial because analyses within the same category should have the same *Output*. We used these characteristic kinds to analyze the approaches again to receive detailed information. Through the new and detailed knowledge we had to rearrange the analysis categories on necessary points. New identified characteristics have been verified on correctness and necessity. After this step the final categorization of the analyses was received. Every analysis has multiple and complex requirements. Therefore a table including all characteristics of a category was not feasible, because of the amount of details. To provide an insight of this amount of different characteristics we present short segments of categories and their requirements.

3.3   Functional Categorization

In the following we present the categories of the functional classification. Therefore we will list them combined with an example of an assigned analysis approach. Additional a short description of the characteristics is be given. The complete assignment of all identified analyses to the categories can be found in (Rauscher 2015). However only a few characteristics are given and it does not present the whole amount of identified requirements in detail.

System Analyses (e.g. Närman et al. 2008) check partial or holistic systems and encompass the analysis types 'Quality Analysis' and 'EID'. Mostly time quality aspects and their optimization are in the main focus. Analyses that are contained in this category are often also part of other functional categories because of possible sub-goals. Examples are an analysis of single quality attributes without considering other parts of a system or an analysis determining a possible impact. Analyses in this functional category have very different realization approaches, thus various different techniques are utilized. Possible techniques are PRM or EID (see Sect. 3.4 for further details).

For instance, specific attributes and their values are analyzed by **Attribute Analyses** (e.g. Razavi et al. 2011). Ten analysis types are joint in this category. The observation and management of attributes is the focus such approaches. For instance the different states of attributes with changing input can be analyzed or the availability of attributes can be observed. This category contains many approaches, because of the high demand of attributes in EAM. Following there exist numerous different field of applications as wells different realization techniques. But the focus lies always on attributes. Through the various fields of application, most of contained analyses are also a part of another functional category.

Analyses which prove the relations between the elements are classified as **Dependencies Analyses** (e.g. Saat 2010). The main goal of these approaches is the identification of dependencies in EAs and relations of single components to receive an understanding of the whole architecture. Therewith critical relations are identified and observed. Additionally a risk analysis addresses also financial aspects beside the relations. The methods range from comparison of scenarios to a weak point analysis of the relations.

Quality Analyses have the main focus on various quality questions regarding attributes, systems, architectures and other components and target subjective and measurable goals (e.g. Närman et al. 2008). Altogether 13 different analysis approaches target quality issues. This category is based on ISO 9126 standard of software quality metrics and analyzes maintainability, maturity, usability, accuracy, security, efficiency and interoperability. Based on the high variety of contained analyses types, also the possible techniques differ. For instance, PRM and EID can be used to analyze service quality. In most cases this category tries to observe subjective quality through comparisons of alternatives or the usage of metrics.

Another category represents the analysis of architecture design (**Design Analyses**), examples are (Aier et al. 2011; Kazienko et al. 2011). Through receiving an overview of the architecture construct all design variants can be identified.

Beside the analysis of holistic or partial design, business entities, procedures and components can be analyzed and used to optimize the architecture. An example for the concentration on a single part is the analysis of interfaces. Without this analysis a holistic overview of the architecture would not be possible. Therefore it is indispensable for EAM. Analysis in this category utilize specific techniques with rare reuse like social network analysis.

All approaches which control impacts in architectures and actions are joint in **Effect Analyses** (e.g. de Boer et al. 2005). This includes 'Gap Analysis' and 'Sensitivity Analysis'. In contrast to dependencies analyses these approaches observe the direct impact and effects of changes in architecture elements. To conduct the effect the change of an artifact is simulated in the model. These artifacts can be data, attributes and quality features. The simulation is done identifying different perspectives and comparisons or using the method of extended influence diagrams.

Requirements Analyses identify the requirements to achieve states or goals (e.g. Aier et al. 2009). Therefore the specific conditions have to be determined. Results are either specified values or features and specific business entities, like operations. The main goal of this category is to identify all requirements of an enterprise architecture. Examples are 'Security Analysis' and 'Survival Analysis'. If requirements are not analyzed, processes can not be aligned optimal and goals are not achievable. It's possible to additionally analyze a life cycle and its changing requirements.

To identify costs and benefits **Financial Analyses** are used (e.g. Niemann 2006). On top financial weak points and possible impacts can be discovered. These analyses present a measurement with mathematical calculations. Therefore key figures and metrics determine the outcome. However receiving affected entities is a side effect of the result. Consequently financial analyses observe too high costs or uncertainty and hence are an indicator of necessary architecture and procedure changes. While costs and benefits are only calculated in this analyses, weak points and risks can also be identified for example with dependencies analyses. Financial analyses evaluate the economical success through assessing the costs and benefits architecture and trigger actions to improve them.

However **Data Analyses** cover all kinds of data (e.g. Närman et al. 2009). The focus lies on quality and accuracy, because data is a critical factor in enterprises. This category has only one technical category, EID. Thereby the data values are analyzed for evaluation purposes. **Data Analyses** target mainly the data quality because the accuracy of data is fundamental for all EA operations.

Finally the category **Business Object Analyses** was identified. Approaches like (Della Bordella et al. 2011) are included. Business objects of every kind, e.g. operations, artifacts and entities, which are part of the architecture are addressed here. This category analyzes single business artifacts and whole operations. Example for measurement procedures are the evaluation of time and therewith an optimal operation or the creation of views. Next to 'Business Process Support Analysis' and 'Business Entity Analysis' also 'Social Network Analysis' belong to this category.

3.4   Technical Categories

In the following we describe the 17 technical categories. Therefore we use the introduced characteristic kinds with their properties and goals. For the description we chose the most important and marked characteristics (see Sect. 3.2). Again only special chosen characteristics will be presented and not all necessary steps for the execution are conducted. Since nearly all technical categories require an architecture model, scenarios and goals as *Input* we won't mention it below.

The first technical category represents analyses conducted with **Bayesian Networks** (e.g. Närman et al. 2008). Analyses of this category utilize this technique to analyze the quality of systems and architectures. It is reused in other analyses as part of their procedures, e.g. **PRM** analyses. Requirements of the *Input* are a meta model with entities, attributes and references, different architectural layers and at least two scenarios. These requirements are the most common *Input* prerequisites. The *Condition* are defined attribute states and connection types. They must have discrete areas and are either a causal relation or a definitional relation. In the *Construct*, firstly a model with Bayesian Networks is built, including all nodes and connections of the architecture. A node represents a variable with conditional probability distribution. Therefore in the next step probabilities of attributes and the whole model can be calculated while creating matrices with discrete ranges, connections and weighted attributes. In conclusion this category has probability values as *Output* and can answer questions about the probability of an attribute's status.

Business Entities are a method to receive artifacts on the one hand and on the other hand to analyze quality (e.g. Della Bordella et al. 2011). Here it can be distinguished between analyzing single entities, combined entities or their quality. As *Input* and *Condition* BMM and UMD diagrams with all relations and processes, the goal type, strategies and quality features have to be determined. The first step of the *Construct* detects advantages, operations and elements of strategies. As a second step, influencer and strategies are combined to observe the goals. Additionally matching operations and their entities are identified and assigned. The *Measurement* quantifies the goal. Dependent on the chosen goal type, the strategy elements are evaluated. For instance an observation of maturity can be conducted by weighting elements with a scale. Therewith the strategy with the highest efficiency is identified. The *Output* contains valued strategies, quality values and identified operations and entities.

Probabilistic Relational Models (PRM) contains 14 analyses and is therewith the most used technique (e.g. Buschle et al. 2011). For instance dependency and quality analyses can be conducted with PRM. Therefore artifacts and effects are the main focus. An EA model, scenarios, problems and goals are the *Input*. *Conditions* require controllable attributes and determinable goals and criteria for the later determination of metrics. As a prestep of the *Construct* connections are defined and uncertainties are formalized. Hereafter a concrete model is built and the PRM is used to calculate the conditional probability of all scenarios and of the dependencies and attributes. PRM can be seen as template of an architecture model. This model has a set of classes. Every class has attributes, values and references. The connections can be one out of five states. This model is conducted with every scenario of the input data. Therefore it is possible to calculate the probability of every scenario. Additional the probability of attributes is determined by using Bayesian Networks. The *Output* contains a probability for attribute values, scenarios and uncertainty values.

Social Network analyses (e.g. Kazienko et al. 2011) differ deeply from the other categories. For their conduction questionnaires and all available documents, like bills and connections are required. For the *Input* all available nodes (= entities), connections and needed data sources have to be defined. Entities are persons, groups and companies which can have roles. Only if the methods are accepted, the analysis can be successful, because of the needed support of employees. As *Construct* clusters are built and properties can be checked. Additional new entities and connections are found. One method is combining the socio metric data analysis, questionnaires and other data sources to identify new entities and connections and to evaluate them afterwards. For the *Measurement* a matrix with entities and factors is created for quantitative evaluation with factors or for identification of weak points. An overview of the whole architecture model and its entities and connections on a social basis is found in the *Output*.

Analytic Hierarchy Process (AHP) can be used for analyzing attributes and quality aspects and is one of the most elaborated EA analysis technique (e.g. Razavi et al. 2011). Therefore the requirements for execution as well as the procedure of the identified approaches are described detailed. Typical requirements for execution are a model, scenarios and uncertainties values. *Conditions* are expert knowledge, which is used for weighting, as well as quality attributes and their level of success. First in the *Construct* and *Measurement* the quality attributes with their criteria, subcriteria and level of importance are determined. Then the quality attributes are weighted through a pairwise comparison according to the architectural layers by experts. All weightings of the importance level are summarized in a vector and in the next step a prioritized vector of the layers is created. This prioritized list of quality attributes is used for a concrete definition of the scenarios. These scenarios are also compared pairwise to each other, which concludes in a table with the priorities of the scenarios according to the quality attributes. Finally the most suitable scenario is selected and the level of suitability and uncertainty of the selection is calculated. The results are described in the *Output* as prioritized lists of quality attributes and scenarios.

The method of **Time Evaluation** (e.g. Lankhorst 2013) observes the quality of business entities and operations through the calculation of time values. Analyses which try to optimize the performance utilize this technical category. For example processes and entities are checked for weak points. As additional information to the common requirements, trigger and arrival times are required as *Input*. Rules are necessary to cut the architecture in views and conclude with five perspectives for single time measurements (*Condition*). In this category *Construct* and *Measurement* are combined and require specific time values and calculation metrics. For each view the specific time values are calculated. Examples are "Costumer View" and "Process View" with "Processing Time" and

"Response Time". First, the workload calculation is conducted with a top-down approach. Afterwards the calculation will be applied backwards with a bottom-up approach. Finally all calculated times are summed up to a total time.

Trees are used to analyze and identify dependencies, coherence's and quality features. The *Output* of those analyses delivers the probability for the occurrence of a failure or specific quality attribute. All necessary operations, procedures, scenarios and time values are included in the *Input* dependent on the goal type. In the beginning of the *Construct* the goals, entities and relations are defined. Afterwards a fault tree is built using Bayesian Networks, containing all steps or events required for the execution. Thereby all given scenarios have to be conducted. For every component of this tree a conditional probability matrix is created to receive the probability of failures or quality attributes (Närman et al. 2011). For the *Measurement* the time values are summed up or probabilities are calculated.

The technique of **KPI** (Key Performance Indicator) is used in most analyses with quantitative measurement. Because of the high variety of contained analyses, a high level of abstraction was developed. As *Input* an UML meta model with layers is required. The *Condition* is very important for this kind of analysis. A goal has to be defined according to the SMART criteria: It has to be specific, measurable, achievable, realistic and time-bound. The *Construct* starts with the identification of all artifacts that have to be analyzed and with the determination of the matching KPIs. In the *Measurement* the artifacts are evaluated and the determined values are compared. It is possible to measure single artifacts or to summarize them and evaluate the whole system. Another method for measurement is the usage of matrices, where two different dimensions have to be selected. For example a matrix can present the costs dependent to different organization units. The result in this analysis category represents the goal achievement, unsatisfied quality constraints or the financial situation (Niemann 2006).

Comparison is a simple but powerful method (e.g. de Boer et al. 2005). Next to whole alternatives, also single scenarios, processes, attributes and dependencies can be compared to each other. It is possible to compare different state in times, i.e. the as-is with the to-be, but also different alternatives, i.e. potential future scenarios. Requirements constraint the alternatives and support the achievement of the desirable vision. Additional rules are used to create a consistent model with all requirements and suitable to the end product. First in the *Construct* viewpoints are chosen and a model is created containing all components which should be analyzed. This model can differ dependent on the analysis object. Afterwards the models are compared with a previous state or another alternative. In addition the single elements will be changed and the impacts observed. On this way all possible states can be observed and the best alternative to achieve the goals is identified. The results of the *Output* show what is required to achieve the to-be state and the different impacts dependent on the input.

The technique **Views** is used to analyze aspects in detail or to create different perspectives. It is a powerful tool for EAM, nevertheless only a few analyses use this technique explicitly. However we identified several analyses utilizing the concept of views in their procedure (e.g. Sasa and Krisper 2011). The necessary *Input* and *Conditions* are chosen views, a distinct goal and determinable connections. Criteria and their desirable perspective have to be specified in the *Construct*. Examples are time measures like response time or processing time. After this the views can be built with all required components. A definite *Measurement* is not contained in this category. However, views can be evaluated with criteria to observe whether the view can achieve its goals, for example focus on the processing time.

A less popular methodology is the observation of **Lifecycle** (e.g. Saat 2010; Aier et al. 2009). These analyses ascertain requirements and dependencies through consideration of different lifecycle phases. Therewith changes are identified and it is possible to determine the state of an artifact at a specific point in time. For the conduction the life cycle phases (states) of the artifacts have to be given as attribute assignments and time values in the *Input*. In the analysis *Construct* the lifecycle of the artifacts in the respective architecture part is determined. Afterwards, to check the state of an artifact at a specific point in time the life table method is used. Thus the change cycles are preserved and the validity of dependencies can be determined. In the *Measurement* the probability for an artifact being in a specific state at a specific point in time is calculated. The *Output* is either this probability or the change cycle.

Using **Ontologies** is an uncommon analysis technique in the domain of EAM (e.g. Sunkle et al. 2013). The contained analyses, 'Change Impact Analysis' and 'Structural Analysis' analyze dependencies respectively the architectural construct. A special meta model created with ontological rules is required as *Input* and *Condition*. The meta model defines the entities (i.e. artifacts and dependency types) of the EA model whereas the rules define the dependencies between the elements. The *Construct* analyzes the entities and dependencies in order to determine specific sets of them. Afterwards dependencies, viewpoints and special factors are evaluated for the outcome.

EID (Extended Influence Diagram) is the third most technique in order to conduct EA analyses (e.g. Johnson et al. 2007a). Possible results can be statements about maintainability, security and availability. Therefore systems, attributes, quality aspects, impacts and data are analyzed. The steps of the procedure are independent of the analysis type. The scenarios and alternatives have to be conducted and a goal must be defined. As *Condition* it has to be secured that the contained components can be built with EID. Afterwards all scenarios, goals and entities are represented as EID nodes and connections. For *Measurement* Bayesian Networks are used to calculate the probabilities of the attributes. Thus it is possible to analyze dependencies by inferring changes and altered values.

For the identification of **Weak Points** and their costs the following requirements can be determined (e.g. Xie et al. 2008). *Input* data are workflows and resources as well as their availability requirements. In the *Construct* a matrix of the workflows and resources is created, which is used for the availability calculation. Whenever the availability is higher as the availability requirement, the condition is fulfilled. If this is not the case a enhancement parameter helps to calculated the current level of availability. Afterwards the expected availability for every workflow is calculated. In addition it is possible to weight resources and receive alternatives with higher availability. The *Output* is the assignment of availabilities to resources.

Another identified technique is the usage of a **Matrices** (e.g. Szyszka 2009). Application fields are for instance 'Coverage Analysis' or 'Maturity Analysis'. Matrices can be used in various ways, mostly for the presentation of results. The *Input* is a common architecture model with classes, types and relations. Additional the goal and application area is required. In order to built and evaluate the matrix, the dimensions and the kind of measurement have to determined. Additionally the elements have to be aligned within the matrices. Dependent on the measurement method a quantitative evaluation or a scale for discrete areas is conducted. The results can vary from quantitative outcomes to weak points, redundant artifacts and functional dependencies.

Analyses joint in the category **Design** are able to observe architecture design in a specific way (Aier et al. 2011). The analysis identifies strengths and weaknesses of the architecture. As *Condition* the considered factors and expert knowledge is required. In the main *Construct* items and data are determined, factors are checked with questionnaires and a cluster analysis is conducted. Similarities and clusters are identified through this way. As *Measurement* a matrix of items and factors is built and evaluated. In the *Output* the results of the matrix evaluation represent the potential of a cluster.

The last technical category contains an analysis with a **Structural** procedure (Buckl et al. 2009a). This analysis tries to observe design through displaying obstacles of different architecture versions. Therefore a documentation of the EA is required as *Condition* and the main part of the analysis consists of an observation of changes. The *Output* type is unique and represents potential obstacles caused by different versions.

4   Formalization of Analysis Requirements

The identified requirements for the 10 functional categories and the 17 technical categories are formalized using a domain specific language. Therewith we can elaborate the integrity and correctness of the requirements, i.e. if they are sufficient to describe the analyses in an adequate way. The language provides a uniform description possibility for EA analyses. This supports the decision making about the implementation of an analysis since their requirements and goals are obvious the uniform description makes them comparable. For the language development we used Xtext[1], a framework that comprises a powerful language for the description of textual languages. The framework generates the model as well

---

[1] Xtext https://eclipse.org/Xtext/index.html.

a parser, linker, type checker and compiler. The DSL was developed according to the meta model development process for abstract syntax development from (Brambilla et al. 2012). This incremental and iterative process consists of three phases: The Modeling Domain Analysis phase, elaborating the purpose and content, the Modeling Language Design phase, defining the meta model, and the Modeling Language Validation phase, verifying the correctness and integrity. For the last step we select representative EA analyses for each category and formalize them using our modeling language. Difficulties and mistakes during modeling trigger a new iteration of the development process. The concrete syntax is developed simultaneously with the abstract syntax due to the nature of Xtext.

The developed DSL is structured in a general and in a categorization specific part. Figure 3 shows the main rule for the analysis language and the realization of the dimensions. General requirements that occur in all categories are summarized at beginning in the main rule. This is the name of the analysis, the required meta model and potential scenarios to evaluate. For description of the meta model and the scenarios we developed a language construct that allows to specify them similar to a UML model. The goal of an analysis is modeled using a string and its type is defined with an enumeration. Possible goal types are: percentage, matrix, probability, dependency, object, effect, scenario, number or boolean. The choice of the analysis dimensions is realized considering the later usage behavior. The user can choose first either the functional dimension or

```
MetaLanguage:
  'EAM Analysis Language' '{'
  //Domain Definition: General Requirements
    'Performing Analysis' analysis=STRING
    'Metamodel' model+=UMLModel ('{'
      'Scenarios:' scenarioName+=NameIdentifier (scenarioModel+=UMLModel)*
              (";" scenarioName+=NameIdentifier (scenarioModel+=UMLModel)*)*
    '}')?
    'Goal' goal=STRING
    'Goal Type'':' goalType+=GoalType ('&' goalType+=GoalType )*
  '}'
  //Choice of Dimensions
    ('Category functional Dimension' ':' functional+=Functional)?
    ('Category technical Dimension' ':' technical+=Technical)? ;

//----------Functional Categories------------------------------------//
Functional:
  SystemAnalysis | AttributeAnalysis |     ...     | BusinessObjectAnalysis;

//----------Technical Categories-------------------------------------//
Technical:
  BayesianNetworks | BusinessEntities | ... | Structural ;

//Choice of a possible technique matching to the chosen functional Category
SystemAnalysis:
  'System Analysis' (':')?
  ('Technique' analysisTechnique+=SystemAnalysisTechnique)? ;

SystemAnalysisTechnique:
  EID | PRM | BayesianNetworks ;
```

Fig. 3. DSL for EA analyses - main rule

the technical one. The rule system of the DSL restricts the second dimension to those that are feasible. For example the functional dimension **System Analysis** has realizations with the technical dimensions **EID**, **PRM** and **Bayesian Networks**. The rule *SystemAnalysisTechnique* ensures the integrity of the selection according to the matrix (Fig. 2). If the achievement of a planned goal is most important, the functional dimension is decided first. Thereby decisions about the function and purpose of the analysis have to be made, how the analysis is conducted is not in the main focus of the user. As second option the user decides first about the utilized technique. This option is used in case only a specific method or technique should be used, e.g. because of a tool restriction or availability issues. After choosing the technical category, it is possible to discover which goals can be achieved with it (i.e. decide about the functional category).

```
BayesianNetworks:{BayesianNetworks}
    'Bayesian Networks'
    ('Function' analysisFunction+=BayesianNetworksAnalysisFunction)?
    'INPUT'          '{'  ...  '}'
    'CONDITIONS'     '{'  ...  '}'
    'CONSTRUCT'      '{'  ...  '}'
    'MEASUREMENT'    '{'  ...  '}'
    'OUTPUT'         '{'  ...  '}'
;

BayesianNetworksAnalysisFunction:
    SystemAnalysis | DependenciesAnalysis | QualityAnalysis
;
```

Fig. 4. Excerpt of the description of Bayesian Network analysis using the DSL

For each technical category a rule is implemented that satisfies the requirements specified in Sect. 3. The rules comprise statements for defining the input, the conditions and construct, the measurement and the output (see Sect. 3.2). Figure 4 shows an excerpt of this part of the DSL. Inside the five blocks the specific characteristics of the analysis are defined. According to the complexity of the conducted analysis two blocks can be summarized into one combined block or a block can also be omitted.

To illustrate the structure of a category definition Fig. 5 shows an example description of the Information Security Analysis from (Johnson et al. 2007a). This analysis evaluates the architecture by calculating the probability of quality attributes for security. Corresponding to the main rule the description starts with the analysis name followed by a specification of the meta model and two scenarios. The meta model describes the classes, relationships and attributes that are necessary for the analysis. The two scenarios represent different alternatives that should be evaluated. The scenario description is followed by the goal statement and the goal type, in this case *percentage*. Then the functional and technical dimension is defined. The functional dimension is **Attribute Analysis** and the technical one is **Extended Influence Diagram**. The remaining structure of the analysis specification is specific for analyses of the category **EID**. The input of the analysis is here straightforward the defined meta model and both scenarios. The construct part defines the requirements in order to create extended

```
EAM Analysis Language{ Performing Analysis "Information Security Analysis"
    Metamodel Model"Architecture of Information Security"{
        Class "Application"{ ... }
        ...
    }
    {Scenarios:
        "Scenario 1" Model "UML Model Scenario 1"{      ...      };
        "Scenario 2" Model "UML Model Scenario 2"{      ...      }
    }
    Goal"Probability of quality attributes for security"        Goal Type :Percentage
    }
    Category functional Dimension:Attribute Analysis:
    Technique Extended Influence Diagram
        INPUT{ Metamodel "Architecture of Information Security"{
                Scenario"Scenario 1", Scenario"Scenario 2"
        }
    }CONSTRUCT{
        EID MODEL ELEMENTS{ Chosen Scenario "Scenario 1"
            //Value assumptions
            Scenario Node:  type: Decision Node "Scenario Selection" Value: 0."90"
            Goal:           type: Utility Node "Profit" Value: 0."0"
            Attributes:     type: Chance Node"User Training Process" Value: 0."75"
                            ...
            Relations:      "Scenario Selection" as Causal Relation to "User Training Process"
                            ...
        }}
    MEASUREMENT{
        //Example calculation for one node for one scenario
        Chance Node Selection:"User Training Process"
        Scenario Name "Scenario 1"->"Present":
        Calculation of Section: P("User Training Process")= ...
        Result="0.95"
        Goal Calculation: P(A|B)=P(B|A)P(A)/P(B)
        Result: "Usage of Bayesian network analysis tool GeNIe"
    }
    OUTPUT{
        Results: Best Scenario "Scenario 1"
    }
```

Fig. 5. Excerpt of the description of EID analysis using the DSL

influence diagrams. First the chosen scenario is set, and then the nodes, goals and attributes with their types and values are defined. Finally the EID specific relations are declared. In the measurement part for each node in each scenario a matrix with the conditional probability is specified. This is exemplary shown in Fig. 5. The value of the node 'User Training Process' is defined with a EID calculation. This calculation determines the probability of the node to be in a specific discrete range, here 'present', in dependency from further nodes. Finally the result and the goal calculation according to the bayesian theorem are declared. Such a calculation can also be done for a quality attribute to have a specific value in one scenario. The output contains the scenario with the best values according to the measurement.

5   Evaluation and Discussion

We evaluated our DSL through formalizing existing analysis approaches from literature. The experiences and limitations are presented below, followed by a discussion about the categorization as well as related work.

All identified categories, functional as well as technical, are integrated in the language and it was possible to formalize a representative from each category. Figure 5 shows an excerpt of the definition of the Information Security Analysis (functional dimension: attribute analysis, technical dimension: extended influence diagram). The language can be reused for the development of new analyses, since it provides a sound foundation of requirements that have to be extended. After further development the language can also be used as an entry point for the specification and execution of analysis. The analysis language itself provides a high abstraction grade that enables also the application for example in service-oriented architectures or business analyses. Additionally the language is easy extendable and without special knowledge understand- and usable.

Most of the requirements for the technical categories are realized in the language. A few requirements are determined as given and not further mentioned, since these requirements are obviously. Examples are the possibility to raise data, i.e. whether data can be used or be accessible. In addition requirements, which are not verifiable couldn't be included. For instance, it is not verifiable whether the meta model can be used to achieve the goals, whether artifacts can be mapped to EID components or whether used nodes are controllable. Additionally the acceptance of a used technique or the availability of expert knowledge is not verifiable and thus not integrated in the language. Requirements that are defined in a graphical way, for example matrices, are difficult to realize in a textual language. Also the definition of patterns is only specified with limitations in the language. The lower number of functional categories in contrast to the technical ones can be explained with the focus on one field of interest. Since we concentrate on pure EA analyses the analysis goals were repetitive. A problem during categorization was the issue that not all aspects from the analyses are described in detail in the available publications. At this point we were only able to identify limited requirements or we had to make assumptions in order to proceed. A interrelated problem is the fact of the low amount of available descriptions of conducted analyses to evaluate our language. Additional some analyses use very specific techniques or modeling approaches. Here, it was not possible to consider all details in order to create a sound categorization. We abstracted from some specifics in order to define the general requirements for a category. We received the general valid requirements by focusing on the approach with the highest level on elaboration and abstracting from it considering the issues of the other approaches. An example is the technical category **KPI** with a high abstraction level. The contained analyses differ deeply in measuring values with different formulas. Therefore the mathematical computation cannot be described in full detail in our language.

Encountered categorization approaches in related work tried to focus on the meta level. However, in contrast to our target they designed an analysis framework independent from the meta model (Langermeier et al. 2014), developed a category independent meta language (Buckl et al. 2011) or had the main focus on characteristics (Buckl et al. 2010). Additional EA analyses can be distinguished between the point of execution time. Therefore the analyses are sorted in ex-ante and ex-post to determine whether an analysis will be conducted before or after the adoption of an architecture. It is also possible to separate the analyses according to their execution technique: expert-based, rule-based or indicator-based (Buckl et al. 2009b). However, both classifications are not detailed enough to identify characteristics and most of the analyses can't be strictly classified within these divisions. Lankhorst (2013) conducted an initial categorization with four dimensions: Quantitative and functional differ at the input and output data. The functional dimension can be further distinguished in static and dynamic. However this division is not detailed enough to identify the explicit requirements of classified analyses and four categories is a rough classification. Therefore an advantage of categorization cannot be accomplished. Regarding the varieties of containing approaches, the existing categorizations are not sufficient.

6   Conclusion

In this paper we presented a two-dimensional categorization of EA analyses, based on the characteristics of the approaches found in literature. The first dimension addresses the functional aspect, the second one the technical aspect. Altogether we identified 105 analyses, which are classified in 10 functional categories and 17 technical categories. Using this categorization we can identify 40 different analysis types used in EA. The dependencies between the approaches of the functional and technical dimensions are visualized in a matrix. The dependencies as well as the characteristics of the analysis categories are formalized with a domain specific language. The language provides a structural way to represent the preconditions of an analysis, the technical requirements for execution and also the outcome of it. Additionally the enterprise architecture can use the language to decide whether the outcome of an analysis is from interest for his question, if the analysis is applicable on his EA model and how great the effort of adaption is in order to execute the analysis. The idea of such an EA analysis catalog is the support of reuse of existing work in the domain of EA. Therefore future work has to investigate techniques for context independent execution of those analyses. This could be the development of tool support for the usage of the categories and the DSL. Thus, computations, which need further tools, can be included, new analyses could be created simplified and requirements are checked automatically. Additionally a higher abstraction level of the category characteristics would be conceivable to make the requirements general valid.

References

Aier, S., Buckl, S., Franke, U., Gleichauf, B., Johnson, P., Närman, P., Schweda, C. M., and Ullberg, J. A survival analysis of application life spans based on enterprise architecture models. In: 3rd Workshop on EMISA, pp. 141–154 (2009)

Aier, S., Gleichauf, B., Winter, R.: Understanding enterprise architecture management design-an empirical analysis. In: Proceedings of 10th Conference on Wirtschaftsinformatik (2011)

Brambilla, M., Cabot, J., Wimmer, M.: Model-driven software engineering in practice. Synth. Lect. Softw. Eng. **1**, 1–182 (2012)

Buckl, S., Buschle, M., Johnson, P., Matthes, F., Schweda, C.M.: A meta-language for enterprise architecture analysis. In: Halpin, T., Nurcan, S., Krogstie, J., Soffer, P., Proper, E., Schmidt, R., Bider, I. (eds.) BPMDS/EMMSAD -2011. LNBIP, vol. 81, pp. 511–525. Springer, Heidelberg (2011). doi:10.1007/978-3-642-21759-3_37

Buckl, S., Matthes, F., Neubert, C., Schweda, C.M.: A wiki-based approach to enterprise architecture documentation and analysis. In: Proceedings of ECIS 2009, pp. 1476–1487 (2009a)

Buckl, S., Matthes, F., Schweda, C.M.: Classifying enterprise architecture analysis approaches. In: Poler, R., Sinderen, M., Sanchis, R. (eds.) IWEI 2009. LNBIP, vol. 38, pp. 66–79. Springer, Heidelberg (2009b). doi:10.1007/978-3-642-04750-3_6

Buckl, S., Matthes, F., Schweda, C.M.: A meta-language for EA information modeling – state-of-the-art and requirements elicitation. In: Bider, I., Halpin, T., Krogstie, J., Nurcan, S., Proper, E., Schmidt, R., Ukor, R. (eds.) BPMDS/EMMSAD -2010. LNBIP, vol. 50, pp. 169–181. Springer, Heidelberg (2010). doi:10.1007/978-3-642-13051-9_15

Buschle, M., Ullberg, J., Franke, U., Lagerström, R., Sommestad, T.: A tool for enterprise architecture analysis using the PRM formalism. In: Soffer, P., Proper, E. (eds.) CAiSE Forum 2010. LNBIP, vol. 72, pp. 108–121. Springer, Heidelberg (2011). doi:10.1007/978-3-642-17722-4_8

Davis, F.D.: Perceived usefulness, perceived ease of use, and user acceptance of information technology. MIS Q. **13**(3), 319–340 (1989)

de Boer, F. S., Bonsangue, M.M., Groenewegen, L., Stam, A., Stevens, S., Van Der Torre, L.: Change impact analysis of enterprise architectures. In: IEEE International Conference on Information Reuse and Integration, pp. 177–181 (2005)

Bordella, M., Liu, R., Ravarini, A., Wu, F.Y., Nigam, A.: Towards a method for realizing sustained competitive advantage through business entity analysis. In: Halpin, T., Nurcan, S., Krogstie, J., Soffer, P., Proper, E., Schmidt, R., Bider, I. (eds.) BPMDS/EMMSAD -2011. LNBIP, vol. 81, pp. 216–230. Springer, Heidelberg (2011). doi:10.1007/978-3-642-21759-3_16

Johnson, P., Lagerström, R., Närman, P., Simonsson, M.: Enterprise architecture analysis with extended influence diagrams. Inf. Syst. Front. **9**(2), 163–180 (2007a)

Johnson, P., Nordström, L., Lagerström, R.: Formalizing analysis of enterprise architecture. In: Doumeingts, G., Müller, J., Morel, G., Vallespir, B. (eds.) Enterprise Interoperability, pp. 35–44. Springer, London (2007b)

Kazienko, P., Michalski, R., Palus, S.: Social network analysis as a tool for improving enterprise architecture. In: O'Shea, J., Nguyen, N.T., Crockett, K., Howlett, R.J., Jain, L.C. (eds.) KES-AMSTA 2011. LNCS (LNAI), vol. 6682, pp. 651–660. Springer, Heidelberg (2011). doi:10.1007/978-3-642-22000-5_67

Krcmar, H.: Informationsmanagement. Gabler (2015)

Langermeier, M., Saad, C., Bauer, B.: A unified framework for enterprise architecture analysis. In: 18th IEEE International EDOC Conference Workshops, pp. 227–236 (2014)

Lankhorst, M.: Enterprise Architecture at Work: Modelling, Communication and Analysis. The Enterprise Engineering Series. Springer, Heidelberg (2013)

Matthes, F., Monahov, I., Schneider, A., Schulz, C.: Eam kpi catalog. Technical report v 1.0, Technical University Munich (2011)

Närman, P., Buschle, M., Ekstedt, M.: An enterprise architecture framework for multi-attribute information systems analysis. Softw. Syst. Model. **13**, 1–32 (2012)

Närman, P., Franke, U., König, J., Buschle, M., Ekstedt, M.: Enterprise architecture availability analysis using fault trees and stakeholder interviews. Enterp. Inf. Syst. **8**(1), 1–25 (2011)

Närman, P., Johnson, P., Ekstedt, M., Chenine, M., König, J.: Enterprise architecture analysis for data accuracy assessments. In: 13th IEEE International EDOC Conference, pp. 24–33 (2009)

Närman, P., Schonherr, M., Johnson, P., Ekstedt, M., Chenine, M.: Using enterprise architecture models for system quality analysis. In: 12th IEEE International EDOC Conference, pp. 14–23 (2008)

Niemann, K.D.: From Enterprise Architecture to IT Governance. Springer, Heidelberg (2006)

Rauscher, J.: Analysen in Unternehmensarchitekturen - Ziele, Techniken, Anwendungsbereiche. Bachelor thesis, University Augsburg (2013)

Rauscher, J.: Anforderungen an und Definition von einer Analysesprache für das Enterprise Architecture Management. Bachelor thesis, University Augsburg (2015)

Razavi, M., Aliee, F.S., Badie, K.: An AHP-based approach toward enterprise architecture analysis based on enterprise architecture quality attributes. Knowl. Inf. Syst. **28**(2), 449–472 (2011)

Saat, J.: Zeitbezogene Abhängigkeitsanalysen der Unternehmensarchitektur. In: MKWI, pp. 119–130 (2010)

Sasa, A., Krisper, M.: Enterprise architecture patterns for business process support analysis. J. Syst. Softw. **84**(9), 1480–1506 (2011)

Sunkle, S., Kulkarni, V., Roychoudhury, S.: Analyzable enterprise models using ontology. In: CAiSE Forum, vol. 998, pp. 33–40 (2013)

Szyszka, B.: Analysis and classification of maturity models in enterprise architecture management. Bachelor thesis, Technical University Munich (2009)

Van Lamsweerde, A.: Goal-oriented requirements engineering: a guided tour. In: 5th IEEE International Symposium on Requirements Engineering, pp. 249–262 (2001)

Wan, H., Carlsson, S.: Towards an understanding of enterprise architecture analysis activities. In: Proceedings of 6th ECIME (2012)

Winter, R., Fischer, R.: Essential layers, artifacts, and dependencies of enterprise architecture. In: 10th IEEE International EDOC Conference Workshops (2006)

Xie, L., Luo, J., Qiu, J., Pershing, J., Li, Y., Chen, Y., et al.: Availability "weak point" analysis over an SOA deployment framework. In: IEEE Network Operations and Management Symposium, pp. 473–480 (2008)

Zia, M.J., Azam, F., Allauddin, M.: A survey of enterprise architecture analysis using multi criteria decision making models (MCDM). In: Chen, R. (ed.) ICICIS 2011. CCIS, vol. 135, pp. 631–637. Springer, Heidelberg (2011). doi:10.1007/978-3-642-18134-4_100

A Framework for Visualization of Changes of Enterprise Architecture

Robert Bakelaar[1], Ella Roubtsova[2(✉)], and Stef Joosten[2]

[1] Royal Vopak, Global IT, Westerlaan 10, 3016CK Rotterdam, The Netherlands
[2] Open University of the Netherlands, Valkenburgerweg 177,
6401DL Heerlen, The Netherlands
Ella.Roubtsova@ou.nl

Abstract. An innovation that is substantial enough to change the enterprise architecture poses a problem for a system architect. Enterprise architecture modeling methods and tools do not support the distinction between the As-Is architecture and the To-Be architecture in one view model. Recognizing the changes becomes similar to a game of "finding changes in two drawings". As the size of architectures and number of architectural view pairs grows, the changes can be overlooked. In order to support the recognizing of changes by the implementation teams, the changes need specific visualization means.

In this paper, we use the modern cases of transformation of ERP (Enterprise Resource Planning) systems to the Best of Breed solutions and an architecture modeling language ArchiMate to propose a framework for visualization of changes. The framework includes a new abstraction called "Gap of Changes", artifacts, principles and means for visualization. The new abstraction is defined on a metamodel that makes it reusable in different enterprise and software architecture description languages. The framework is tested with real cases of changes of ERP using the Best of Breed strategy.

1 Introduction

Modern enterprises are systems of business processes, software applications and technology. The enterprise architecture description languages include software architecture languages and allow for presentation the snapshots of concepts/relations of an enterprise architecture at one specified moment.

Enterprises are often changed or transformed in order to survive and preserve their market positions [8]. The changes of enterprises that should be implemented, are reflected by two enterprise architectures: As-Is and To-Be; or by two sets of architectural views: As-Is and To-Be. Understanding the changes becomes similar to a game of "finding changes in two drawings". As the size of the enterprise architecture and the number of view pairs grows, the changes can be overlooked or ambiguously understood by several implementation teams. In order to support the unambiguous understanding of changes by the implementation teams, the changes need specific visualization means.

© Springer International Publishing AG 2017
B. Shishkov (Ed.): BMSD 2016, LNBIP 275, pp. 140–160, 2017.
DOI: 10.1007/978-3-319-57222-2_7

In this paper, we use the popular enterprise architecture language Archi-Mate [10] to explore the difficulties during the visualization process, and the abstractions needed for it. Our choice of the ArchiMate modeling language is explained by several reasons.

- First, ArchiMate follows to the TOGAF (the abbreviation of "The Open Group Architecture Framework"). It is a standard for enterprise architecture [11].
- Second, ArchiMate is based on a metamodel that contains a layered structure in which the business, application and technology architectures are covered and the modeling of relations between the different layers is supported. Having means to model different domains of the same business, ArchiMate fills the gap between the different domain architectures and the missing relationships between these architectures, as they are most of the time created by separate architects in different modeling languages [5].
- Third, the ArchiMate language is used in industry, and it is supported with some open-source tools, for example, Archi 2.4. [4]

We investigate the ArchiMate and its extensions.

As a result, we propose a visualization framework based on the ArchiMate and its extensions. The proposed framework is tested with the cases of transformation of ERP (Enterprise Resource Planning) systems using the Best of Breed strategy to illustrate the visualization of changes.

Our framework contains a new abstraction for visualization of changes, artifacts, principles and means for visualization. We explain the new abstraction on a metamodel extending the metamodel of ArchiMate. Such an approach makes our result applicable in other architecture description languages based on the TOGAF standard.

The structure of the paper is the following.

Section 2 describes some characteristics of ArchiMate and its extensions relevant to the visualization of changes.

Section 3 presents our framework, the definition and the metamodel of a new abstraction called *"Gap of Changes"* for visualization of changes.

Section 4 describes a test case of transformation of an ERP system using the Best of Breed strategy.

Section 5 visualizes the strategic views on the test case.

Section 6 uses our framework to visualize the test case at the application layer.

Section 7 visualizes the test case at the technological layer.

Section 8 discusses the principles, means and abstractions used for visualization and the scalability issues.

Section 9 concludes the paper.

2 ArchiMate and Its Extensions

ArchiMate is one of the popular tools for visualization of enterprise architecture [3,5]. Mostly, it is because it supports visualization of three related layers of the enterprise architecture:

1. the business layer (products, services, actors, processes);
2. the application layer (application components, application functions and data objects) and
3. the technological layer (infrastructure services, hardware, system software).

The visual elements of ArchiMate within the application and technology layers are mostly concepts and relations [6]:

- Active elements performing behavior (i.e. application service, application component).
- Elements describing behavior (i.e. infrastructure service, application function).
- Passive elements on which behavior is performed (i.e. data object).
- Relations between the elements, depicted as connecting lines between elements or boxes.
- The visual elements can be included into other elements by aggregation, composition and grouping relations.

There are also ArchiMate extensions [10] that cover high level concepts used in business implementation. Among them are the motivation extension and the implementation and migration extension. These extensions contain

- Elements describing motivation: goals, requirements, principles;
- Elements describing migration: plateaus and gaps.

The elements used in this paper are listed in Fig. 1.

Our research goal is to define and test a framework for visualization of architecture changes. The notions of plateau and gap in the migration extension should be related to changes.

"A plateau is defined as a relatively stable state of the architecture that exists during a limited period of time" [10]. Plateaus can be used to present the As-Is and To-Be view.

"A gap is defined as an outcome of a gap analysis between two plateaus" [10]. Figure 2 is a fragment of the ArchiMate metamodel. It shows that a gap is only associated with core elements combined in different plateaus. So, it is supposed that an analysis of the differences between the As-Is and To-Be architectures results only a set of changed elements. In this paper, we show that not only changed elements should be captured to visualize architectural changes.

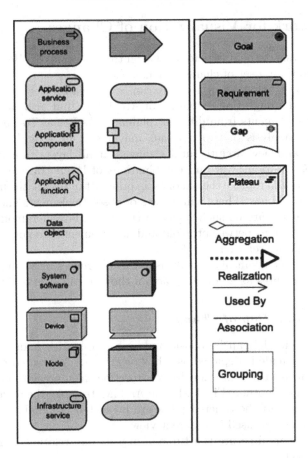

Fig. 1. Visual elements of ArchiMate [10] and its extensions used in this paper

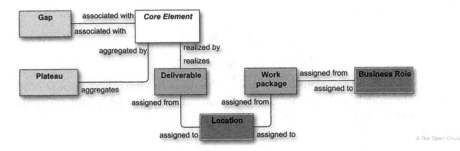

Fig. 2. A fragment of the metamodel for the migration extension: Gap, Plateau and Core Elements [10]

3   Framework for Visualization of Changes

In fact, an analysis of the differences between the As-Is and To-Be architectures results in more than a set of changed elements.

First, we suggest that a gap not only can *be associated with core elements* as it is defined in the migration extension of ArchiMate, but also can *aggregate* a selection of core elements from different plateaus (As-Is and To-Be plateaus).

Second, the analysis of two plateaus may result in several sets of tuples combining old and new architectural elements at all layers from the business layer to implementation layer and combinations of layers. In one set of tuples the new elements will replace the old ones, in other set of tuples, the new elements will modify the old ones. There will be sets of obsolete elements and completely new elements. There are no such tuples in the ArchiMate metamodel.

Third, the relations between the old and new elements are not defined in the set of the ArchiMate relations.

We formalize the result of an analysis of the differences between an As-Is and an To-Be architectures as a new abstraction that we call *Gap of Changes*.

3.1   Abstraction *Gap of Changes*

Each ArchiMate-model can be considered as a graph with nodes and ordered pairs of nodes. A node is depicted as a box or an area. A directed pair of nodes has different forms of presentation from arrows between areas to depicting one node in the area of another (Fig. 1). In the ArchiMate-tools, the nodes are maintained as objects and the ordered pairs are presented as binary relations in a "repository". They are used in different views.

An enterprise architecture is a tuple of objects and relations defined on the set of these objects.

$$Arch = (O, R).$$

In case of a transition, we distinguish two ArchiMate-models: an As-Is model and a To-Be model.

$$AsIs = (O_{AsIs}, R_{AsIs}),$$
$$ToBe = (O_{ToBe}, R_{ToBe}).$$

Some objects and relations exist only in the As-Is model, others appear only in the To-Be model, and, usually, a significant amount of objects and relations exists in both models.

We distinguish:

- An object or a relation is called *obsolete* if it exists in the As-Is model and not in the To-Be model.
- An object or a relation is called *new* if it exists in the To-Be model and not in the As-Is model.
- An object is called *changed* if it exists in both models, and it is linked (by relations) in the To-Be model to another set of objects than in the As-Is model.

– An object is called *unchanged* if it exists in both models, and it is linked (by relations) in the To-Be model to the same set of objects as in the As-Is model.

In Archimate, we designate some views as "As-Is". We make sure that an "As-Is" view contains no new elements. We can also designate views as "To-Be", making sure that an "To-Be" view contains no obsolete elements.

An abstraction called *Gap of Changes, Gch*, is a view that

– combines the obsolete, new, changed objects and relations,
– annotates them with new relations <Replaced-By> and <Extended-By> and
– positions the obsolete and changed objects in the As-Is architecture and the new and changed objects in the To-Be architecture by showing a subset of unchanged objects related to the obsolete, new and/or changed objects.

A *Gap of Changes* is a tuple:

$$Gch = (O_{obsolete}, O_{new}, O_{unchanged}, O_{changed},$$
$$R_{obsolete}, R_{new}, R_{replaced-by}, R_{extended-by}, R_{border})$$

– $O_{obsolete} = \{o|\ o \in O_{AsIs}\ and\ o \notin O_{ToBe}\}$
  is a set of obsolete objects from the As-Is architecture.
– $O_{new} = \{o|\ o \notin O_{AsIs}\ and\ o \in O_{ToBe}\}$
  is a set of new objects from the To-Be architecture.
– $O_{unchanged} = \{o|\ o \in O_{AsIs}\ and\ o \in O_{ToBe}\ and$
  $\forall x : (o, x) \in R_{ToBe} \Leftrightarrow (o, x) \in R_{AsIs}\}$
  $O_{unchanged}$ is a subset of all unchanged objects. They have the same relations in the To-Be model in comparison with the As-Is model.
  These objects are included to relate the *Gap of Changes* to the As-Is and To-Be architectures.
– $O_{changed} = ((O_{AsIs} \cap O_{ToBe}) \setminus O_{unchanged})$
  is a set of changed objects that appear in both models and do not have the same relations in both models.

All sets of objects are disjoint.

– $R_{obsolete} = \{(a, b)|(a, b) \in R_{AsIs}\ and\ (a, b) \notin R_{ToBe}\}$
  is a set of obsolete relations that appear in the As-Is model and do not exist in the To-Be model. $R_{obsolete}$ relate obsolete and/or changed objects.
– $R_{new} = \{(a, b)|(a, b) \notin R_{AsIs}\ and\ (a, b) \in R_{ToBe}\}$
  is a set of new relations defined on the sets of new and changed objects.
– $R_{<replaced-by>} \subseteq O_{obsolete} \times O_{new}$
  is a set of annotations, being relations of type $< Replaced - By >$.
  These relations are added during the analysis of the difference between the As-Is and To-Be models.

Not all obsolete elements are necessarily replaced by new elements.
Not all new elements replace the obsolete ones.

- $R_{extended-by} \subseteq O_{changed} \times O_{new}$
  is a set of annotations, being relations of type
  $< Extended - By >$.
  These relations are added by analysis of the difference
  between the As-Is and To-Be models.
- $R_{border} \subseteq (O_{unchanged} \times O_{changed}) \cup (O_{changed} \times O_{unchanged})$
  is a set of relations between the changed elements and
  the unchanged elements within the As-Is and To-Be
  architectures.

Note that $O_{obsolete}$ or O_{new} can be empty.

3.2   Metamodel of a *Gap of Changes*

Figure 3 shows the metamodel of our framework for visualization of changes.

We separate the As-Is Plateau and To-Be Plateau conceptually. Each of those plateaus aggregates own set of core elements: As-Is Core Element and To-Be Core Element. The intersection of those sets is usually not empty.

A *Gap of Changes* aggregates: the <obsolete> and <changed> Core Elements from an As-Is plateau and the <new> and <changed> Core Elements from a To-Be plateau.

We add new types of relation between the Core Elements aggregated by a *Gap of Changes*: <Replaced−By> and <Extended−By>.

Such an approach allows one to select an abstraction representing changes in a *Gap of Changes*, so that the communication teams do not need to find differences in two architectures As-Is and To-Be.

Relations between the As-Is and To-Be Core Elements aggregated in the *Gap of Changes* provide the possibility to associate the constraints, requirements and principles with the gap elements and, in such a way, visualize them.

Separation of two plateaus also allows one to associate goals and drivers of transformation with the To-Be plateau. The concepts of goals and drivers are also taken from the motivation extension of ArchiMate [10].

3.3   Visual Means: Colors and Labels

Our framework suggests to use colors and labels to visually separate the new, changed and the obsolete elements of a gap of changes. We suggest to use colors and show

- new objects in green;
- changed objects in orange;
- obsolete objects in grey.

However, we have found, that when a model contains a large number of objects and even objects over multiple layers, the use of colors can be distracting and can make the visualization unclear, due to the fact that the layers in ArchiMate are distinct by color. So, we suggest to include the labels <*new*>, <*changed*> and <*obsolete*> in the objects name.

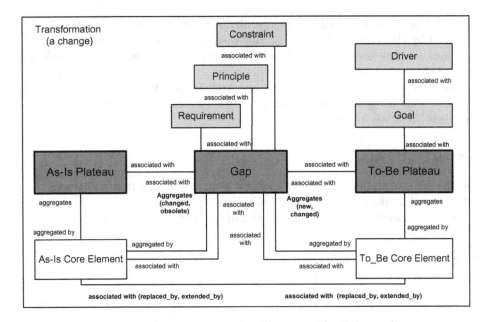

Fig. 3. The metamodel of a framework for visualization of changes

3.4   Border Relations

The abstraction *Gap of Changes* includes the border relations for reminding the place of the gap elements in the As-Is and To-Be architectures.

The relations used for reminding are often fall into the categories of group, aggregation, composition and derived relations. For example, the reminder may show that the elements of a *Gap of Changes* belong to a specific layer or a component. Let us recall that "the grouping relationship is used to group an arbitrary group of model objects, which can be of the same type or of different types. In contrast to the aggregation or composition relationships, there is no "overall" object of which the grouped objects form a part. Unlike the other language concepts, grouping has no formal semantics. It is only used to show graphically that model elements have something in common. Model elements may belong to multiple (overlapping) groups." [10] Aggregation and composition in ArchiMate have the formal semantics inspired by the UML. [9] When elements belong to other elements by an aggregation or composition relation, elements can be *rolled up to the aggregated or composed element*.

Derived relations. It may be convenient to a skip the intermediate relations and elements in a certain chain and show only a very well known element of a component. This can be done using the derived relations of ArchiMate. The structural relations in ArchiMate are divided into four categories of strength, where "association is the weakest structural relationship; composition is the strongest. Part of the language definition is an abstraction rule that states that two relationships that join at an intermediate element can be combined and replaced by the weaker of the two." [10] Using this abstraction rule of derived relations, a view may abstract from the intermediate elements of a chain of related elements (make some intermediate elements invisible). Elements can be rolled up, using the derived relationship of ArchiMate, where the chain of related elements can be generalized by relating two elements in the chain using the "weakest" relation in the chain.

3.5   Visual Artifacts

On the basis of the metamodel of the new abstraction, our framework selects a set of visual artifacts needed for visualization of changes.

All visual artifacts of our framework fall into three categories:

1. Strategies views,
2. As-Is views, To-Be views and
3. Views on a *Gap of Changes*.

Any change depends on the chosen strategy and on the given requirements. Therefore, we need a goal/requirements view associated with a change presented as one transition from an abstract As-Is to an abstract To-Be.

The As-Is views, To-Be views and views on a *Gap of Changes* may be visualized at different system layers: the business process layer, at the application layer and at the technology layer. The elements of the views on a *Gap of Changes* at different layers may be related in order to form the visualization at a combination of layers. For example, it is good to remind that the changes are implemented for business. Therefore, the relations between a *Gap of Changes* at the application and implementation layers are related to the business layer.

4   Testing Case: Transformation of ERP Using the Best of Breed Strategy

In order to test the proposed framework, we set an experiment for visualization of the ERP implementation within Royal Vopak (https://www.vopak.com/) modified using the Best of Breed strategy [7].   •

4.1   Best of Breed

Business processes often contain some parts of functionality that are well supported by standard solutions. The Best of Breed strategy is directed to use the most suitable standard software and to develop only the parts that are not supported by standard software [7]. This approach promises flexible application implementation, low costs of maintenance and changes [2].

Many companies have ERP systems that provide all the applications for an enterprise and integrate them in a superior solution where every module may

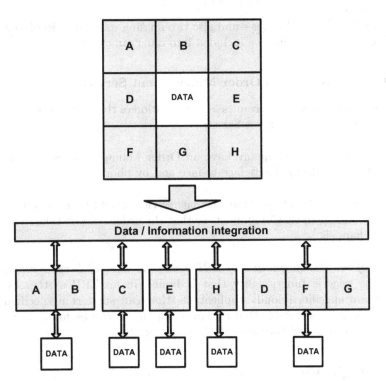

Fig. 4. From ERP to Best of Breed: The ERP implementation of functions (A, B, C, D, E, F, G, H) are decomposed into the best applications available on the market (A, B), (D, F, G), C, E and H.

not be the best of its class. If a company has an implemented ERP system and wants to change it in order to use the best standard solutions, the company should examine and change its architecture.

Ideally, the transformation is the decomposition of the application functionality and the data, as it is shown in Fig. 4. In reality, the elements are not only decomposed, but also removed, added and changed. Because of that, we have studied several cases of architectural changes.

We consider the following business situations that cover the transformation from ERP to Best of Breed:

1. The business process remains unchanged, but the changes should be made in the application and the technological layers by adding, changing and removing elements.
2. The relations between applications may change.
3. The relations between technological elements and applications may change.

For each of the situations, we analyse what should be visualised. Doing the experiment, we have discovered the repeated steps, artifacts, principles and means useful for visualization of changes e and also two missing relations <Replaced−By> and <Extended−By> that we included into our Framework.

4.2   Replacement of an Order Management Service

In this paper, we present the results of visualization of the testing case of replacement of an Order Management Service.

As-Is situation. Let a company have an Order Management Service allowing one to take orders from clients face-to-face and by phone.

To-Be situation. The Order Management Service should be replaced with the new Order Management Component, so that the orders can be taken via e-mail and B2B channels.[1]

The goal of the transformation of ERP using the Best of Breed strategy is to replace the generic functionality that is bound in an ERP system by separate, domain specific, (cloud) applications that can support a specified business process. It is preferable that all new components can be found as the best components in terms of the user interface and performance.

5   Strategic Views

The strategic views usually assign a name to a transformation and formulate the goals of transformation.

  Figure 5 visualises the "Replacement of an Order Management Service" using plateaus and gap elements from the migration extension of ArchMate.

Fig. 5. Strategic view on the "Replacement of an Order Management Service"

  Figure 6 visually presents the requirements for the transformation.

  The set of strategic views may be extended in the correspondence with the well accepted goal-oriented approaches [1]. The goal views and views on requirements may be related with the gap or with the To-Be architecture. The visual means for the strategic views on the transformation are available in the migration extension of ArchiMate.

---

[1] Business-to-business (B2B) means that the services or goods are sold to other businesses, not to private customers. B2B channels provide wider negotiation opportunities in comparison with the Business-to-Customer channels.

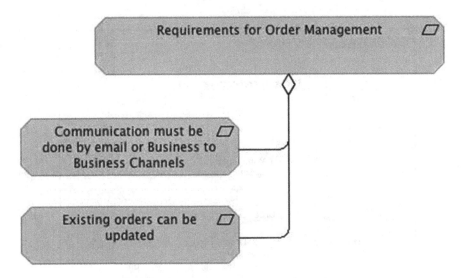

Fig. 6. Requirements for the "Replacement of an Order Management Service"

6   Visualization at the Application Layer

A view of the As-Is architecture may be given before any transformation. In practice, it is often not the case, so in a transformation project both views should be found or depicted.

The As-Is and To-Be architectures can be visualized at selected layer.

In Figs. 7 and 8 the two architectures of the Order Management Service are visualized on the application layer.

For the sake of simplicity, we select only the application layer. All figures are made using the tool Archi [4].

The As-Is architecture is shown in Fig. 7.

The To-Be architecture is depicted at Fig. 8.

The abstraction *Gap of Changes* is shown in Fig. 9. The new architectural elements are shown in green, the obsolete elements are grey.

The `External Communication` is an obsolete module. It is <Replaced-By> the new elements `E-mail Communication` and `B2B Communication`.

The `Order Entry Module` belongs to both the As-Is and To-Be architectures. It is <Extended-By> the new element `Order Updating`.

In order to position the *Gap of Changes* in the As-Is architecture, the component `Order Entry Module` is used. The component `Order Entry Module` groups the obsolete element `External Communication` and the new element `Order Updating`.

In order to relate the *Gap of Changes* with the To-Be architecture, the component `Communication Application` is included into the abstraction to group

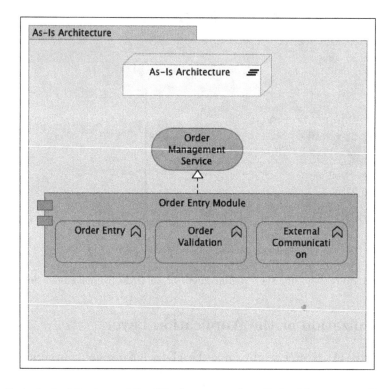

Fig. 7. As-Is Architecture of the "Replacement of an Order Management Service"

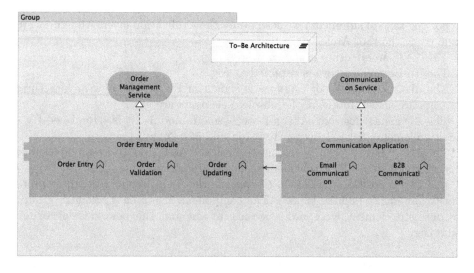

Fig. 8. To-Be Architecture of the "Replacement of an Order Management Service"

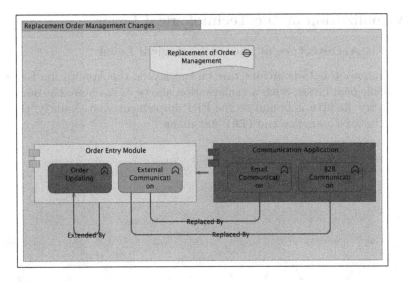

Fig. 9. Gap of changes with focus on relations between the old and new application functions (Color figure online)

E-mail Communication and B2B Communication. In order to minimize the number of elements in the Gap of Changes, the software architects have not shown the Communication Service and the Order Management Service.

The abstraction *Gap of Changes* is defined by the following tuple of sets:

- $O_{obsolete}$ = {External Communication}.
- O_{new} = {E-mail Communication,
             B2B Communication,
             Order Updating,
             Communication Application}.
- $O_{changed}$ = {Order Entry Module}.
- $R_{obsolete}$ = {(Order Entry Module, External Communication)},
- R_{new} = {(Communication Application, Order Entry Module),
             (Communication Application, E-mail Communication),
             (Communication Application, B2B Communication),
             (Order Entry Module, Order Updating)}.
- $R_{<replaced-by>}$ =
             {(External Communication, E-mail Communication),
             (External Communication, B2B Communication)}.
- $R_{<extended-by>}$ =
             {(Order Entry Module, Order Updating)}.

The sets of unchanged objects and border relations are empty in this example.

7   Visualization at the Technological Layer

7.1   As-Is Architecture at the Technological Level

Figure 10 shows the As-Is architecture on two layers: the Application Layer and the Technological Layer. Such a visualisation allows us to show that our service Order Entry Module is bound to the ERP implementation. Namely, the PERI infrastructure service and PERI database.

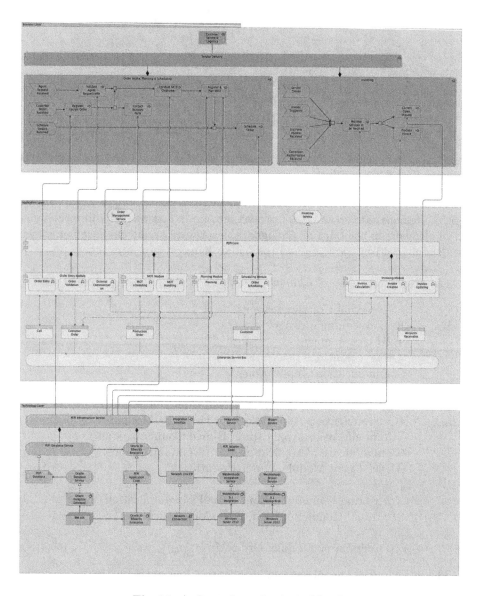

Fig. 10. As-Is at the technological level

7.2   To-Be Architecture at the Technological Layer

The technological goal of the transformation of ERP to Best of Breed is to support the new applications, replacing the generic functionality that is bound in an ERP system, with the cloud access. Figure 11 shows that all services should become the cloud applications.

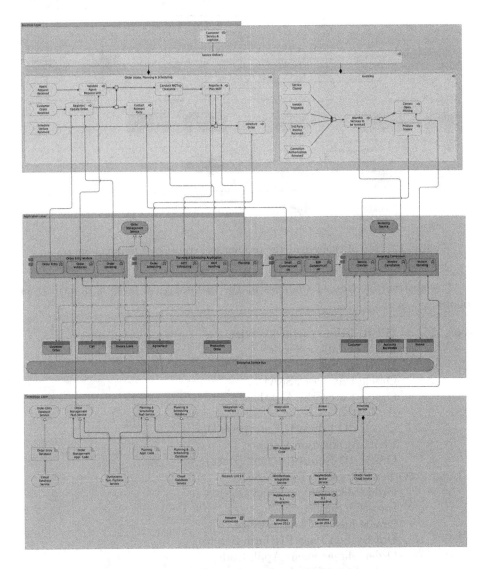

Fig. 11. To-Be at the technological level

7.3   Gap of Changes at the Technological Layer

Summarising the observation of the As-Is and To-Be architectures, we result in the *Gap of Changes* shown in Fig. 12.

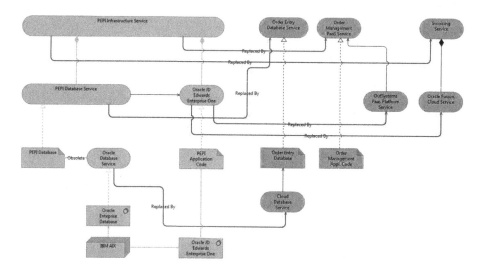

Fig. 12. Gap of changes at the technology level (Color figure online)

The abstraction *Gap of Changes* at the technological layer is described as follows:

– $O_{obsolete}$ = {PERI Infrastructure Service,
        PERI Database Service,
        PERI Database,
        Oracle Databases Service,
        Oracle Enterprise Database,
        IBM AIX,
        Oracle JD Edwards Enterprise One,
        PERI Application Code,
        Oracle JD Enterprise One (Data)}.
– O_{new} = {Order Entry Database Service,
        Order Management PaaS Service,
        Invoicing Service,
        Oracle Fusion Cloud Service,
        Out System Paas Platform Service,
        Order Management Appl. Code,
        Order Entry Database,
        Cloud Database Service}.
– $R_{<obsolete>}$ - all relations between obsolete (grey) objects in Fig. 12.
– $R_{<new>}$ - all relations between new (green) objects Fig. 12.

- $R_{<replaced-by>} = \{$
  - (PERI Infrastructure Service, Invoicing Service),
  - (PERI Infrastructure Service, Order Management PaaS Service),
  - (PERI Database Service, Order Entry Database Service),
  - (Oracle JD Edwards Enterprise One, Out System Paas Platform Service),
  - (Oracle JD Edwards Enterprise One, Oracle Fusion Cloud Service),
  - (Oracle Databases Service, Cloud Database Service)}.
- Other sets are empty in this case.

In the case of automation of visualization of a *Gap of Changes*, the type of each relation can be added to each relation as a description attribute.

8 Discussion

8.1 Visualization Principles

Our visualization principles are the minimum visual elements and the focus on changes. In order to follow these principles, we sought for means for separation the changes and unchanged elements and for visualization of relations between unchanged elements and new elements at the business, application and technology layers. We explored available means of visualization in ArchiMate.

8.2 Omitting Unchanged Elements

The unchanged elements can be sometimes omitted from the model. When a model contains unchanged elements and those elements are part of a more generic element (that is required for clarity in the model), the elements can be left out and only the generic element can be a part of the model, using the generalization method.

In Fig. 12 we omit the element representing the planning functionality `Planning and scheduling application`. This application and its implementation is not relevant for the applications `Order Entry Module` and `Communication Module` and may be omitted.

8.3 New Relations Between Changed Elements and Motivation

We have found it very useful that the core elements of ArchiMate can be related to motivational elements (goals, principles, requirements etc.) [10] For example, the principle, ``Cloud unless`` can be chosen to motivate the prosed technological elements `Oracle Fusion Cloud Service` and `Cloud Database Service` (Fig. 12).

8.4 Relations <Extended-By>, <Replaced-by>

The core of the transformation of ERP using the Best of Breed strategy is the decomposition of functionality and data, as it is shown in Fig. 4. However, in reality, this pure transformation is rare. Usually, even when following the Best of Breed strategy of changes, some functions are deleted; the new functions replace the old ones, and the new functions are often added. Therefore, we have found it useful to introduce the relations between the new and old functions and groups of functions.

Relations like <Extended-by> and <Replaced-by> are definitely needed for the visualization of changes. As the current ArchiMate language and the corresponding tools do not have such relation types, we reuse the directed relations of types <used-by> or <triggering relationship> and replace their labels by <Extended-by>, <Replaced-by>.

8.5 Scalability of Visualization

In all cases, the visualization of changes is a very creative activity that demands good abstraction and generalization skills. The comprehensible views of a system with large amount of elements cannot be produced without abstractions. In particular, the ability to make groups of elements and the ability to responsibly omit elements are the key techniques for visualizing of changes in a comprehensible way.

Three types of abstractions have been found useful for visualization of changes:

1. the abstractions from the unchanged elements;
2. the abstraction from the elements that are out of focus of particular view;
3. the abstractions from relations and elements in a chain using the derived relationships of ArchiMate.

For example, the derived relationship rule allows us to show in Fig. 13 only the access relations between the services the *Order Entry Module* and the *Communication Application* and the messages (data objects) sent via the *Enterprise Service Bus*. All other technological components are omitted. Indeed, at the border of the application and technological layers, there is the Enterprise Service Bus. The new and modified services suppose to subscribe for and publish messages using the Enterprise Service Bus. Therefore, we present a *Gap of Changes* view with the focus on communication elements. Figure 13 shows that the `Communication service` are subscribed for the `Customer Orders` and `Invoice Lines` published by the `Order Management Service`.

Another way of making the visualization of changes scalable is showing a sequence of gaps. As changes within a system are often implemented in steps, the visualization of each step as a *Gap of Changes* may restrict the number of changed elements and relations and make the visualization of each gap comprehensible.

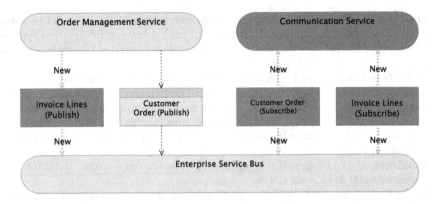

Fig. 13. Gap of changes with focus on communication elements

9   Conclusions and Future Work

This paper presents a framework for visualization of changes in ArchiMate. Our framework defines an abstraction of two architectures, As-Is and To-Be. This abstraction is called *Gap of Changes*. The new abstraction uses two architectures and two new relations to express a replacement or an extension of one element (or a group) from As-Is architecture by an element (or a group) in the To-Be architecture. The advantage of the proposed abstraction is the separation of the analysis of changes in two architectures as a directed business activity that results in a view on a *Gap of Changes*. This view can be unambiguously understood by implementation teams and can be used for planning and management. The proposed abstraction has been precisely defined to be built into the tools for visualization of enterprise architectures.

The framework has been tested with cases of transformation of ERP using the Best of Breed strategy. We expect that different combination of layers may be used for visualization of changes driven by different strategies. However, the core of the proposed framework, the abstraction *Gap of Changes* will remain the same. In the future work, we are going to apply this framework in new projects of changes with different strategies. We also plan to use the abstraction *Gap of Changes* to capture the patterns of changes corresponding to different strategies.

References

1. van Lamsweerde, A.: Requirements Engineering: From System Goals to UML Models to Software Specifications. Wiley, Chichester (2013)
2. Cardoso, J., Bostrom, R.P., Sheth, A., Sheth, C.I.A.: Workflow management systems and ERP systems: differences, commonalities, and applications. Inf. Technol. Manage. **5**, 319–338 (2004)

3. Fritscher, B., Pigneur, Y.: Business IT alignment from business model to enterprise architecture. In: Salinesi, C., Pastor, O. (eds.) Advanced Information Systems Engineering Workshops. Lecture Notes in Business Information Processing, vol. 83, pp. 4–15. Springer, Heidelberg (2011)

4. Institute of Educational Cybernetics, Archi 2.4 (2012). http://archi.cetis.ac.uk/

5. Lankhorst, M.M., Proper, H.A., Jonkers, H.: The architecture of the archimate language. In: Halpin, T., Krogstie, J., Nurcan, S., Proper, E., Schmidt, R., Soffer, P., Ukor, R. (eds.) Enterprise, Business-Process and Information Systems Modeling. Lecture Notes in Business Information Processing, vol. 29, pp. 367–380. Springer, Heidelberg (2009)

6. Lankhorst, M.M., Proper, H.A., Jonkers, H.: The anatomy of the ArchiMate language. IJISMD **1**(1), 1–32 (2010)

7. Light, B., Holland, C.P., Wills, K.: ERP and best of breed: a comparative analysis. Bus. Process Manag. J. **7**(3), 216–224 (2001)

8. Mckeown, I., Philip, G.: Business transformation, information technology and competitive strategies: learning to fly. Int. J. Inf. Manag. **23**(1), 3–24 (2003)

9. OMG, Unified Modeling Language: Superstructure version 2.1.1 formal/2007-02-03 (2003)

10. The Open Group. ArchiMate 2.1 Specification (2013). http://pubs.opengroup.org/architecture/archimate2-doc/chap03.html

11. The Open Group. TOGAF, The Open Group Architecture Framework, Version 9.1, an Open Group Standard (2016). http://pubs.opengroup.org/architecture/togaf9-doc/arch/

Towards a Thorough Evaluation Framework of Software Tools Suitable for Small and Medium Size Enterprises Focusing on Modelling and Simulating Business Processes

Rallis C. Papademetriou[1] and Dimitrios A. Karras[2(✉)]

[1] Faculty of Technology, School of Engineering, University of Portsmouth, Anglesea Building,
Anglesea Road, Portsmouth, PO1 3DJ, UK
[2] Automation Department, Sterea Hellas Institute of Technology, 34400 Psachna, Evoia, Greece
dakarras@teiste.gr, dimitrios.karras@ieee.org,
dimitrios.karras@gmail.com

Abstract. Although Business process modelling is an increasingly popular research area for both organisations and enterprises due to its usefulness in optimizing resources management, business reengineering and business performance, it is not yet widely accepted in Small and Medium size Enterprises (SMEs), which are vital for sustainable economy development. The understanding of Business Process is an essential approach for an Organization to achieve set objectives and improve its operations. It has been able to show Business Analysts, and Managers where bottleneck exists in the system, how to optimize the Business Process to reduce cost of running the Organization, and the required resources needed for an Organization. This is clear for large scale organizations and enterprises but under research investigation for SMEs. Business Process Modelling (BPM) is a representation of the processes of the Organization. Several modelling techniques have been proposed and used to capture the characteristics of business processes. However, limited guidelines exist for selecting appropriate modelling techniques based on the characteristics of the problem and its requirements. This is even more accurate in the case of selecting proper BPM software tools to achieve those BPM modelling and simulation goals. This paper aims at presenting a comparative analysis of some relatively popular business process modelling techniques focusing on the associated software tools. The comparative framework proposed is based on the following major criteria: data flow capability, logical reasoning and understandability, specification of roles, and capability of simulation, flexibility and ease of use, simulation support and scope. However, the emphasis of this investigation is put on SME applicability of these tools and techniques. Therefore, the first goal is to define proper selection criteria for the application of BPM tools to SMEs. The proposed framework can serve as the basis for evaluating further modelling techniques and generating selection procedures focusing on a comparison of existing tools to implement these techniques properly for SMEs. This is to enable a potential user/modeller choose the right technique and tool in modelling critical SME Business Processes in order to analyse and optimize its operations.

Keywords: Business process · Modelling requirements · SMEs · Software evaluation · Business process modelling tools

© Springer International Publishing AG 2017
B. Shishkov (Ed.): BMSD 2016, LNBIP 275, pp. 161–182, 2017.
DOI: 10.1007/978-3-319-57222-2_8

1   Introduction

BPM has gained prevalence during the last decade. It evolved from a series of approaches to improving business performance including Total Quality Management, Business Process Reengineering and Six Sigma (Harmon 2010). The proliferation of Enterprise Resource Planning systems has been one major reason for BPM's increasing prominence (Al-Mudimigh 2007). While it has inherited many of the principles of the above predecessor approaches, BPM represents a more holistic discipline as opposed to a single structured methodology, toolset or software type (De Bruin and Rosemann 2005). Although BPM is a broad discipline, there are a small number of concepts at its core. BPM recognises the capacity to separate the definition, design, analysis and refinement of processes from their execution. While much of the available research provides good guidance to larger, established organisations, there is less commentary addressing the challenges of and approaches to adoption of BPM within Small Businesses in the early stages of their establishment. Small businesses often operate under considerable cost and time pressure, with constrained human resources and have limited access to skills (Fogarty and Armstong 2009). These characteristics can negatively impact the adoption of BPM within Small Businesses. On the other hand, Small Businesses often have tight integration of activities, a strong work ethic and rapid decisionmaking; factors that can positively impact BPM adoption and effectiveness (Kirchmer 2011). Recently, a number of authors attempted to address this topic with case studies conducted in a number of small and medium businesses (SMEs). Chong (2007) conducted an exploratory study on barriers to adopt BPM techniques within SMEs in the wine industry in Australia. Imanipour et al. (2012a, b) looked into inhibiting factors for BPM adoption within the Iranian E-Retail industry. While Bazhenova et al. (2012) explored the use of BPM and adaptive technologies in SMEs in emerging economies.

Experts in Business analysis and Information System Analysis have both drawn the conclusion that the success of a system starts with a clear understanding and knowledge of the Business process of the organisation (Aguilar-Saven 2003). The Business Process Model provides a platform for the analysis of the processes to be carried out. Business Process Modelling is a method commonly used in organizations to increase awareness of the business process, and to simplify the complexity of the organization by disaggregating the process (Recker et al. 2009).

On its own, Business Process Modelling is not an improvement tool; it is simply a means to an end. It outlines the activities carried out in the organisation, providing a framework for improvement to be carried out. Business Process Modelling techniques are used to design of the process model; and are implemented using software tools.

With the rapid growth and embrace in IT from the 1990s to this present time, BPM has gained more popularity in organisations. This has led to the growing number of Business Process Modelling tools, techniques, and methodologies. These different techniques of Business Process Modelling have their distinct uses and purposes. Due to the lack of guide, and a numerous presence of approaches, selection of the right tool and techniques has become more complex for organisations. One of the major questions that should be answered by the ongoing research in this field is whether mainstream BPM tools, techniques and technologies could be successfully applied in a SMEs Business environment and what are the advantages of applying BPM in SMEs Business.

In view of this, a critical comparison of the Business Process Modelling techniques and tools is attempted in this paper, towards an in depth analysis of their applicability in the SMEs business environment. This is to enable SMEs to understand the right techniques and tools to use, as well as the pitfall of these techniques. Modelling of a Business process is used in detecting constraints of a system and providing a framework for carrying out continuous improvement of an Organization. This is more relevant to large organizations but is yet to be defined in SMEs. This study aims at providing background knowledge on the Business Process Modelling Techniques and especially on the requirements and selection of proper software tools for SMEs. Moreover, it seeks to determine and compare the modern mathematical and Information Systems based techniques and tools of Business Process modelling applicable to SMEs. However, at this stage in the present paper, this investigation aims at providing a proper framework only for such a thorough analysis and not the complete analysis.

2 Business Process Models Comparative Analysis

A business model is a framework used to represent the complex reality of an organization. The business model is used to present a clear description of the objectives, strategies, organizational structure, and operations of an Organization. Business Models such as the Organizational Chart, and financial statements have been used by organizations for decades. In recent times, business models such as the Business Organizational Model, Business Rule Model, Business Motivational Models, and Business Process Model have been introduced (Bridgeland and Zahavi 2009). These newer models do not displace the previous models, but to focus on other parts of the complex reality of a business.

The model of a business system can be classified into two categories (Kalnins et al.);

i. As-is Model: This is a representation of the present state of the Business System which includes the Organizational Structure, the main operations of the organization, the logical behaviour aspects of the system – who carries out a task, when it is to be carried out, and what it aims to achieve

ii. To-be Model: This is an improvement of the As-Is Model after an analysis of the present state has been carried out. It is a representation of what the system can be and how the operations can be optimised.

A branch of Business Model which is considered to be an essential aspect of Business Process Management is the *Business Process Model*.

Business Process Model is used to represent a step-by-step approach in operations of an Organization. The Business Process model is a means to an end; showing what the series of activities aim to achieve, who/what department is to carry out the activities, and what stage the activity is to be carried out in the organizational operations process. The representation of the interactions between the tasks, operations, and processes provides a foundation for the improvement of the efficiency, effectiveness and business process of an organization (Business Process Modelling 2007).

In present times, the research on Business Process Modelling is beginning to gain attention in both the academic and industrial environment. It is not just restricted to Business Process Management; it can be applicable to areas such as web development analysis, software development/engineering, and service-oriented structure (Prezel et al.). Business Process Modelling is not only used in conventional business environment, but also in government agencies, charity organizations, and all process-oriented systems. A Business Process Model can be used repeatedly for similar processes (Yamamoto et al. 2005). The increasing awareness and embrace of Information Technology/Information Systems has heightened the demand for process improvement with the aid of Business Process Modelling. The top priority of modelling a Business Process is to improve the system's performance through the optimisation of the activities carried out to achieve set objectives. Figure 1 illustrates the representation of the present activities of a system (AS-IS), and what the process is to become (TO-BE) order to optimize production/services. Other purposes to model a Business Process includes; communication, training, process reuse, persuasion in sales (Bridgeland and Zahavi 2009).

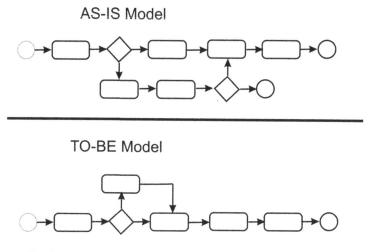

Fig. 1. Example of an AS-IS and TO-BE Business Process Model

The increase in demand of process modelling has equally made it as relevant as existing process optimization tool such as Total Quality Management (TQM). To model a Business Process, different techniques can be used. These techniques have been developed for different purposes and are more suitable in various aspects. Business Process Modelling techniques are concerned with the mapping and workflow of activities in a system in order to be able to carry out analysis, and also provide a framework for change management (Business Process Modelling 2013).

The techniques of Business Process Modelling can be classified into three different set based on their representation of a model (Vergidis et al. 2008);

- *Diagrammatic Model:* At the inception of Business Process Model, these techniques were being solely used. It is a simple and easy-to-communicate graphical representation, originally developed for software analysis and development. Initially, the representation of these techniques was plain graphics.
- *Mathematical Model:* These are referred to as second generation of BPM techniques. These techniques are well defined and precise, and can be analysed mathematically to extract knowledge. Though these models are very appropriate in carrying out quantitative analysis and improvement of a process, they are not suitable in modelling complex constructs based on no emphasis on the diagrammatical representation of the process such as decision points. Representation of a Business process mathematically may prove to be much more complex than diagrammatic representation.
- *Business Process Languages:* The most recent set of BPM techniques to be developed. The development of these set of techniques, like the first generation set, was influenced by software development. Business process languages is an Information Technology based technique in used to represent Business Processes. This latest trend of BPM techniques is dynamic in nature and rapidly evolving.

This section provides a comparative analysis of modern Business Process Modelling techniques. In this chapter, a basis for comparing the techniques is developed; the techniques are reviewed, stating their strengths and weakness (if any). The chapter ends with recent methodologies used in modelling an Enterprise.

In the study carried out, ten techniques were selected. This selection was based on popularity on websites of reputable Business Process Management software developers, and few existing recent journals from publishers such as IEEE, Science Direct.

In carrying out the comparative study of Business Process Model techniques, the answers to the following questions provided guidelines on how to achieve the objective

- What are the bases for comparing the different Business Process Modelling techniques?
- What are the strengths and weakness in using the technique?
- What are the basic focuses of the techniques?

Past researchers have classified and compared the BPM techniques based on different views; in her article, Aguilar-Saven (2003) classified the techniques based on the purpose of the model and model change permissiveness (active and passive).

Another classification based on the representation of the techniques; Mathematical, Diagrammatical, and BP language (Vergidis et al. 2008).

However, most of these techniques make use of the conventional approach, representing Business Process (regardless of the form) as series of activities, emphasizing the structure of the flow of activities, and the resultant output from the activities; and also, used for similar purpose.

Hence, an approach for comparison is proposed based on the different techniques in this project to not only aid Academicians, but also aid BPM practitioners in selecting a technique.

In answering the research questions, four features were proposed; and the strengths and the weakness were stated. The features were based on intensive study of the general characteristics of Business Process Modelling techniques, and purpose of model classification by Aguilar-Saven (2003): *learning description; decision support for process design, control, and execution; Information Technology enactment support.*

The Table 1 below outlines and describes the features that were used in the comparison.

Table 1. Business process general comparison criteria

Features	Description
Data flow approach	All techniques outline the flow of activities in the model; data flow description further explains what information is passed along. In some modelling techniques, text is combined with the visual representation of activities in the process flow. This approach is perhaps regarded as the most important form in the communication of process models to stakeholders. This feature explains the additional description offered by the techniques
Logical approach	In this context, logical reasoning is the process of using statements/ notations/arguments in describing conditions which must be met for an activity to be carried out. This feature adds more structure in the process model, providing alternate routes in achieving the objectives of the process. This feature is highly relevant in making decisions in the Organization
Role approach	In process modelling techniques, this feature is usually a secondary structure included. The use of roles in techniques gives a clear description of who is responsible for the different tasks in the process, providing organization distribution of activities. The role assignment feature targets analysis of administrative procedures, providing a guideline in carrying out structural change in Organizations
Simulation	Simulation is the act of imitating the behaviour or operations of real-world Business Process or systems. This feature is used to carry out virtual analysis of a process

3 Business Process Modelling Software (BPMS) Tools Requirements, Selection Criteria and Comparative Analysis

There are about 150 different BPM Software tools - and might there exist even more. One can get a nice overview at www.businessprocessincubator.com/tools/bpms.html and https://www.businessprocessincubator.com/content/business-process-management-bpm-software-evaluation-report/.

It is, therefore, important to define selection criteria in order to choose the appropriate tool from such a list. One of these criteria is BPMN 2.0 compliance.

Business Process Model and Notation (BPMN) is an ISO/IEC 19510:2013 standard and de-facto standard for business process modeling, which defines a graphical notation for representing business processes in the form of business process diagrams. In order to take the full advantage of the standard, the use of modeling tools is highly recommended. They enable easier and faster modeling, because they support a wide variety of features, such as enforcement of syntactic and semantic rules, support for team modeling, business process simulation, export and import in different formats and many more facilities. Before BPMN 2.0 (https://www.goodelearning.com/courses/business-process/bpmn-training), any tool could claim BPMN compliance, since there was no official criteria. Consequentially, many BPM tools that provided "boxes and arrows" for modeling claimed to be compliant with BPMN. The standard states that the software "can claim compliance or conformance with BPMN 2.0 if and only if the software fully matches the applicable compliance points as stated in the International Standard". However, if the software only partially matches the applicable compliance points, it can only claim "that the software was based on this International Standard, but cannot claim compliance or conformance with this International Standard". Furthermore, the specification introduces four types of conformance: (1) Process Modeling Conformance, (2) Process Execution Conformance, (3) BPEL Process Execution Conformance, and (4) Choreography Modeling Conformance. Any tool that claims Process Modeling Conformance must support the elements and attributes of three subclasses, namely Descriptive, Analytical and Common Executable. The Descriptive and Analytical subclasses address the non-executable models and provide the information, necessary for visual representation of the diagrams (e.g. icons, markers, border styles, shape types). Any description of the data and the corresponding XML and meta-model is part of the Common Executable subclass. A study card of Process Modeling Conformance is available on the Good e-Learning website (https://www.goodelearning.com/downloads/business-process/subclassess-of-bpmn-process-modeling-elements).

A Process Execution Conformance tool must fully support and interpret the semantics and activity life-cycle, as well as fundamental meta-model. Besides, importing process diagrams must also be totally supported. Software claiming BPEL Process Execution Conformance must firstly fully support Process Execution Conformance. Besides, it must completely support mapping from BPMN models to BPEL, as defined in the specifications. Finally, tools that claim to support Choreography Modeling Conformance must provide BPMN Choreography types, elements, visual appearance, semantics and interchange in line with the BPMN specification. The official BPMN homepage (http://bpmn.tools/) listed more than 74 BPMN compliant tools after 2014. There are of course many more on the market, but are not formally registered in the previous list. Consequently, selecting the most appropriate BPMN modeling tool for a Business Process Modeling (BPM) project can be a laborious task having high risk factors in terms of time and cost.

While medium-to-large sized projects may conduct extensive studies to select such tools smaller modeling teams cannot afford such procedures and is more proper to have a less formal but swift tool selection process based on, however, a methodical procedure. To this end, in this section, we will present one of the suggested approaches (http://bpmn.tools/select-bpmn-modeling-tool/) adapted via the previous section concerning BPM comparison criteria that might be viable for application in SMEs. It should be emphasized that the Table 2 below proposes a set of criteria focusing mainly on SMEs, extending previous evaluation methodologies (http://bpmn.tools/select-bpmn-modeling-tool/) and (Rolóna et al. 2015).

Table 2. Business Process Modelling Software (BPMS) Tools general weighted selection criteria for SMEs

Criteria	Definition	Weight	Value
Cost	All buying, maintenance and implied costs should be taken into account. Free/Open Source, that is BPMS of minimal cost take on value of 100 (Moderate budget required for license, maintenance, support, training and implementation)	0.9	0–100
Learning curve	The easiest to learn building complex models take on values of 100	0.8	0–100
Usability	The ones having the most friendly user interface take on values of 100	0.9	0–100
Focus on SME market	The tool must be intended for the SME-market	0.9	0–100
Hardware and software Infrastructure requirements and ease of installation with minimal technical requirements	BPMS demanding minimal infrastructure and change of infrastructure, regarding both software and hardware, requirements take on value of 100. Minimal technical development expertise needed at workflow creation (forms, data definition, API)	0.8	0–100
Good documentation	The existence of suitable documentation for both advanced and novice users	0.6	0–100
Localization possibility	Availability in the English language and possibility of localization of the end-user interface	0.7	0–100
Possibility of adaptation to customer SME needs	Possibility to implement tool and adapt internal processes according to SME processes within very short time	0.6	0–100
Financial stability of the provider	Financial stability of the provider by a proven installed record (with references that can be contacted, especially from the SME market, not large scale organizations)	0.8	0–100
BPMN Syntax checking errors	The software tool can parse and check the model for syntactical errors	0.7	0–100
BPMN agreement	Compliance with BPMN 2.0, or above, four types of conformance and preferably browser based modelling	0.9	0–100
Interoperability	Capability to import and export models in different formats	0.4	0–100
BPM simulation	Native execution and simulation of BPMN 2.0 modelled processes	0.9	0–100

Step 1: definition of functional and non-functional requirements

Both functional and non-functional requirements of a software tool in examination need to be specified. While BPMS functional requirements address BPM criteria defined in Sect. 2, Non-functional requirements should address usability and user interface friendliness, proper documentation, performance characteristics, minimal hardware considerations and of course cost etc., which are obviously vital for application of BPM techniques to SMEs.

Step 2: definition of selection criteria and their relevant weights

Step two, proper selection criteria must be defined to determine which BPMS tools satisfy SME requirements. Besides, we need objective criteria for measuring such characteristics and a threshold, beyond which BPMS tools are not appropriate for our needs. This threshold is of course user defined but for its full definition weights are needed for each criterion. The weighted sum of values from this table, that is, Sum_of (weight * Value) defines the score of each evaluated BPMS tool.

Table 2 below represents an example of selection criteria along with their corresponding definitions and example only proposed weights, proper for SMEs. As it can be seen from the table, each of the criteria is ranked from 0 (no support) to 100 (full support) per evaluated software. However, these values can take any given numerical range, depending on the decision maker's preferences. The relevant weights range from 0.0 to 1.0 usually and are given according to the experience of the decision maker.

Step 3: Identification of candidate BPMS tools

In Step three, identification of candidate BPMS tools must be performed by the decision maker. As already mentioned, the official BPMN homepage http://www.bpmn.org/ lists more than 74 BPMN tools. Evaluating each of those would be too time-consuming. There is, however, a shorter list of popular BPMN tools as defined in Table 3 adapted from https://bpmnmatrix.github.io/. Even in this case, however, the identification of BPMS candidate task still remains laborious.

One of the methods that addresses these issues was proposed by (Kannengiesser 2007). Author introduced a number of filters, which reduce the input to the full evaluation process. The method can be summarized as follows:

1. Acquire a demo or free version of a BPMS tool on the list of Table 3 below or an extended list, e.g. from the site
   www.businessprocessincubator.com/tools/bpms.html
2. Evaluate the ease of installing the selected tool in light of installation or configuration problems and in general evaluate mainly usability.
3. Evaluate the operability and interoperability problems, in accordance with the ISO/IEC 9126-1 quality model.
4. Analyse the minimum support for BPMN in the tool. This is an essential prerequisite for accepting the tool for further evaluation.

After the initial input of BPMS tools has been reduced, the BPMS tool requirements are applied, which furthermore filter the number of candidate tools. The list of potential candidates should be reduced to a five or fewer software tools list in order to further proceed with the proposed evaluation process.

Step 4: Evaluate best candidates according to Table 2

In the fourth step, when a short list of candidates has been conducted, we can furthermore evaluate the BPMS tools. In this step, we systematically apply the weighted evaluation criteria we introduced in Table 2 above

Table 3. Popular Business Process Modelling Software (BPMS) Tools adapted from https://bpmnmatrix.github.io/, supporting and compliant to BPMN 2.0

Name	Creator	Platform/OS	First release	Latest release	Licence type
Activiti Modeler	Alfresco and the Activiti community	Cross-platform	2010-05-17	2014-12-18	Free, proprietary, Open Source
ADONIS (software)	BOC Information Technologies Consulting AG	Windows	1995	2012	Free, proprietary
ARCWAY Cockpit	ARCWAY AG	Windows, Mac (Linux unofficially)	2005	2014	Free, proprietary
ARIS Express	Software AG	Windows (and Linux, Mac unofficially)	2009-07-28	2012-12-19	Free
AuraPortal	AuraPortal	Windows	2001	2016	Free, proprietary
BeePMN	ESTECO SpA	Cloud	2016-02-01	2016-04-11	Free, proprietary
Bizagi Process Modeler	Bizagi	Windows			Free
bpmn.io	Camunda Services GmbH	Cloud	2014-02	2016-07-29	Free, Open Source
Bonita BPM	Bonitasoft	Windows, Linux, Mac	2001	2014-07-02	Free, Open Source
Camunda Modeler	Camunda	Cross-platform	2013	2014-03-31	Free, Open Source
Cubetto Toolset	Semture GmbH	Windows, Mac, Linux	2003	2013-08	Free
Eclipse BPMN2 Modeler	Eclipse.org. Eclipse SOA project	Cross-platform	2011	2014	Free, Open Source
HEFLO	Venki Tecnologia	Cloud (browser based)	2015-10-15	2016-7-25	Free, proprietary
GenMyModel	Axellience	Cross-platform (browser based)	2015	March 2015	Free, proprietary
INNOVATOR for Business Analysts	MID GmbH	Windows	2010	2012	Free, proprietary
jBPM (6.5)	Redhat	Cross-platform (in java)		2016-10-25	Free
jBPMN	NetBeans Community project.	Cross-platform	2013	2014	Free
LucidChart	Lucid Software Inc.	Cross-platform (browser based)	2011	Twice a month	Free, proprietary
RunaWFE	Runa Consulting Group	Cross-platform	2004	2014-08-01	Free, Open Source
simpl4	Transparent solutions GmbH	Java, Cloud-Platform PaaS/SaaS	2014-09	2016-05	Free, Open Source
SYDLE SEED Community	SYDLE Systems	Cloud (browser based)	2012-07	2012-07	Free
Yaoqiang BPMN Editor	史耀强 (Blenta) (Sourceforge ID)	Java/Windows, Linux, Mac, Solaris	2010-05-27	2014-11-16	Free, proprietary, Open Source
yEd	yWorks	Windows, Mac, Linux/Unix		2016-07-15	Free
yEd Live	yWorks	Windows, Mac, Linux/Unix	2016-07-25	2016-07-25	Free

(1) To ensure evenness across the selected tools, the same BPMN testing model should be used. It is recommended to use a model with moderate complexity, which consists of at least 100 activities, 20 data objects and 10 swim-lanes (Kannengiesser 2007).

(2) Additionally, all BPMN 2.0 diagram types defined in the BPMN specification should be involved. If all steps are conducted in accordance with this approach, we will end up with a list of maximum three software tools, that their weighted scores exceed the predefined decision maker's score threshold.

Step 5: Select the winner BPMS tool
The final step of the proposed procedure, the selection of the most suitable tool is performed. To achieve this, a fine-tuning of requirements and weighted evaluation criteria should be performed and applied to the existing short list of potential candidates defined after step 4.

However, should we decide that a criterion of Table 2 is more important to our project than another, a fine-tuning of weights is necessary at this step. Therefore, step 5 herein involves a project based reconsideration of Table 2 criteria. In such a case the general case weights proposed in Table 2, could be increased, decreased or remain the same, as in Table 2, accordingly, based on a careful attention to detail of current major SME project requirements.

Brief Analysis of Mainly Free Open Source BPM Platforms with Suitability for SMEs. Business Process Modelling/Management software is the platform used in the implementation of the techniques discussed.

From researches on existing Business Process Modelling software available, BPM software are developed based on two distinct key functions:

1. Modelling of a Business Process
2. Simulation of Business Process Model.
   i. Analysis
   ii. Optimization

Based on researches carried out in this work, it has been observed that some BPM software tools are just restricted to the design of the model, while some others have the capabilities of both functions. Some of the software applications have more than one technique embedded in them. In designing the Business Process Model, a modeller chooses the technique provided by the available software. For example, ARIS architecture discussed previously provides its own software which uses BPMN and EPC in the design of a Business Process Model. With the simulation function of the software, the results of the operations can be determined without necessarily spending huge capital of running the actual process in real-world. There are certain essential features which a Business Process Model should have;

- Complete Information: The resources, organizational units, idle time and operating time and everything related to the process should be stated.
- Realistic & Executable: The AS-IS model should be a real representation of the process, and also the TO-BE model should be achievable.
- Ability to be Partitioned: This is to enable analysis of a unit of a process to be carried out
- Traceability: No activity should be without a connection to the start event.

Simulation mimics the actual process of a system. In Business Process context, simulation goes beyond imitating the system; simulation of a Business Process Model is carried out to achieve this given objectives in the Organization;

- Process and resource analysis and optimization
- Identification of Bottleneck
- Human resources planning
- Risk assessment and risk minimization.

The consideration whether Simulation of the Business Process is important in the organization is dependent of; the effort in preparing the process model and the aims to be achieved from simulation. The output of the simulation is a result of the model designed.

In carrying out the simulation, the following pieces of information are first determined;

- Processing time per function/activity
- Number of available resources/equipments
- Additional information in getting a precise result. E.g. interruptions due to pause in activities, parts replacement in the cause of the process.

The more detailed the information gathered, the more precise the simulation output.

In the search for Business Process software, at least fifty software applications were discovered. A question posed by Organization is "What is the best modelling software to choose?"

Based on researches carried out, below are different characteristics which are to be considered in choosing a business process modelling software;

Notation and Technique, Cost, Operating System Capability, Functionality and Documentation format.

Discussed below is a brief summary of some BPM software. The software discussed here is a mixture of both freeware and commercial version, therefore not all were tested. For this reason, some pieces of the information here are retrieved from the BPM software companies and third-party vendors. But we are focusing this analysis, mainly to usability for SMEs and whether they are free as well as open source BPM software tools.

(1) **Activiti** (https://www.activiti.org/) is a lightweight workflow and Business Process Management (BPM) tool focused at business people, developers and system administrators. Its core is a fast and solid BPMN 2.0 process engine for Java. It's open-source and distributed under the Apache license. Activiti runs as a standalone Java application, on a server, on a cluster or in the cloud. It integrates perfectly with **Spring framework** (https://projects.spring.io/spring-framework/) and is based on simple concepts.

Activiti supports all aspects of Business Process Management (BPM) in the full context of software development. This includes analysis, modeling and optimizing business processes as well as aspects of creating software support for business processes. Activiti's primary purpose and focus is to implement the general purpose process language BPMN 2.0 but also, provides a Process Virtual Machine architecture where any custom process language can be build on top of it.

(2) **Bonita BPM** (http://www.bonitasoft.com/) enhances business operations by connecting people, processes, and information systems into easily managed applications. SMEs could involve Bonita Studio to map their organization, define the data structure, build the user interface, and create actionable reports. Bonita Portal creates a central location to perform tasks, monitor case completion, search for information, and collaborate with peers.

(3) **Camunda** (https://camunda.org/) is an open source platform for workflow and business process automation and management, where the decision maker could model and execute BPMN 2.0, CMMN 1.1 and DMN 1.1 It is very light-weight and scales very well. Camunda is written in Java and a perfect match for Java EE and the Spring framework (https://projects.spring.io/spring-framework/), while providing a powerful REST API and script language support. The decision maker can use Camunda BPM for system integration workflows as well as for human workflow and case management, adding Camunda to his Java application as a library, or using it as a container service in Tomcat, JBoss etc. So it can be used by multiple applications which can be redeployed without shutting down the process engine. Although very large companies in the world use it as well as most trusted public institutions rely on Camunda, it is not of prohibitive complexity for SMEs.

(4) **jBPM** (https://www.jbpm.org/) is a free and flexible Business Process Management (BPM) platform. It makes the bridge between business analysts and developers. Traditional BPM engines have a focus that is limited to non-technical people only. jBPM has a dual focus: it offers process management features in a way that attracts both business users and developers. The core of jBPM is a lightweight, scalable workflow engine written in Java that allows executing business processes using the latest BPMN 2.0 specification. It can run in any Java environment, embedded in decision maker's application or as a service.

(5) **jSonic BPM** (http://jsonic.org/) platform enables enterprise owners to align business processes with the dynamic market conditions, statutory compliances and, customer and partner requirements. It is a comprehensive solution that improves the bottom line of organization, even of small to medium scale organizations, but mainly of large ones, by increasing process efficiency, optimizing resource utilization and automating human workflow system. jSonic BPM suite, is a free and Open Source BPM Software that offers an integrated solution covering process designing, modeling, executing, automating and monitoring as per the business needs and desires. The major components of the suite include Process Management, Workflow Management and the Interface Designer.

(6) **Orchestra** (http://orchestra.ow2.org/xwiki/bin/view/Main/WebHome) is a complete solution to handle long-running, service oriented processes. It provides out of the box orchestration functionalities to handle complex business processes. It is based on the OASIS standard BPEL (Business Process Execution Language). Orchestra's objectives: enhancement and control of processes, Services communication, Productivity and agility of the company. Orchestra is fully Open Source and is downloadable under the LGPL License.

(7) **ProcessMaker** (http://www.processmaker.com/) is a cost effective and easy to use open source business process management (BPM) or workflow software application. Workflow software such as ProcessMaker can assist organizations of any size with designing, automating and deploying business processes or work-flows of various kinds. We consider it well suited for SMEs. ProcessMaker work-flow software features an extensive toolbox which provides the ability to easily create digital forms and map out fully functioning workflows. The software is completely web based, making it simple to manage and synchronize workflows throughout an entire organization of any size– including user groups and depart-ments. ProcessMaker workflow software can also interact with other applications and systems such as ERP, business intelligence, CRM and document management. Therefore, we think that Processmaker needs further analysis and elaboration for SMEs.

(8) **Red Hat JBoss BPM** platform (https://www.redhat.com/en/services/training/jb427-developing-workflow-applications-red-hat-jboss-bpm-suite#) is the JBoss platform for Business Process Management (BPM). It enables enterprise business and IT users to document, simulate, manage, automate and monitor business processes and policies. It is designed to allow business and IT users to collaborate more successfully, so business applications can be changed more easily and quickly. Create, test, deploy and monitor BPMN2-based business processes to optimize enterprise workflows and automate critical processes. Red Hat JBoss BPM includes all the business rules and event processing capabilities of Red Hat JBoss BRMS. Easily create real-time dashboards to monitor key performance indicators for running processes and activities. It is well suited for large scale organizations but further investigation is needed for its suitability for SMEs with no IT department.

(9) **Eclipse STP BPMN Modeler/Intalio Designer** (https://eclipse.org/proposals/bpmn-modeler/), was developed in 2006 by Intalio which donated the BPMN modeler to the Eclipse foundation. The main website of the project is http://www.eclipse.org/bpmn/ but so far the modeler is not automatically integrated into Eclipse and the installation needs to be done via the STP site, fully described on the projects website. As alternative to the BPMN modeler plugin for Eclipse 3.5.1 the company Intalio offers community edition of its commercial BPMN modeler which already included the needed Eclipse runtime files (http://www.intalio.com/downloads). All versions are available for Windows, Linux and Mac. The instal-lation is not too easy, however.

(10) **TIBCO Business Studio** (http://www.tibco.com/products/automation/business-process-management/activematrix-bpm/business-studio), is neither open source or under an open license like the GPL, but the tool is at least free. The official website of the tool is http://www.tibco.com/products/bpm/process-modeling/business-studio/default.jsp where it is available as a download for Windows and Linux after completing a short registration form. Again, there are some difficulties in the installation process due to not full documentation but it seems very powerful, although not designed as a pure modeler, supporting additional diagrams within the BPMN project. e.g. organizational structure. However, Drawing is very

difficult, all icons have by default a given color (yellow) and there is no graphical export functionality for BPMN diagrams.

(11) **Yaoqiang BPMN Editor** (https://sourceforge.net/projects/bpmn/), is a very small java application especially designed to support BPMN 2.0. The project is hosted on SourceForge.net: http://sourceforge.net/projects/bpmn/. The application looks a little like MS Visio regarding the layout of the modules of the GUI and the idea to display and draw processes. It presents some advantages: very small application, No installation needed, Exports diagrams into a lot of different graphic formats, it's Open Source, with Clear colors for the different symbols. But, on the other hand, all symbols are displayed on the same level, there is no real control of connections and lines from one symbol to another and there are limitation of a process drawing size, limited by page size.

(12) **Aris Express** (http://www.ariscommunity.com/aris-express) is the light version of the classic Aris BPMS Tool. Aris Express is not available under an open source and open license but the usage is free and supported by a community. Aris Express is written in Java and starts every time via Java Webstart.

Investigating many BPMS tools from the lists above, a decision maker would not find the perfect BPMN modeler/tool. However, some important characteristics of the software described so far are:

Open source and free software, the majority using an open license like GPL, Apache, BSD, CDDL, etc., Support of BPMN 2.0, Graphical modeler which support BPMN diagrams and does the syntax check, Visual presentation of drawing shall be nice; good looking diagrams, Easy to go, Windows or/and Linux support.

In the sequel some BPMS tools brief description is provided, which are mainly commercial.

1. **ADONIS:** This software was created and first released in 1995 by BOC Information Technologies Consulting, supporting Business Process Management based on a framework – BPMS which was developed at the University of Vienna. This software is free but a closed source which makes use of BPMN tool and with the commercial version providing simulation function. ADONIS software is created in an easy-to-use style so a beginner can easily understand how to use.

2. **Enterprise Architect Suite:** This software was developed by Sparx Systems based on UML. The Enterprise Architect was initially released in 2000 and supported just UML, but subsequent releases has seen it supporting basically all Object-Oriented technique – UML, BPMN, BPEL, SPEM. Aspects covered by this software not only include Business Process Modelling design, but also Simulation, Development Life-cycle, requirements management, project management. The software is a complete BPM suite which can be useful for software developers, modellers, Business Analyst, and other Organization entities.

3. **Microsoft Visio 2013:** The Microsoft Visio is more of a diagramming application which supports the design of a Business Process Model. This application first developed in 1992 by Shapeware Corporation, the product was later acquired by Microsoft. Microsoft Visio is not particularly based on a particular notation or technique. It provides different notation and techniques like IDEF0, BPMN2.0, UML; its own

flowchart technique – Microsoft SharePoint workflow; and different software and database diagrams. Using the Microsoft Visio, a modeller can decide to also design his notations.

4. **BIZAGI BPM Suite**: Bizagi BPM Suite was developed by Bizagi Ltd., a privately owned company founded in 1989. Bizagi BPM Suite consists of three tools – Process modeller, Studio, and Server. The Business Process are drawn and documented in the Process Modeller; the process applications are built in the studio and stored in a database, the execution and control of the built Process application takes place in the server. This all-in-one suite provides a graphical real- time tracking, simulation and monitoring of the process, providing Business Process management to companies such as Schlumberger, Adidas Group, Audi, and Petrobas. Bizagi supports BPMN, and also compatible with XML Definition Process Language (XPDL).

5. **Enterprise Dynamics:** The Enterprise dynamics software was developed by InControl Simulation Solutions. This application is a platform for carrying out simulation of a Business process. Models in this application are built by a drag- and-drop method. This software does not necessarily make use of any of the notations discussed, but it supports the model of Business Process through workflow technique. The main function of this software is to carry out simulation of a serial model. Though it is mainly used in the manufacturing sector, it can also be useful in other aspects of Industries. In the Enterprise Dynamics, the activities and roles are represented as servers. When simulated, the efficiency of the server (in %) is shown. Representing how the performance of each activity. A graph and simulation report is generated to carry out analysis.

   This software makes use of a petri net - like and workflow technique in the representation of processes carried out, the blue circles represents the nodes in this process, moving from one server to another as the Business Process takes place.

   This software is best suitable if a modeller is just concerned about the serial flow of activities and not concerned about the roles in carrying out the activities. Depending on the number of employees in carrying out tasks, the modelling of a process using this software can be very complex.

6. **Accuprocess Modeller:** The Accuprocess software is developed as an Easy-to- Use application compared to most other process modelling software. Accuprocess makes use of only one notation, BPMN 1.0 (similar to the flow chart) which has few notations in carrying out a modelling exercise. This software provides free documents and trainings in which a new user can quickly learn how to use the software.

7. **ARIS Toolset**: Relevant to Aris Express, the ARIS toolset is made up of different products developed by IDS Scheer, a company established by Prof. August-Wilhem Scheer, whose academic research brought about Architecture of Integrated Information Research (ARIS). IDS Scheer was developed to in1984 to market the ARIS reference framework, but the company was later acquired by Software AG in 2010. The ARIS product was first released in 2009. Business Process Modelling on ARIS products is based on BPMN2.0 and EPC.

To further explain the techniques and tools of Business Process Modelling based on the above comparative analysis, the modelling and simulation process in this subsection is carried out using software which makes use of a technique easily communicated and with simulation capability. Compared to other Business Process Software, Accuprocess Modeller provides full functionality (modelling & simulation) in its trial version.

4   Preliminary Case Study and Simulation Scenarios

In this case scenario, only the activities directly involved with the receipt of goods of an organization are modelled. Ten actions are carried out with two decision points to determine the path to take. The scenario is outlined in Table 4. In the decision points, probability of getting a defective batch is 20%, good batch 80%; second decision point, probability of being damaged after being received (due to poor handling) is 10%, and being the fault of the supplier, 90%. The average time for the longest activity is 20 min, while the least activity takes 2 min. This process runs 600 times (i.e. 600 batches of goods are received).

Accuprocess Modeller. The Accuprocessor modeller is divided into two aspects; modeller and Simulation. In the modeller section, all the necessary notations to model the system are provided in a canvas. The modelling of the system is done by a drag-and-drop method.

A drag-and-drop canvas is provided, selecting the different objects to use in mapping the Business Process. In the Accuprocess, the simulation is further sub-divided into two areas; the resource area, where the Organizational unit in which the roles can be assigned to are situated – and the scenario- in which the simulation is to be carried out. Each activity is assigned to a role which is in the simulation resources. The vital activities to be part of the simulation exercise are included in the scenario, the execution time of each of these activities are further specified. Accuprocess gives the modeller option to specify the type of distribution, for purpose of the simulation carried out, a normal distribution is used.

After the AS-IS configuration has been completed, a simulation is run to determine the state of operations in the Organization. A brief simulation run summary is displayed on the application interface. To view a detailed report to carry out analysis, an html file is generated displaying all the parameters and configurations. The complete steps in modelling and the simulation of the Business Process using the Accuprocess Modeller are discussed in (Papademetriou and Karras 2016).

Graphs generated from the simulation run are shown in Fig. 2 depicting the result of the simulation carried out after 600 runs. The first graph shows the average utilization of the different units of the process in percentage, with Incoming Goods unit being more utilized. The run time graph depicts the maximum, minimum, and average time taken for one run to be completed in hours.

Table 4. Business Process Modelling Software comparative characteristics evaluation

	Notation/ Techniques	Functionality	Operating system	Application mode	Documentation format
Adonis (Community Ed.)	BPMN 2.0	Model design, simulation	Windows	Stand-alone	Pdf, html
Enterprise Architect 11.1 Suite (Ultimate)	UML, SysML, BPMN 2.0, BPEL	Model design, simulation, code Execution	Windows, Linux, Mac	Web, Stand-alone	Pdf, html, docx, rtf
Microsoft Visio 2013 (Professional)	BPMN 2.0, UML, IDEF0, Flowchart	Model design, simulation	Windows	Web, Stand-alone	vsdx, vsdm
Bizagi BPM Suite	BPMN 2.0	Model design, simulation, Code Execution.	Windows	Web	docx, xlsx
Enterprise Dynamics	Workflow, Petri net	Simulation	Windows	Stand-alone	Mod, bmp
ARIS Express	BPMN 2.0, EPC	Model design	Windows, Linux, Mac	Stand-alone	Adf, pdf, rdf
ARIS Business Simulator	BPMN 2.0, EPC	Model design, simulation	Windows, Linux, Mac	Stand-alone, web	Adf, pdf, rdf
Accuprocess (Professional Ed.)	BPMN 1.0	Model design, simulation	Windows, Mac	Stand-Alone	Pm, Html, pdf, docx, jpg

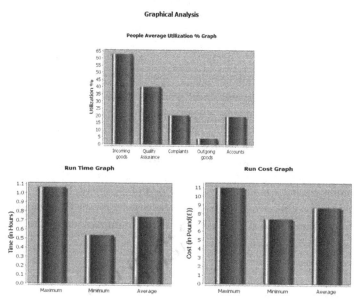

Fig. 2. Graphical analysis of the model

Advantages and disadvantages of Accuprocess Modeller are discussed in (Papademetriou and Karras 2016)

ARIS Business Simulator. A similar process is being modelled and simulated using ARIS Business Simulator. This is done to show the ability to optimize process automatically. The optimization aim is to determine the least number of employees to carry out each run of the process at a faster time with less cost. It should be noted that the simulation exercise using the ARIS Business Simulator was not carried by the author. It was obtained from the ARIS forum to carry out the comparison. Therefore some parameters and configurations will have some slight changes, but still similar approaches.

The type of Business Process Model technique is specified, in this case EPC is used; the database to use is selected; and the model in which to carry out the simulation is defined. In carrying out the experiment, the attribute of the objects are varied, the highest and lowest limits of the objects (in this case, all the Organizational Units) are specified; the low and high text field. This is referred to as Factor Variation.

Depending on the configuration in the Factor Variation, many scenarios are created discussed in (Papademetriou and Karras 2016).

The next step is to specify the responses to be saved, in this case scenario, the throughput time for the model (Receipt of Goods), and the idle time cost for the objects (the Organizational units).

In carrying out the simulation, the optimization configuration has to be specified according to what is to be achieved. In this case, minimization of the model and objects is specified.

In the ARIS software, one of the documentation format used is Microsoft Excel; this makes the analysis to be carried out easier. After all parameters has been set in the simulation the output format- Excel- is specified, and a file is created for the result to be viewed and saved.

The generated output Microsoft Excel file of the simulation is displayed, showing the values for the different objects, the factors, and responses based on the amount of possible configuration being run.

The optimization configuration is compared from the values in the objective column which is generated automatically. These values are further compared to idle time cost of the different responses. This process can be made easier by sorting the values according to ascending or descending order, or by generating a graph based on the values.

The lowest objective value which is the idle time cost provides the result for the factors. From Fig. 3 above the result was gotten. Advantages and disadvantages of ARIS Modeller are discussed in (Papademetriou and Karras 2016).

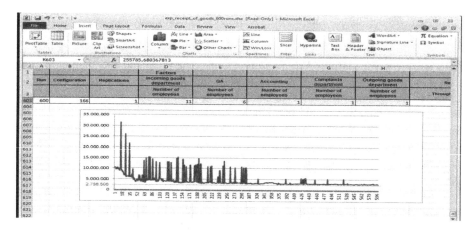

Fig. 3. ARIS software provided optimization graph

5   Discussion - Conclusions

Business Process Model as a topic aims at improving the operations of an Organization. However, the presence of numerous techniques and tools has created a setback to modelling a Business Process. In this study, a comparison have been carried out to enable a potential user understand the usability of these techniques and tools.

The techniques were compared using features necessary for having a complete Business Process Model; *data flow, logical reasoning, specification of roles, and capability of simulation*. A technique possessing all the features will be effective for use in these four target areas of an Organization;

- Production Planning: Goods/services to be produced – the conversion of the input into output.
- Organizational Structure: With the structural view, the management determines the relationship between the tasks and equipment/personnel/units; useful for the Human resource unit of an Organization.
- Logistics: The flow of products; not only how it's being produced in the Organization, but also to the point of consumption, how the requirements are met.
- Strategic Planning: The strategic planning involves a futuristic plan for the Organization. Using the techniques and tools, the AS-IS model is analysed, improved upon to generate the TO-BE model. Simulation is carried out to determine the result of the future plan. This is done to reduce cost of actually implementing a plan that might be a failure.

Though techniques such as EPC, IDEF, WORKFLOW, and BPMN all have the features mentioned, it is necessary for a modeller to consider one which is easily understandable to stakeholders; easy in the communication of processes involved in the business, and to also facilitate learning. From the study, the EPC and the BPMN technique clearly states the activities, roles, the flow of messages (in BPMN), documents to be read, and requirements for a task to be carried out. These two techniques also give a clear outline of the structure of an Organization ranging from large scale ones to SMEs.

Apart from the discussion of BPMN techniques, however, a major contribution of this paper is an investigation of selection criteria for BPMS tools focusing on SMEs. Actually, a new framework has been proposed, targeted on SMEs aiming at evaluating proper BPMS tools.

Some major software tools were analysed in this study to determine what requirements to look out for in choosing Business Process software, especially for SMEs, focusing on free and open source software but, also, on some classic commercial software. The comparison showed that most software packages make use of BPMN technique in the modelling of a Business Process. Judging from the outcome of this study, it is best to choose a software tool which not only models a system, but, also, it is able to carry out its simulation. It was shown that some software tools with the simulation functionality do provide only analysis of the AS-IS model, while others go further to enable optimization of the Business Process to be carried out producing the TO-BE Business Process Model. Then relevance to SMEs should be further explored.

This study ended with simple simulation scenarios carried out to show the importance of modelling and simulating a Business Process to improve the operations of an Organization. However, this study is incomplete and needs improvement with more comparisons targeted to SMEs.

References

Aguilar-Saven, R.S.: Business process modelling: review and framework. Int. J. Prod. Econ. **90**, 129–149 (2003)

Al-Mudimigh, A.S.: The role and impact of business process management in enterprise systems implementation. Bus. Process Manag. J. **13**(6), 866–874 (2007)

Bazhenova, E., Taratukhin, V., Becker, J.: Towards on business process management on small-to medium enterprises in the emerging economies.In: 7th International Forum on Strategic Strategic Technology (IFOST), pp. 1–5 (2012)

Bridgeland, D.M., Zahavi, R.: Business Modelling - A Practical Guide to Realizing Business Value. Morgan Kaufmann, Burlington (2009)

Business Process Modelling (2007). From Business Process Modelling, http://www.businessprocessmodelling.co.uk. Accessed 21 June 2014

Business Process Modelling (2013). From BusinessBalls.com, http://www.businessballs.com/business-process-modelling.htm. Accessed 24 June 2014

Chong, S.: Business process management for SMEs: an exploratory study of implementation factors for the Australian wine industry.J. Inf. Syst. Small Bus. **1**(1–2), 41–58 (2007)

De Bruin, T., Rosemann, M.: Towards a business process management maturity model. In: Proceedings of the 13th European Conference on Information Systems, CD Rom, Paper presented at the ECIS 2005 (2005)

Fogarty, G., Armstrong, D.B.: Modelling the interactions among factors that influence successful computerisation of small business.Australas. J. Inf. Syst. **15**(2) (2009)

Harmon, P.: The scope and evolution of business process management. In: vom Brocke, J., Rosemann, M. (Eds.) Handbook on Business Process Management 1. International Handbooks on Information Systems, pp. 37–81, Springer, Heidelberg (2010). doi: 10.1007/978-3-642-00416-2_3

Imanipour, N., Talebi, K., Rezazadeh, S.: Business process management (BPM) implementation and adoption in SMEs: inhibiting factors for Iranian e-retail industry. J. Knowl. Process Manag. (2012a)

Imanipour, N., Talebi, K., Rezazadeh, S.: Obstacles in business process management (BPM) implementation and adoption in SMEs (2012b). Available at SSRN. http://ssrn.com/abstract=1990609. Accessed 29 July 2012

Kirchmer, M.: Small and medium enterprises also benefit from MPE. In: Kirchmer, M. (Ed.) High Performance Through Process Excellence, pp. 147–157. Springer, Heidelberg (2011). doi: 10.1007/978-3-642-21165-2_10

Kalnins, A., Kalnina, D., Kalis, A. (n.d.): Comparison of Tools and Languages for Business Process Reengineering. http://citeseerx.ist.psu.edu/viewdoc/download?doi=10.1.1.127.1036&rep=rep1&type=pdf

Kannengiesser, U.: Evaluation of BPMN Tools. National Information Communications Technology Australia (2007)

Papademetriou, R. Karras, D.A.: An in depth comparative analysis of software tools for modelling and simulating business processes. In: BMSD 2016 - Proceedings of the 6th International Symposium on Business Modeling and Software Design, pp. 124–133 (2016)

Prezel, V., Gašević, D., Milanović, M. (n.d.): Representational Analysis of Business Process and Business Rule Languages. From OntoRule Project, http://ontorule-project.eu/attachments/075_buro2010_paper_2.pdf

Recker, J., Indulska, M., Rosemann, M., Green, P.: Business process modelling - a comparative analysis. J. Assoc. Inf. Syst. **10**(4), 333–363 (2009)

Rolóna, E., Chaviraa, G., et al.: Towards a framework for evaluating usability of business process models with BPMN in health sector. In: Procedia Manufacturing, 6th International Conference on Applied Human Factors and Ergonomics (AHFE 2015) and the Affiliated Conferences, AHFE 2015, vol. 3, pp. 5603–5610 (2015). http://dx.doi.org/10.1016/j.promfg.2015.07.748

Vergidis, K., Tiwari, A., Majeed, B.: Business process analysis and optimization beyond reengineering. IEEE Trans. Syst. Man Cybern. Part C Appl. Rev. **38**, 69–82 (2008)

Yamamoto, R., Yamamoto, K., Ohashi, K., Inomata, J.: Development of a business process modeling methodology and a tool for sharing business processes. In: 12th Asia-Pacific Software Engineering Conference (APSEC 2005). IEEE (2005)

Microflows: Automated Planning and Enactment of Dynamic Workflows Comprising Semantically-Annotated Microservices

Roy Oberhauser[✉]

Computer Science Department, Aalen University, Aalen, Germany
`roy.oberhauser@hs-aalen.de`

Abstract. Businesses are under increasing pressure to quickly and flexibly adapt their business processes to external and internal software and other changes. Furthermore, to address the rapid change and deployment of software functionality, microservices have emerged as a popular architectural style for partitioning business logic into small services accessible with lightweight mechanisms, resulting in a higher degree of dynamic integration of information services with processes. Current process-aware information systems tend to rely on manually pre-configured static process models and during process enactment exhibit challenges in reacting to unforeseen dynamic changes. This paper presents Microflows, an automatic lightweight declarative approach for the workflow-centric orchestration of semantically-annotated microservices using agent-based clients, graph-based methods, and the lightweight semantic vocabularies JSON-LD and Hydra. A case study shows approach's advantages for automating workflow modeling and enactment in a dynamic microservice environment.

Keywords: Workflow management systems · Microservices · Service orchestration · Agent systems · Semantic technology

1 Introduction

A trend towards increased automation can be observed in many areas of society today. One area affecting organizations and businesses in particular is the area of business processes or workflows. The automation of a business process according to a set of procedural rules is known as a workflow (WfMC 1999). In turn, a workflow management system (WfMS) defines, creates, and manages the execution of workflows (WfMC 1999). These workflows are often rigid, and while adaptive WfMS can handle certain adaptations, they usually involve manually intervention to determine the appropriate adaptation. As one indicator of its importance to business, spending on Business Process Management Systems (BPMS) is forecast at $2.7 billion in 2015 (Gartner 2015).

Moreover, there is an increasing trend toward applying the microservice architecture style (Fowler and Lewis 2014) for an agile and loosely coupled partitioning of business logic into small services accessible with lightweight mechanisms. They can be deployed independently of each other and conform to a bounded context. As the dynamicity of

© Springer International Publishing AG 2017
B. Shishkov (Ed.): BMSD 2016, LNBIP 275, pp. 183–199, 2017.
DOI: 10.1007/978-3-319-57222-2_9

the service world grows, the need for more automated and dynamic approaches to service orchestration becomes evident.

Service orchestration represents a single executable process that uses a flow description (such as WS-BPEL) to coordinate service interaction orchestrated from a single endpoint, whereas service choreography involves a decentralized collaborative interaction of services (Bouguettaya et al. 2014), while service composition involves the static or dynamic aggregation and binding of services into some abstract composite process.

While automated and dynamic workflow planning can remove the manual overhead for workflow modeling, a fully automated semantic integration process remains challenging, with one study indicating that only 11% of Semantic Web applications achieve it (Heitmann et al. 2012). Rather than pursuing the fairly heavyweight service-oriented architecture (SOA) and semantic web standards, we chose to investigate the viability of a lightweight approach. Analogous to microservices principles, we use the term Microflow to mean lightweight workflow planning and enactment of microservices, i.e. a lightweight service orchestration of microservices.

This paper explores an approach we call Microflows for automatically planning and enacting lightweight dynamic workflows of semantically annotated microservices. It uses a declarative paradigm with cognitive agents leveraging current lightweight semantic and microservice technology and investigates its viability. It extends (Oberhauser 2016) and contributes more detail on its branching and error handling capabilities. Note that this approach does not intend to address all facets of BPMS support, but is focused on a narrow area addressing the automatic orchestration of dynamic workflows given a multitude of microservices using a pragmatic lightweight approach rather than a theoretical treatise.

This paper is organized as follows: the next section discusses related work. Sections 3 and 4 describe the solution approach and its realization respectively. Section 5 describes the evaluation, followed by the conclusion.

2 Related Work

While the term Microflow has been used in IBM business process manager documentation to mean a transient non-interruptible BPEL process (IBM 2015), in our terminology a Microflow is independent of any specific BPMS or any choreography or orchestration language.

Work related to the orchestration of microservices includes (Rajasekar et al. 2012), who describe the integrated Rule Oriented Data System (iRODS) for large-scale data management, which uses a distributed event-condition-action rule engine to orchestrate micro-services into conditional chain-oriented workflows, maintaining transactional properties through recovery micro-services. (Alpers et al. 2015) describe a microservice architecture for BPM tools, highlighting a Petri Net editor to support humans with BPM.

As to web service composition, (Sheng et al. 2014) provides a survey of current research prototypes and standards in the area of web service composition. While the web service composition using the workflow technique (Rao and Su 2005) can be viewed having similarity to ours, our approach does not explicitly create an abstract composite service but rather can be viewed as automated dynamic web service orchestration using the workflow technique.

Declarative approaches for process modeling include DECLARE (Pesic et al. 2007). A DECLARE model is mapped onto a set of LTL formulas that are used to automatically generate automata that support enactment. Adaptations with verification during enactment are supported, typically via GUI interaction with a human, whereby the changed model is reinitiated and its entire history replayed. As to inputs, DECLARE facilitates the definition of different constraint languages such as ConDec and DecSerFlow.

Concerning the combination of multi-agent systems and microservices, (Florio 2015) proposes a multi-agent system for decentralized self-adaptation of autonomous distributed components (Docker-based microservices) to address scalability, fault tolerance, and resource consumption. These agents known as selfLets mediate service decisions using partial knowledge and exchanging messages. (Toffetti et al. 2015) provide a position paper focusing on microservice monitoring and proposing an architecture for scalable and resilient self-management of microservices by integrating management functions into the microservices, wherein service orchestration is cited to be an abstraction of deployment automation (Karagiannis et al. 2014), microservice composition or orchestration are not addressed.

Related standards include OWL-S (Semantic Markup for Web Services), an ontology of services for automatic web service discovery, invocation, and composition (Martin et al. 2004). Combining semantic technology with microservices, (Anderson et al. 2015) present an OWL-centric framework to create context-aware applications, integrating microservices to aggregate and process context information. For a more lightweight semantic description of microservices, JSON-LD (Lanthaler and Gütl 2012) and Hydra (Lanthaler 2013) (Lanthaler and Gütl 2013) provide a lightweight vocabulary for hypermedia-driven Web APIs and enable the creation of generic API clients.

In contrast to the above work, our contribution specifically focuses on microservices, proposing and investigating an automatic lightweight declarative approach for the workflow-centric orchestration of microservices using agent-based clients, graph-based methods, and lightweight semantic vocabularies like JSON-LD and Hydra. Furthermore, adaptations during enactment do not require a complete reinitiation of the workflow and branching logic can be included to support automation.

3   Solution Approach

The principles and process constituting the solution approach described below reference the solution architecture of Fig. 1.

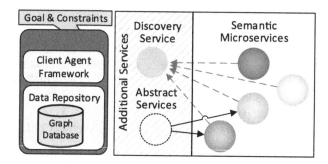

Fig. 1. Solution concept.

3.1 Microflow Solution Principles

The solution approach consists of the following principles:

Semantic self-description principle: microservices provide sufficient semantic meta-data to support autonomous client invocation. For example, in our realization this was done using by using JSON-LD with Hydra.

Client agent principle: Intelligent agents exhibit reactivity, proactiveness, and social ability, managing a model of their environment and can plan their actions and undertake goal-oriented behavior (Wooldridge 2009). Nominal WfMS are typically passive, executing a workflow according to a manually determined plan (workflow schema). Because of the expected scale in the number of possible microservices, the required goal-oriented choices in workflow modeling and planning, and the autonomous goal-directed action required during enactment, agent technology seems appropriate. Specifically, we chose Belief-Desire-Intention (BDI) agents (Bratman et al. 1988) for the client realization, providing belief (knowledge), desire via goals, and intention utilizing generated plans that are the workflow.

Graph of microservices principle: microservices are mapped to nodes in a graph and can be stored in a graph database. Nodes in the graph are used to represent any workflow activity, such as a microservice. Nodes are annotated with properties. Directed edges depict the directed connections (flows) between activities annotated via properties. To reduce redundant resource usage via multiple database instances, the graph database could be shared by the clients as an additional microservice.

Microflow as graph path principle: A directed graph of nodes corresponds to a workflow, a sequence of operations on those microservices, and is determined by an algorithm applied to the graph, such as shortest path. The enactment of the workflow involves the invocation of microservices, with inputs and outputs retained in the client and corresponding to the client state.

Declarative principle: any workflow requirement specifications take the form of declarative statements, such as the starting microservice type, end microservice type, and constraints such as sequencing or branch logic constraints.

Microservice discovery service principle (optional): we assume a microservice landscape to be much more dynamic in microservices coming and going than heavyweight services, and therefore utilize a microservice registry and discovery service. This could be deployed in different ways, including centralized, distributed, or having it embedded within each client, and utilize voluntary microservice-triggered registration or multicast mechanisms. For security purposes, there may be a wish to avoid discovery (of undocumented microservices) and thus maintain a whitelist. Clients may or may not have a priori knowledge of a particular microservice. Various broadcast services could be used.

Abstract microservices principle (optional): microservices with similar functionality (search, hotel booking, flight booking, etc.) can be grouped behind an abstract microservice. This provides an optional level of hierarchy to allow concrete microservices to only provide a client with link to the next abstract microservice(s), since the actual concrete microservices can be numerous and rapidly change, while determining exactly which one is appropriate can best be done by the client in conjunction with the abstract microservice.

Path weighting principle (optional): any followers of a service, be it abstract or concrete, can be weighted with a potentially dynamic cost that helps in quantifying and comparing one path with another in the form of relative cost. This also permits the navigation from one to another to be dynamically adjusted should that path incur issues such as frequent errors or slow responses. The planning agent can determine a path that minimizes the cost.

Logic principle (optional): if the path weighting is insufficient and more complex logic is desired for assessing branching or error conditions, these can be provided in the form of constraints referencing scripts.

Note that the Data Repository and Graph Database could readily be shared as a common service, and need not be confined to the Client.

3.2 Microflow Lifecycle

The Microflow lifecycle involves three stages as shown in Fig. 2.

Fig. 2. Microflow lifecycle.

The *Microservice Discovery* stage involves utilizing a microservice discovery service to build a graph of nodes containing the properties of the microservices and links to other microservices. This is analogous to mapping the landscape.

In the *Microflow Planning* stage, an agent takes the goal and other constraints and creates a plan known as a Microflow, finding an appropriate start and end node and using an algorithm such as shortest path to determine a directed path.

In our opinion, a completely dynamic enactment without any planning (no schema) could readily lead to dead-end or circular paths causing a waste of unnecessary invocations that do not lead to the desired goal and can potentially not be undone. This is analogous to following hyperlinks without a plan, which do not lead to the goal and require backtracking. Alternatively, replanning after each microservice invocation involves planning resource overhead (CPU, memory, network), and since this is unlikely to dynamically change between the start and end of this lifecycle, we chose the pragmatic and hopefully more lightweight approach from the resource utilization perspective: plan once and then enact until an exception occurs, at which point a necessary replanning is triggered. Further advantages of our approach in contrast to a thoroughly adhoc approach is that the client is assured that there is at least one path to the goal, and validation of various structural, semantic, and syntactic aspects can be readily performed.

In the *Microflow Enactment* stage, the Microflow is executed by invoking each microservice in the order of the plan, typically sequentially but it could involve parallel invocations. A replanning of the remaining Microflow can be performed if an exception occurs or if notified by the discovery service of changes to the set of microservices. A client should retain the Microflow model (plan) and be able to utilize the service interfaces and thus have sufficient semantic knowledge for enactment.

The *Microflow Analysis* stage involves the monitoring, analysis, and mining of execution logs in order to improve future planning. This could be local, in a trusted environment, or this could be distributed. Thus, if invocation of a microservice has often resulted in exceptions, future planning for this client or other clients could avoid this troublesome microservice. Furthermore, the actual latency incurred for usage of a microservice could be tracked and shared between agents and taken into account as a type of cost in the graph algorithm.

4   Realization

A realization of the solution concept as a prototype involved mapping technology choices onto the solution concept (Fig. 3) and explained below.

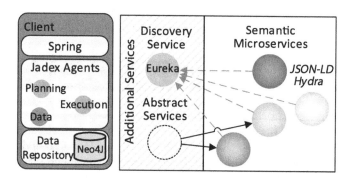

Fig. 3. Microflow solution realization technologies.

The prototype integrates the following, especially for REST (REpresentational State Transfer) and HATEOAS support (Fielding 2000): Spring-boot-starter-web v. 1.2.4, which includes Spring boot 1.2.4, Spring-core and Spring-web v. 4.1.6, Embedded Tomcat v. 8.0.23; Hydra-spring v. 0.2.0-beta3; and Spring-hateoas v. 0.16. For JSON (de)serialization Gson v. 2.6.1 is used. Unirest v. 1.3.0 is used to send HTTP requests. As a REST-based discovery service, Netflix's open source Eureka (Eureka 2016) v. 1.1.147 is used.

4.1 Microservices

To support a larger-scale evaluation of the prototype, we created virtual microservices that differentiate themselves semantically but provide no real functionality. Microservice descriptions use Hydra based on JSON-LD, an example of which is shown in Fig. 4.

```
{
  "@context": {
    "@vocab": "http://schema.org/"
  },
  "@type": "Service",
  "serviceType": "Preferences",
  "serviceOutput": {
    "@type": "ItemList",
    "itemListElement": {
      "@type": "PropertyValue",
      "unitText": "",
      "value": "",
      "name": ""
    },
    "numberOfItems": 0
  },
  "offers": {
    "@type": "Offer",
    "businessFunction": "http://purl.org/goodrelations/v1#ProvideService"
  },
  "availableChannel": {
    "@type": "ServiceChannel",
    "serviceUrl": "http://192.168.0.14:8333/execute"
  },
  "description": "Get preferences service",
  "@id": "http://192.168.0.14:8333/",
  "hydra:followers": {
    "@id": "http://localhost:8333/followers",
    "hydra:operation": [
      {
        "hydra:method": "GET"
      }
    ]
  },
  "hydra:execute": {
    "@id": "http://localhost:8333/execute",
    "hydra:operation": [
      {
        "hydra:method": "PUT",
        "hydra:expects": {
          "@type": "URL",
          "hydra:supportedProperty": []
        }
      }
    ]
  }
}
```

Fig. 4. Example microservice description with Hydra.

Abstract microservices with similar functionality (hotel searching, payment, etc.) can be grouped behind an abstract microservice. This provides an optional level of hierarchy to allow concrete microservices to only provide a client with link to the next abstract microservice(s), since the actual concrete microservice can change.

4.2 Microservice Clients

Microservice Client Agents. For an agent framework, the microservice clients uses the BDI agent framework Jadex v. 3.0-SNAPSHOT (Pokahr et al. 2005). Jadex's BDI nomenclature consists of Goals (Desires), Plans (Intentions), and Beliefs. Beliefs can be represented by attributes like lists and maps. Three agents were created: the Data-Agent is responsible for providing for and maintaining data repository, the Planning-Agent generates a path through the graph as a Microflow, while the ExecutionAgent communicates directly with microservices to invoke them according to the Microflow. Neo4j and Neo4j-Server v. 2.3.2 is used as a client Data Repository.

Microflow Goals and Constraints. The goals and constraints for a MicroFlow are referred to as PathParameters and consist of the startServiceType (e.g., preferences), endServiceType (e.g., payment), and constraint tuples in JSON. Each constraint tuple consists of the target of the constraint (the service type affected), the constraint, and a constraint type (required, beforeNode, afterNode).

As an example, let us assume we have a process in mind such as that depicted in simplified form using Business Process Modeling Notation (BPMN) in Fig. 5 (whereby a BPMN model is not used or required by our solution). Let us assume that a search should determine the minimum total price for both flight and hotel within +/− 2 days of a given starting and ending date before booking. Here we assume the Search, Booking, and PaymentSpecification services are abstract and that one or more concrete services of their respective types are available (in BPMN subprocesses (not shown) could be used to determine these). After the booking, the type of payment service used should be determined based on total price (e.g., if > $2000 should use a billing service, between $500–$2000 should use a credit card service, and otherwise prepayment).

Fig. 5. Equivalent BPMN process desired.

The Microflow textual constraint specification for this example is shown in Fig. 6. For instance, target = "Hotel Search", constraint = "Book Hotel", and constraint type = "beforeNode" would be read as: "Hotel Search" before "BookHotel", implying the Microflow sequencing must ensure that "Search Hotel" precedes "Book Hotel" (but must not be directly before it).

```
1  {  "startServiceType":"Get preferences",
2     "endServiceType":"Completion",
3     "constraints":[
4        { "type": "RequiredNode", "target": "Book Flight"},
5        { "type": "RequiredNode", "target": "Book Hotel"},
6        { "type": "BeforeNode", "target": "Flight Search", "constraint": "Book Flight"},
7        { "type": "BeforeNode", "target": "Hotel Search", "constraint": "Book Hotel"},
8        { "type": "AfterNode", "target": "Payment Specification", "constraint": "Abstract Booking"},
9        { "type": "BranchAfterExecution", "target": "Abstract search", "constraint": "<PathToGroovyScript>"},
10       { "type": "BranchAfterExecution", "target": "Payment Specification", "constraint": "<PathToGroovyScript>"},
11       { "type": "IncreaseCostOnError", "target": "All", "constraint": "4"}
12    ]}
```

Fig. 6. Goal and constraints inputs in JSON.

By default, branching occurs based on a minimization of total path cost across all path segments. However, to flexibly support branching logic independent of the microservice implementation, branching constraints can be provided consisting of the type "BranchAfterExecution", the target node, with the constraint consisting of the path to a Groovy script consisting of program logic that dynamically determines and returns a target node to branch to as a JSON string. As input, the script is passed all next follower nodes (potential branch targets) as a JSON string and the workflow state (consisting of the inputs and outputs from all previously invoked nodes) as a map. For example, the groovy script could be used to branch.

In order to specify error or exception handling, a constraint type "IncreaseCost OnError" is provided, with either a specific target node or "All", and a constraint consisting of a multiplication factor with which to dynamically adjust the cost weighting of a problematic segment of a path to that node (e.g., the credit card has expired, or the node did not respond in time, etc., that can be used to constrain the number of retries). This factor can also be set to "MaxInt" to essentially ensure a problematic segment will not be retried. HTTP response status code of 5xx server errors cause a Microflow to navigate back to the previous abstract node and permit another attempt from there, under the assumption that the client is OK and the that particular service had an issue. Furthermore, if an "IncreaseCostOnError" factor exists it penalizes that segment's cost weighting by the given multiplication factor, and then reinvokes any branching logic script if any was specified, otherwise it triggers a replanning that minimizes the total remaining path cost. On 4xx client errors, a restart of the Microflow from the beginning is initiated, under the assumption that perhaps some changes in the resource environment are causing the client to make erroneous requests, and the entire plan and its enactment should be reinitialized. An "OnError" type constraint with a groovy script can be used for more complex error handling scenarios where increasing a path segment alone is insufficient.

The set of constraint tuples are analyzed on Microflow initialization, whereby any AfterNode is converted to a BeforeNode by swapping target and constraint, then ordered, and then checked if any constraint is redundant. Then RequiredNode constraints are also converted to BeforeNode constraints. A PathWrapper is used because of occasional issues incurred when passing Path objects in the Neo4J format between agents.

4.3 Microflow Lifecycle

We now describe the various microflow lifecycle stages.

Microflow Discovery Stage. The *Microservice Discovery* stage involves the interactions shown in Fig. 7, where Microservices first register themselves with the DiscoveryService. On client initialization, the DataAgent has the DataRepository fetch (via its DatabaseController) the registered services from the DiscoveryService and retrieve the service description from each microservice rather than a central repository. This avoids the issues of the discovery service retaining duplicate or incorrect (stale) semantic data.

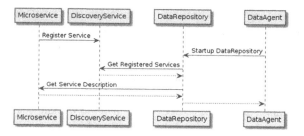

Fig. 7. Microservice Discovery stage interactions.

In Fig. 8, the semantic description of the microservice is retrieved and, if a node does not yet exist, a node is inserted in the graph along with its properties. All followers are also inserted (if not already) and their association with this microservice is annotated as a directed edge. If any microservices are detected that were not (yet) registered with the discovery service, these are also tracked in a list.

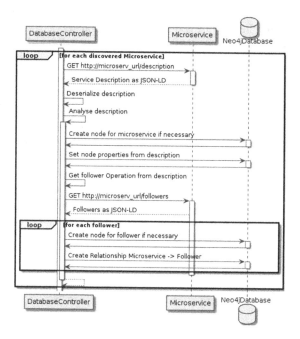

Fig. 8. Microservice description collection interactions.

Microservice Planning Stage. During the *Microservice Planning* stage, the Planning-Agent plans a Microflow. It has two Beliefs: PathParameters (the input) and the Path (see Fig. 9). The annotations show that anytime PathParameters changes, Jadex triggers a planning.

```
1 @Plan(trigger = @Trigger(factchangeds = "pathParameters"))
2 public void pathParametersChanged(ChangeEvent event) {
3  if (algorithmService != null) {
4     validPaths = algorithmService.getShortestPaths(param);
```

Fig. 9. Microflow planning triggering in Jadex.

Although Neo4 J offered native graph algorithms, they did not completely fulfill our requirements. While we utilize them, we generate Microflows with our own algorithm as shown in Fig. 10. After converting the constraints (Line 1–3) as described above, the set of possible starting microservices matching the starting type are determined (Line 4). Then this set is iterated over using the shortestPath algorithm, trying to find a path to the start of the next pathPart, which is either the target of the next constraint or the endServiceType, which is iterated (Line 7) since multiple nodes are possible. Then a recursive calculation of pathParts is initiated (Line 10), which either ends due to a deadend (Line 17) or the path to a valid endServiceType being found (Line 15).

```
1 constraints = analyze(constraints);
2 // list of constraints
3 cList = orderConstraints(constraints);
4 startList = findServicesForServiceType(startType);
5 foreach(service in startList) {
6   nextTargetList = findServicesForServiceType(cList[0]);
7   for(target in nextTargetList){
8     path = findPath(service, target);
9     if(path.isValid()){
10       pathPartList = calculateNextPathPart(target,
11         cList[1...cList.length()-1]);
12       if(pathPartList.isValid()){
13         pathPartList.prepend(path);
14         possiblePathsList.add(pathPartsToPath(pathPartsList));
15         break; // Stop, valid path from a start found
16       }
17     }
18   }
19 }
20 calculatedPath = findBestPath(possiblePathsList);
21 return calculatedPath;
```

Fig. 10. Microflow generation algorithm (pseudocode).

The Microflow schema is currently only applicable for the current enactment, so that future enactments involve a replanning. However, the Microflow schema (sequence plans) could be retained and reused if desired - for instance, if nothing changed in the environment. If multiple clients and thus agents coexisted in a trusted environment, then they could utilize their social communication ability to request and share Microflows.

Although support for gateways (forking and merging) and intermediate events are feasible in this approach, are prototype did not yet realize this functionality at this time. Support for using costs with graph paths is implemented but not utilized in our evaluation, since with virtual microservices it appeared artificial for the focus of our investigation.

In focusing on a lightweight approach, and not requiring interoperability, we chose to avoid the XML-centric BPEL and BPMN, which would only have added extra overhead in our case study without any benefit.

Microservice Enactment Stage. For the *Microflow Enactment* stage, the Execution-Agent is primarily responsible. It has three beliefs: pathWrapper, currentNode (points to which node is either active or about to be executed), and path (the planned Microflow), and similar to Fig. 9, the ExecutionAgent's plan is triggered by a change to the path variable (by the PlanningAgent), as shown in Fig. 11.

```
1 @AgentArgument
2 @Belief
3 protected PathWrapper pathwrapper;
4 @Belief
5 protected int currentNode = -1;
6 @Belief
7 protected Path path;
8
9 @Plan(trigger = @Trigger(factchangeds = "path") )
10 public void startPathExecution(ChangeEvent event) {
```

Fig. 11. ExecutionAgent (snippet).

The Microflow enactment algorithm is shown in Fig. 12. Line 7 shows that abstract nodes are skipped. Line 12 is a loop for the case when a microservice takes more than one input. In Line 15 the output of this invocation is retained for possible input as client state during further Microflow processing. Because the microservice invocations are asynchronous, a Java CountDownLatch is used for synchronization purposes. Line 21 shows that a new Microflow planning starting with the current node is triggered when an error occurs with avoidance of the problematic microservice if possible (e.g., if other identical microservice types are available) - otherwise a retry can be attempted. In addition, the initial constraints are readjusted since certain constraints may no longer be applicable (e.g., if they were already fulfilled in the partial Microflow already executed). Line 28 determines a new workflow plan after a branch. For the non-branching case the next node in the plan is taken (Line 30).

```
1  // toBeExecutedNode = index of node in workflow/path
2  // possibleInputList = list of available inputs generated by previous services
3  if (!isNodeValid(toBeExecutedNode))
4    return; // stop execution
5  serviceDescription = getServiceDescription(toBeExecutedNode);
6  if (isNodeAbstract(serviceDescription)){
7    toBeExecutedNode++; // continue with next node in workflow
8    return;
9  }
10 if (!isValidInputAvailable(serviceDescription))
11   return; // stop execution
12 for each (input in getValidInputList(serviceDescription)){
13   response = executeServiceWithInput(serviceDescription, input);
14   if (response.OK()){
15     possibleInputList.add(response.getBody());
16   }else{
17     // On 5xx error, go back to the last abstract node, else restart WF
18     // The new WF contains all previously visited nodes up to the last abstract one
19     // Optionally: transition to current node is penalized by given cost factor
20     // Keep inputs up to the last abstract node
21     toBeExecutedNode = generateNewWorkflowAfterError(toBeExecutedNode);
22     return;
23   }
24 }
25 // The branching is encoded in the constraints.
26 // The new WF contains the already visited nodes up to the current one.
27 if(isBranchingNode(serviceDescription, constraints))
28   toBeExecutedNode = generateNewWorkflowAfterBranching(toBeExecutedNode);
29 else // normal non-branching case is the next node in the plan
30   toBeExecutedNode++;
```

Fig. 12. Microflow enactment algorithm (pseudocode).

Figure 13 shows the interactions when a Microflow is enacted. Within a loop a PUT is used to invoke each virtual microservice in the Microflow for testing purposes, this would be adjusted for real microservices. When an error occurs, a replanning is done from the prior abstract node, and the transition path segment cost to the current node is penalized by a factor if given. If a branch is involved, a new path is calculated from the branch taken.

While the service description could be retrieved directly from the microservice, we currently use the internal copy stored during the discovery stage to avoid the additional network and microservice overhead of retrieving this information again. If the description is expected to be highly dynamic, the current description could be retrieved from the microservice during enactment.

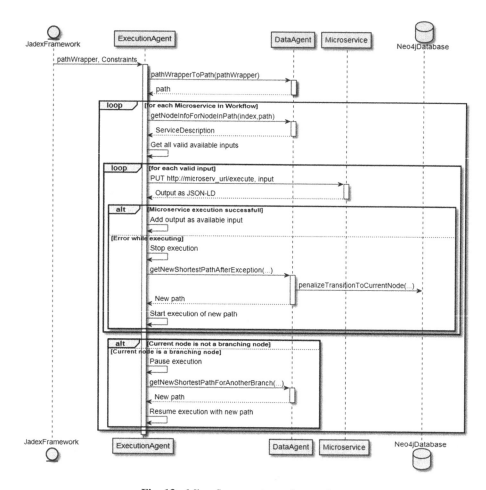

Fig. 13. Microflow enactment interactions.

5   Evaluation

In our prior paper (Oberhauser 2016), we evaluated resource utilization and scalability to validate the lightweight nature and performance of Microflows. We also compared the typical standard BPM modeling approach vs. the constraint-based declarative automated planning approach of Microflows as far as modeling efficiency.

Here we provide a case study that illustrates the solution approach including the use of path costs and branching.

5.1   Case Study

In this case study, we utilize a Microflow example comparable to standard workflows based on the previously described BPMN model Fig. 5 and the Microflow equivalent constraints of Fig. 6. Based on the Neo4j graph, the annotated Microflow is shown in Fig. 14. The Microflow consists of 12 nodes: Get preferences (node 1), Abstract search (node 2), Search for Flight service (node 3), Search for Hotel service (node 4), Abstract Booking (node 5), Execute Flight Booking (node 6), Execute Hotel booking (node 7), Payment Specification (node 8), which can be followed by a conditional Branch to either Prepayment (node 9), Bill Payment (node 10), or Credit Card Payment (node 11), followed by a Merge to the Completion (node 12). Let us assume the following path segment costs: a = 30, b = 6, c = 8, d = 2, e = 10, f = 7, g = 4, h = 3, i = 19, j = 20, k = 3, l = 10, m = 30, n = 20, o = 10, p = 10, q = 10. Prepayment is the cheapest and least risky form of transaction, credit card is a more expensive transaction with little risk, while billing the customer involves the most risk and longest wait for funds.

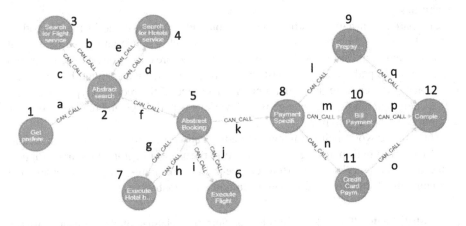

Fig. 14. Microflow example shown in Neo4j as nodes and call options (annotated with node numbers and path segment letters).

If branching logic is provided in the constraints, then this logic in the form of a groovy script determines the next node to attempt. If branch logic is provided by "BrachAfter-Execution" after Abstract search via a groovy script, then a loop of additional search invocations to determine the total minimum cost within two days before and after the given date preference can be attempted before continuing to Abstract Booking. If branch logic is provided at Payment Specification, then it determines the choice (e.g., based on total price, if > $2000 should use a billing service, between $500–$2000 should use a credit card service, and otherwise prepayment, or based on various risk factors associated with the customer profile).

Without branching logic, the path costs are used. The total path cost up to node 8 (Payment Specification) is 112. Absent any such branching logic, then Payment Specification is an abstract node that provides the possible followers. In this case, since Prepayment (node 9) is the least costly (cost 10), it invokes it but receives an error (e.g., due to insufficient funds). Because of the given "IncreaseCostOnError" factor 4, the new cost is calculated to be l = 40. The least cost path is now calculated to be via node 11, which is invoked and also receives an error (e.g., credit card expired). The cost of the path segment is increased by the factor to n = 80. The cheapest path is now via node 10 (Bill Payment), and this is invoked and succeeds with a cost of 30. The total path costs were 182 including the erroneous invocation paths taken.

6   Conclusions

We described Microflows, an automatic lightweight declarative approach for the workflow-centric orchestration of semantically-annotated microservices using agent-based clients, graph-based methods, and lightweight semantic vocabularies. Microflow principles and its lifecycle were presented and its prototype realization described. A case study demonstrated the branching, path segment cost weighting, and error handling capabilities.

Compared to a naive Restful approach, one advantage we see in the Microflow approach is that the plan (or workflow) is not thoroughly adhoc and dynamic, so that validation and verification checks can be performed before execution and one is assured that at least one path to the goal exists before beginning with enactment. For instance, if all microservices were there, but a payment service of the required type is missing, then a client without this knowledge would work its way through and realize at the very end that it has no way to pay.

Thus, future work includes integrating advanced verification and validation techniques for the automatic planning, optimizing resource usage, integrating semantic support in the discovery service, supporting compensation and long-running processes, and enhancing the declarative and semantic support and capabilities.

Acknowledgments.   The author thanks Florian Sorg and Sebastian Stigler for their assistance with the design, implementation, evaluation, and diagrams.

References

Alpers, S., Becker, C., Oberweis, A., Schuster, T.: Microservice based tool support for business process modelling. In: 2015 IEEE 19th International Enterprise Distributed Object Computing Workshop (EDOCW), pp. 71–78. IEEE (2015)

Anderson, C., Suarez, I., Xu, Y., David, K.: An ontology-based reasoning framework for context-aware applications. In: Christiansen, H., Stojanovic, I., Papadopoulos, George A. (eds.) CONTEXT 2015. LNCS (LNAI), vol. 9405, pp. 471–476. Springer, Cham (2015). doi: 10.1007/978-3-319-25591-0_34

Bouguettaya, A., Sheng, Q.Z., Daniel, F.: Web Services Foundations. Springer, New York (2014)

Bratman, M.E., Israel, D.J., Pollack, M.E.: Plans and resource-bounded practical reasoning. Comput. Intell. **4**(3), 349–355 (1988)

Eureka. https://github.com/Netflix/eureka/wiki. Retrieved 20 April 2016

Fielding, R.T.: Architectural Styles and the Design of Network-based Software Architectures. Doctoral dissertation, University of California, Irvine (2000)

Florio, L.: Decentralized self-adaptation in large-scale distributed systems. In: Proceedings of the 2015 10th Joint Meeting on Foundations of Software Engineering, pp. 1022–1025. ACM (2015)

Fowler, M., Lewis, J.: Microservices a definition of this new architectural term (2014). http://
martinfowler.com/articles/microservices.htm. Retrieved 15 April 2016

Gartner: Gartner Says Spending on Business Process Management Suites to Reach $2.7 Billion
in 2015 as Organizations Digitalize Processes (2015). https://www.gartner.com/newsroom/id/
3064717. Retrieved 15 April 2016

Heitmann, B., Cyganiak, R., Hayes, C., Decker, S.: An empirically grounded conceptual
architecture for applications on the web of data. IEEE Trans. Syst. Man Cybern. Part C: Appl.
Rev. **42**(1), 51–60 (2012)

IBM: IBM Business Process Manager V8.5.6 documentation (2015). http://www.ibm.com/
support/knowledgecenter/SSFPJS_8.5.6/com.ibm.wbpm.wid.bpel.doc/topics/
cprocess_transaction_micro.html. Retrieved 2 May 2016

Karagiannis, G., Jamakovic, A., Edmonds, A., Parada, C., Metsch, T., Pichon, D., Bohnert, T.M.:
Mobile cloud networking: virtualisation of cellular networks. In: 2014 21st International
Conference on Telecommunications (ICT), pp. 410–415. IEEE (2014)

Lanthaler, M.: Creating 3rd generation web APIs with hydra. In: Proceedings of the 22nd
International Conference on World Wide Web Companion. International World Wide Web
Conferences Steering Committee, pp. 35–38 (2013)

Lanthaler, M., Gütl, C.: On using JSON-LD to create evolvable RESTful services. In: Proceedings
of the Third International Workshop on RESTful Design, pp. 25–32. ACM (2012)

Lanthaler, M., Gütl, C.: Hydra: A vocabulary for hypermedia-driven web APIs. In: Proceedings
of the 6th Workshop on Linked Data on the Web (LDOW2013) at the 22nd International World
Wide Web Conference (WWW 2013), vol. 996 (2013)

Martin, D., et al.: OWL-S: Semantic markup for web services. W3C (2004). http://www.w3.org/
Submission/OWL-S/. Retrieved 24 March 2017

Oberhauser, R.: Microflows: Lightweight automated planning and enactment of workflows
comprising semantically-annotated microservices. In: Proceedings of the Sixth International
Symposium on Business Modeling and Software Design (BMSD 2016), pp. 134–143.
SCITEPRESS (2016)

Pesic, M., Schonenberg, H., van der Aalst, W.M.: Declare: Full support for loosely-structured
processes. In: 2007 11th IEEE International Enterprise Distributed Object Computing
Conference, EDOC 2007, pp. 287–287. IEEE (2007)

Pokahr, A., Braubach, L., Lamersdorf, W.: Jadex: A BDI reasoning engine. In: Bordini, R.H.,
Dastani, M., Dix, J., El Fallah Seghrouchni, A. (eds.) Multi-agent Programming. Multiagent
Systems, Artificial Societies, and Simulated Organizations, vol. 15, pp. 149–174. Springer,
Heidelberg (2005)

Rajasekar, A., Wan, M., Moore, R., Schroeder, W.: Micro-Services: A service-oriented paradigm
for. data intensive distributed computing. In: Challenges and Solutions for Large-scale
Information Management, pp. 74–93. IGI Global (2012)

Rao, J., Su, X.: A survey of automated web service composition methods. In: Cardoso, J., Sheth,
A. (eds.) SWSWPC 2004. LNCS, vol. 3387, pp. 43–54. Springer, Heidelberg (2005). doi:
10.1007/978-3-540-30581-1_5

Sheng, Q.Z., et al.: Web services composition: A decade's overview. Inf. Sci. **280**, 218–238 (2014)

Toffetti, G., Brunner, S., Blöchlinger, M., Dudouet, F., Edmonds, A.: An architecture for self-
managing microservices. In: Proceedings of the 1st International Workshop on Automated
Incident Management in Cloud, pp. 19–24. ACM (2015)

WfMC: Workflow Management Coalition: Terminology & Glossary. WFMC-TC-1011, Issue 3.0
(1999)

Wooldridge, M.: An Introduction to Multiagent Systems. Wiley, New York (2009)

Software Configuration Based on Order Processes

Andreas Daniel Sinnhofer[1]([✉]), Peter Pühringer[1,2], Klaus Potzmader[2],
Clemens Orthacker[2], Christian Steger[1], and Christian Kreiner[1]

[1] Institute of Technical Informatics, Graz University of Technology, Graz, Austria
{a.sinnhofer,steger,christian.kreiner}@tugraz.at
[2] NXP Semiconductors, Gratkorn, Austria
p.puehringer@inode.at, {klaus.potzmader,clemens.orthacker}@nxp.com

Abstract. Business processes have proven to be essential for organisations to be highly flexible and competitive in today's markets. However, good process management is not enough to survive in a market if the according IT landscape is not aligned to the business processes. Especially industries focused on software products are facing big problems if the according processes are not aligned to the overall software system architecture. Often, a lot of development resources are spent for features which are never addressed by any business goals, leading to unnecessary development costs. In this paper, we will present a framework for an automatic, order process driven, software configuration. For this, modern software product line engineering techniques are used to provide a systematic way to align the variability of the order processes with the software architecture.

Keywords: Software product lines · Feature oriented modelling · Business processes · Tool configuration

1 Introduction

Business Process (BP) oriented organisations are known to perform better regarding highly flexible demands of the market and fast production cycles (e.g. [1–3]). This is achieved through the introduction of a management process, where business processes are modelled, analysed and optimised in iterative ways. Nowadays, business process management is also coupled with a workflow management, providing the ability to integrate the responsible participants into the process and to monitor the correct execution of it in each process step. To administer the rising requirements, so called business process management tools are used (BPM-Tools) which cover process modelling, optimization and execution. In combination with an Enterprise-Resource-Planning (ERP) system, the data of the real process can be integrated into the management process.

In the domain of software products, different choices in business processes lead to different software configurations. To handle variability automatically is a

© Springer International Publishing AG 2017
B. Shishkov (Ed.): BMSD 2016, LNBIP 275, pp. 200–220, 2017.
DOI: 10.1007/978-3-319-57222-2_10

challenging task because the variability of the process model needs to be reflected in the software architecture. Further, the actual customer choice during the ordering process needs to be mapped to the according software features. Due to this, software configuration is often done manually which takes a considerable amount of time during production. Particularly for resource constraint devices like embedded systems, it is vital to have a working software configuration process since unnecessary features may occupy a lot of resources. Further, it is important to have a software architecture which is synchronised with the business goals. Otherwise, a lot of resources are spent for developing and maintaining software components which are never used anyway. Especially big companies are facing problems to align the whole development team to the business goals. Thus, process awareness is crucial for an efficient development and production.

Context Aware Business Process modelling is a technique for businesses living in a complex and dynamic environment (Saidani and Nurcan [4]). In such an environment a company needs to tackle changing requirements which are dependent on the context of the system. Such context sensitive business process models are able to adapt the execution of their process instances according to the needs, such that the company can react faster and more flexible. This is achieved by analysing the context states of the environment and mapping these states to the according business processes and their related software system. The problem with such approaches is, that the used software systems are often developed independently from each other, although they share a similar software architecture. Therefore, this work focuses on the development of a framework which covers the variability of process models, and mapping such variable process structures to software configuration artefacts. This allows, that the software system can be adapted automatically with respect to its context. Software product lines have proven to be capable of achieving such flexible architectures. Additionally, the robustness of such systems can be increased, since only one system needs to be developed and maintained for whole product families. In this work, we limited the scope to reflect the variability of the order processes for software products. This includes the automatic detection of variable personalization options of different product configurations, and the automated configuration of the software toolchain responsible for generating the resulting software product. The modelling of business process variability is based on our previous work, which can be found in [5]. In particular, a SPLE Tool was used to systematically reuse expert knowledge in form of valid process variations, designed in an appropriated BPM Tool. The integrity of the process variations is secured by the capabilities of the BPM Tool and a rich cross functional constraint checking in the SPLE Tool. A more detailed description is given in Sect. 3.1. This work will extend the framework in order to be able to map process artefacts to software configurations. Hence, software toolchains can be configured in an automatic way and the architecture can be kept aligned with the business goals.

This work is structured in the following way: Sect. 2 summarizes the related work and Sect. 3 gives an overview over the used design paradigm for business processes modelling and Software Product Line Engineering techniques which were needed for the framework. Section 4 summarizes the concept of our work, giving details about the conceptual design, the used type model and rules which the system applies. Section 5 describes our implementation in an industrial use case and Sect. 6 concludes this work and gives an overview over future work.

2   Related Work

As stated in the survey of Fantinato et al. [6], major challenges in the field of business process variability modelling are related to the reaction time of process changes and of the creation and selection of the right business process variants, which are also main topics in our framework since the time to adopt the IT infrastructure to the changed business processes can be reduced with the new framework.

Derguech [7] presents a framework for the systematic reuse of process models. In contrast to this work, it captures the variability of the process model at the business goal level and describes how to integrate new goals/sub-goals into the existing data structure. The variability of the process is not addressed in his work.

Gimenes et al. [8] presents a feature based approach to support e-contract negotiation based on web-services (WS). A meta-model for WS-contract representation is given and a way is shown how to integrate the variability of these contracts into the business processes to enable a process automation. It does not address the variability of the process itself but enables the ability to reuse business processes for different e-contract negotiations.

While our used framework to model process variability reduces the overall process complexity by splitting up the process into layers with increasing details, the PROVOP project ([9–11]) focuses on the concept, that variants are derived from a basic process definition through well-defined change operations (ranging from the deletion, addition, moving of model elements or the adaptation of an element attribute). In fact, the basic process expresses all possible variants at once, leading to a big process model. Their approach could be beneficial considering that cross functional requirements can be located in a single process description, but having one huge process is also contra productive. The exchange of parts during a process improvement process can be difficult.

The work of Gottschalk et al. [12] presents an approach for the automated configuration of workflow models within a workflow modelling language. The term workflow model is used for the specification of a business process which enables the execution in an enterprise and workflow management system. The approach focuses on the activation or deactivation of actions and thus, is comparable to the PROVOP project for the workflow model domain.

La Rosa et al. [13] extends the configurable process modelling notation developed from Gottschalk et al. [12] with notions of roles and objects providing a way to address not only the variability of the control-flow of a workflow model but also of the related resources and responsibilities.

The Common Variability Language (CVL [14]) is a language for specifying and resolving variability independent from the domain of the application.

It facilitates the specification and resolution of variability over any instance of any language defined using a Meta Object Facility (MOF)-based meta-model. A CVL based variability modelling and a BPM model with an appropriate model transformation could lead to similar results as presented in this paper.

The work of Zhao and Zou [15] shows a framework for the generation of software modules based on business processes. They use clustering algorithms to analyse dependencies among data and tasks, captured in business processes. Further, they group the strongly dependent tasks and data into a software component.

3   Background

3.1   Business Processes

A business process can be seen as a sequence of specific activities or sub-processes which need to be executed in a specific way to produce a specific output with value to the customer [18]. According to Österle [16] the process design on a macroscopic level (high degree of abstraction) is split up into sub-processes until the microscopic level is reached. This is achieved, when all tasks are detailed enough, so that they can be used as work instructions. An exemplary order process is illustrated in Fig. 1. As illustrated, the top layer is a highly abstracted description, while the production steps are further refined on the lower levels. As a result, the lowest level is highly dependable on the concrete product and production environment, providing many details for the employees. Usually, the top

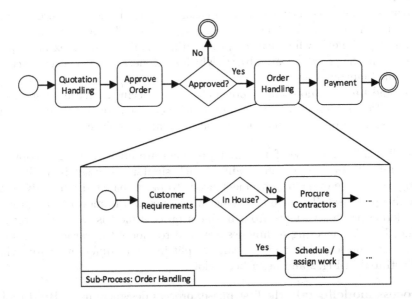

Fig. 1. Exemplary order process to illustrate the basic concepts defined by Österle [16]: A high level description of the process is split into its sub-processes until a complete work description is reached (adapted from [17]).

layers are independent from the concrete plant and the supply chain and could be interchanged throughout production plants. Only the lower levels (the refinements) would need to be reconsidered. Variability of such a process structure can either be expressed through a variable structure of a process/sub-process (e.g. adding/removing nodes in a sequence) or by replacing the process refinement with different processes. One prominent way to design such processes is the use of the *"Business Process Model and Notation"* notation (BPMN; see [19]). The key components of such processes can be classified in the following way:

- **Events**: An Event is something that occurs during the execution of a Process. Such events affect the flow of the Process and usually have a cause and an impact. Examples are the start of an Activity, the completion of an Activity, the start of a Process, etc. According to BPMN [19], events are used only for those types, that affects the sequence or timing of Activities of a process.
- **Activities**: An Activity is work that a company or organization performs during the execution of a process. Two different types of activities can be distinguished: An activity not broken down to a finer level of Process Model is called atomic activity (i.e. a task). Sequences of tasks (e.g. a sub-process) belonging to the same activity are called non-atomic activities.
- **Gateways**: A gateway within a process controls how the process flows through different sequence flows. Each gateway can have multiple input and/or output paths. An example is a decision, where one of many possible alternative paths is selected based on a specific condition. Another prominent example is a parallel gateway which splits a single flow into multiple flows which are executed in parallel.
- **Data**: Data objects represents information flowing through the process such as documents or e-mails. A Data object can be required from a specific activity as input parameter which can be provided internally or by an external party involved in the process. Data objects which are generated by a specific activity are called Output Data.
- **Pool** and **Lanes**: Represent responsibilities for specific activities or sequences of activities in a process. The responsibilities can be assigned to an organization, a specific role, a system or even an dedicated employee.

Traditionally, processes for similar products are created using a copy and clone strategy. As a result, maintaining such similar processes is a time consuming task, since every improvement needs to be propagated manually to the respective processes. To solve this issue, we proposed a framework to automatically derive process variants from business process models (see [5]). Software Product Line Engineering techniques are used to model the variable parts of a process. The presented framework can be split into four different phases which are illustrated in Fig. 2 and described below:

- **Process modelling**: In the first phase, process designers use a BPM tool of their choice and create process templates. That is, defining the sequence of steps of sub-processes using the BPMN notation. Further, they add artefacts to the BPM Tool for required features like documentation artefacts, responsible workers or resources. As indicated in the figure, the design of (sub-) processes and the creation of the according domain model is done hand in hand.

- **Domain modelling**: In the second phase, the created processes are imported into the SPLE tool and added to a feature model (see Sect. 3.2 for a description of feature models). During this process, the domain engineers (Process Designer) chooses the set of available (sub-) processes and defines which parts of these (sub-) processes are variable. Consider the following example, a company responsible for forming metal uses different production planning strategies for different customers. E.g. for customer X the company is using event driven Kanban and for customer Y the company is using Kanban with a quantity signal. As a consequence, the principal sequence of production steps is the same, but the production planning is scheduled differently based on the used Kanban system. Thus, the domain engineer chooses the production plaining strategy to be variable by defining a Variation Point (VP). He deposits the different Kanban implementations as possible variants for this VP such that two process models can be generated. To limit the possible configuration space, the domain engineer can define a comprehensive set of rules and restrictions such that only meaningful and valid process variants can be derived.

- **Feature selection**: In this phase, production experts are using the defined set of process models (within the SPLE tool) to derive process variants for their current needs. This is done by selecting the wished features from the feature model, which was created in the second phase. For example, the production experts could choose event driven Kanban, since they know that customer X has placed an order.

- **Maintenance and Evolution**: In this phase, derived processes are used in the production and observed by production experts. Based on the collected data, the Production Experts can either improve the feature selection of the used process (iteration back to step 3), or issue a process improvement process (iteration back to step 4). For example, during the production for customer X, it was observed that event driven Kanban was to slow to react to the customer needs. As a consequence, the production experts changed the production planning strategy to quantity based Kanban to tackle these problems. Another example could be that it was observed that quantity based Kanban was to general. E.g. the production experts recognized that only one bin Kanban and three bin Kanban are valuable for the production processes. As a consequence, new processes need to be designed and integrated into the existing feature model.

Our today's business environment is focused on creating sustainable value by increasing the revenue of business drivers. The identification of these drivers or, equally important, the identification of drivers capable of destroying value is a crucial step for a process driven organization. Such drivers have a high impact on the organization in order to stay competitive or even survive on the market [20]. The combination of SPLE engineering and business modelling is promising a potential way to improve the identification of the drivers and to react fast to changes of the market.

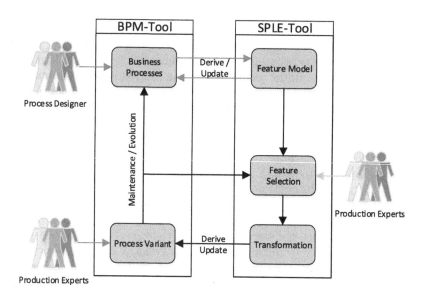

Fig. 2. Used framework for an automatic business process variant generation (adapted from [5]). The grey lines indicate process steps which need to be done manually.

3.2   Software Product Line Engineering

SPLE applies the concepts of product lines to software products [21]. A Software Product Line can be seen as a set of domain features, which are automatically assembled and configured to a whole software project just by choosing the wanted features. Instead of writing code for every individual system, the developer divides the project into small lightweight features which are implemented in so called domain artefacts. For this, a software architecture is required in which the variation points and the respective variants (features) are explicitly modelled. Further, a source code generator is needed which is able to generate the according software products, based on the according feature selection. As identified by Pohl et al. [22] and Weiss et al. [23], the software product line engineering can be split up into two main parts, the *Domain Engineering* and the *Application Engineering*. The domain engineering is the procedure for defining the components, the variabilities and the commonalities of the product line. The application engineering is the procedure where the application itself is built, using some domain artefacts which were created in the domain engineering. The application engineering can be done manually, or automatically by using dedicated generators. This enables the rapid creation of similar software products of a product family.

During domain modelling, *Feature Models* are used to describe all features of a product and to explicitly state their relationships, dependencies and additional restrictions between them. Figure 3 illustrates an explanatory feature model for a car. A car consists of three mandatory variation points ('Engine Type', 'Gear Type', 'Entertainment System'), their respective variants, and an

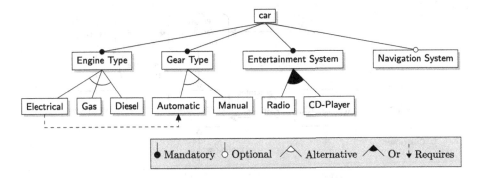

Fig. 3. An exemplary feature model of a car (adapted from [17]).

optional variation point ('Navigation System'). For example, the 'Engine Type' of the car could be Electrical, Gas or Diesel powered. The variants of the 'Engine Type' and 'Gear Type' variation point are modelled as alternative features which means that exactly one variant needs to be chosen. In contrast, the 'Entertainment System' is modelled in such a way, that either one or both options can be chosen. Further restrictions can be defined to ensure that only valid products can be generated. One example is illustrated in Fig. 3; an electrical engine requires that an automatic gear type is selected. Another restriction, which is not illustrated in the figure, could be, that a specific feature cannot be selected if another feature was selected. This allows to implement complex rules to ensure that the generated systems are working as expected.

After defining the set of features, a design is created and the reusable artefacts are implemented. In case of our used process modelling approach [8], the design of the features and the implementation of reusable artefacts is done iteratively. The reason for that is, that the definition of the variable parts and their according restrictions, is the most critical aspect of designing an SPL. This ensures, that the reusable parts can be used in many different contexts.

4   Variability Framework

The goal of the developed framework is to implement a systematic way to keep the customization options of the order processes aligned with the IT infrastructure such that development costs can be reduced and the company is more flexible to changes of the market. For this purpose, we are combining our previously developed product line for business process models (see [5]) with a product line for creating software products. The following Sections summarizes the developed concepts.

4.1   Conceptual Design

The overall conceptual design is based on a feature oriented domain modelling framework and is illustrated in Fig. 4. As shown in the Figure, Domain Experts

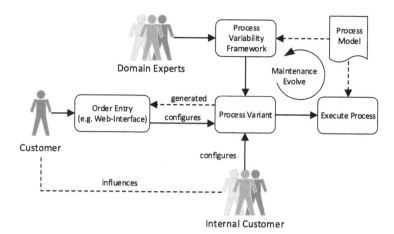

Fig. 4. Overall conceptual design of the framework (adapted from [17]). The "Process Variability Framework" block is described in Fig. 2.

are responsible for operating the "Process Variability Framework" as already described in Sect. 3.1. They design process models based on their domain knowledge and generate process variants for various types of product platforms. Based on this variants, the used SPLE tool also generates an order entry form, stating explicitly which kind of information a customer needs to submit, to be able to order the product. For example, if the customer can decide which applications should run on his device, or if the device can be personalized by adding signatures of the customer.

Complex products usually tend to have a lot of internal stakeholders which can be seen as internal customers. This means that based on the customer needs, specific stakeholders may be addressed to further submit needed information or even parts of the product. For instance, if a product can run on multiple hardware platforms, each of these platforms may be developed by different departments or even different companies which need to be ordered and shipped accordingly.

To be able to automatically generate the order entry forms, additional information needs to be added to the process models. This can be done by either adding this information into the process model itself (i.e. using the BPM tool) or by tagging the process model inside the SPLE tool. The additional type information designed in the SPLE tool is mapped to the according process models using unique identifiers. Using the SPLE tool to add the additional information is the more generic approach. This also has the positive side-effect, that the processes itself are not "polluted" with information that may change in different circumstances. On the other hand, it rises high requirements to the SPLE tool which needs to support product family models such that the process model and the additional information used for the order entry can be kept aligned, but separated.

After all needed data is collected, the process can finally be executed and the ordered products are manufactured. Figure 5 shows a more detailed process of our framework to configure or generate software products. The filled order entry forms of the internal and external customer(s) are collected and converted into a format which can be automatically processed during the following Application Engineering. Here, the given submission files are imported and a feature selection is generated based on the provided input data. The feature model is directly linked to the process model and is maintained by Domain Experts operating the system. The maintenance can be done semi-automatic through the use of mapping rules which are described in Sect. 4.2.

The generated feature selection is verified manually by a Domain Expert against the customer requirements. The verification step is necessary to ensure the configuration safety of the final product. This is also an important topic for process certification, where evidence need to be provided to prove, that the ordered configuration is equivalent to the final product and not confused with any other customer configuration. After the verification, the Domain Experts triggers the "Feature Transformation" process. During this process, the submitted customer data is translated using product specific code generators. The result of this process strongly depends on the intended use case: It could be a binary file which is directly loaded during the production of the IC; another possibility is a set of configuration scripts which are executed to configure the product. In Sect. 5 we will present an industrial case study which generates a set of scripts which are executed to configure the ordered products.

Especially for new products, it is likely that during the manufacturing process knowledge is gained on how to increase the efficiency of the whole process(es) by introducing specific changes to the process model. Further, changes to the generated order entry forms may be identified, leading to more configuration possibilities. This also effects the Feature Model and the code generators used during the application engineering. The advantage of using one core of process models for a specific family of products is, that the gained knowledge can be rolled out in an automatic way for the whole product family. This means that the required changes only need to be implemented once for a whole product family of a product line.

4.2   Type Model

To summarize the findings of the last Section, a type model is required which maps from BPMN nodes to some kind of input data that need to be provided from internal or external customers. Based on this information, order entry forms can be generated for the different stakeholders. As a result, the process model needs to be tagged with additional information such that these order entry forms can be generated automatically for a process variant.

- **Inputs**: Is the abstract concept of different input types which are described below. Additionally, each Input is mapped to an input type defining the format of the input. For example, input data could be delivered as a file (structured or binary) or delivered in form of configuration settings like strings, integers, etc.

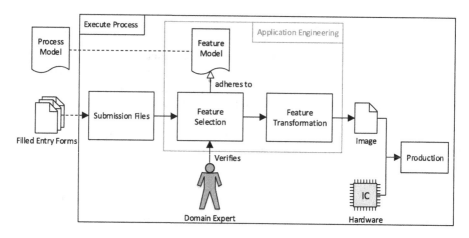

Fig. 5. The zoom-in version of the "Execute Process" task illustrated in Fig. 4. The parts which are executed during the application engineering of the according SPLE workflow are framed grey.

- **None**: No special data needs to be submitted and hence, a node marked with none will not appear as a setting in the order entry form.
- **Customer Input**: Specific data need to be added from a customer. A node marked with this type will generate an entry in the order entry form of a specific type. For example a file upload button will appear if a customer needs to submit a specific file.
- **Internal Input**: Specific data or parts of the product need to be delivered from an internal stakeholder. This information is directly propagated to the internal stakeholder as a separate order.
- **Input Group**: A set of Inputs that are logically linked together. As a consequence, all of these inputs need to be provided for a single feature.

To support the Domain Experts during the tagging of the process model, the following information can be examined automatically from the given process model:

- **Activities**: Non-atomic Activities (i.e. (sub-) processes) can be used to group a specific set of input parameter to a feature. For example a process designed for configuring an application may require several input parameter. For the order entry form, this should be displayed as one group of configuration settings. Any atomic Activity will be automatically tagged as input type "None". This also applies if a non-atomic Activity does not contain any Data nodes.
- **Gateways**: Gateways are used to define the structure of the generated order entry form. An example is a decision where the customer can choose between multiple customization options. Every branch will appear as a separate group that can be selected. If a branch does not contain any data, it will only appear as a checkbox that can be ticked. The system ensures, that only one of the

branches is selected from the possible choices. In contrast, flows in a parallel flow are all mandatory.

- **Data**: Data to be provided by an entity involved in the process. These nodes are tagged as Customer/Internal Input. The type information needs to be added manually by the Domain Experts. Per default, our implementations chooses "string" as a default type since – in our case – "string" is the most frequent type.
- **Pool** and **Lanes**: Gives information about the source of the input file. This means that a file in a company internal lane will be automatically flagged as an "Internal Input". Per default, our implementation chooses "Internal Input" as a default.

4.3 Domain Engineering

An established process management, which is able to generate order entry forms and trigger internal processes, is a big step towards good business management. However, to be successful on the market it is not enough to just focus on well managed processes, but also on an aligned IT infrastructure. Hence, the big remaining challenge is having an IT infrastructure which is able to be configured directly from the according business processes.

For illustration purposes let's consider the following example: A company is developing small embedded systems which are used as sensing devices for the internet of things. The device is offered in three different variants with the following features:

- **Version 1**: Senses the data in a given time interval and sends the recorder signal to a web-server which is used for post-processing.
- **Version 2**: Additionally to the features of **Version 1**, this version allows encryption of the sensed data using symmetric cryptography before it is sent to the web-server. This prevents that third parties are able to read the data. For simplicity, we assume that this key is provided in plain from the customer.
- **Version 3**: Additionally to the features of **Version 2**, this version also allows customer applications to be run (e.g. data pre-processing routines) on the system. This requires that the customer submits a binary file that shall be loaded to the system during the production.

It is economic infeasible to personalize each device manually if it is sold in high quantities. Further, establishing three different order processes using three different versions of customization toolchains will result in higher maintenance efforts. To summarize the findings of this short example, it is fundamental to have a software architecture which is synchronized with the according order process(es). This means that variable parts of the process model need to be reflected by a variable software architecture. Further, minor changes to the process model (e.g. addition of new configuration settings) should not lead to huge development efforts since – ideally – the software architecture does not need to be changed. To be able to define such a stable software architecture it is necessary to understand and identify the variable parts of the processes to be able to define the basic set of features that need to be implemented during the Domain Engineering.

To identify the required features, we will take a second look at the previous example and identify how the order entry is generated: Basically, there are three different customization options, where in the first case a customer can customize a connection string for his web-server. In the second case, he can further submit a key which is stored onto the nodes, and in the third case, executables can be submitted to be loaded to the chip. A very basic process showing these customization options is illustrated in Fig. 6. Applying the rules defined in Sect. 4.2, the default order entry is generated with the following properties: A string input box for defining the IP address of the web server and a decision whether to send the data encrypted or not. In case of encryption, a string input box can be used to specify the plain encryption key and an option will appear that allows a customer to load custom application also as a string input box. In this case, the only problem of the default behaviour is the default string type of the Input "Binary". As a consequence, the Domain Experts need to adapt the default process model by defining the correct input type for the "Binary" Input to get the final process model. If doing so, the system will automatically be able to generate a web form having a file upload button for the custom application. Additionally, the Domain Experts could refine the type of the other inputs to be able to perform automated constraint checks (i.e. verifying that the specified IP-Address is valid, that the given key is valid with respect to its length, etc.). The additional information is directly linked to the processes via the "Process Variability Framework" [5]. This mapping is based on unique identifiers which are unique for each node in every process designed in the BPM tool. Thus, re-factoring of the process sequence does not cause the loss of additional data. Only if the according nodes are deleted, the information is lost. Having this structured view shows that the features can be directly identified that need to be supported by the following software toolchain to generate the different product variants. Thus, the Domain Experts are able to create/derive the according Feature Model consisting of the three features 'Web-Server Configuration' (mandatory), 'Encryption' (optional) and 'Custom Application' (optional; requires 'Encryption').

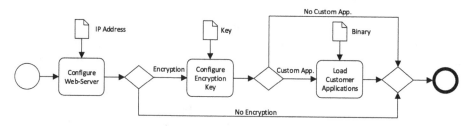

Fig. 6. Simple example process showing the customization process of the described example (Version 1, 2 and 3).

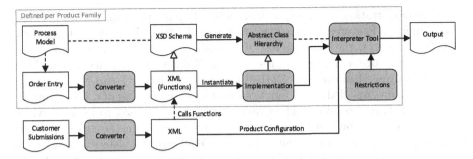

Fig. 7. The architecture of the software tool responsible for generating the wished product outcome (adapted from [17]).

4.4 Application Engineering

Based on the knowledge gained from the Domain Engineering, the goal of the Application Engineering is to automate the process of creating product variants based on the submitted order entry forms. This means, that individual features of the defined Feature Model are automatically selected and assembled to the final product, based on the submitted order entry forms. As a consequence, the submitted order entry forms need to be in a format which is on the one hand easy to read for humans and on the other hand easy to process for the software toolchain. The requirement for a human readable configuration is directly linked to the verification step shown in Fig. 5. If the configuration is not readable, a human won't be able to verify it against the customer requirements. Summing these requirements up, the architecture illustrated in Fig. 7 can be derived. As illustrated, the Extensible Markup Language (XML) is used as the human readable and machine readable file format. But of course, any other markup language can be used as well.

The tool is basically an interpreter which can be "dynamically programmed" for the actual order. This means that variability of the architecture is gained by shifting features from the implementation phase to the configuration phase. To ensure that such freedom is not misused, it is necessary to enforce specific rules in the Interpreter Tool (e.g. security requirements). Based on the Process Model of the Process Variability Framework, a schema file is created which states all possible operations and all additional language primitives (like conditional statements, etc.) the Interpreter Tool can perform. This can be seen as a Domain Specific Language (DSL) which can be used to program the Interpreter Tool. Based on this schema, a XML file is created that reflects the Feature Model which was created from the Domain Experts during the Domain Engineering. Each feature corresponds to a dedicated function which can be called from the according Product Configuration. Each function explicitly states which input parameter need to be provided such that the Interpreter Tool is able to generate the required output. Further, each function contains the sequence of operations that need to be executed by the Interpreter Tool.

For demonstration purposes, we will revisit the example from Sect. 4.3. There, three different Features where identified namely the 'Web-Server Configuration' (mandatory), the 'Encryption' (optional), and the 'Custom Application' (optional; may occur multiple times) feature. Taking this into account and the concept mentioned above, the XML illustrated in Listing 1 can be generated. For each feature, one dedicated functions is created, consisting of a *Configuration* block and a *Translate* block. The Configuration block is used to indicate which data needs to be provided from the order entries (i.e. from the "real" product configuration) and how often they can occur (configuration safety). These Configuration blocks are further used to generate a schema file which is used by the converter tool to convert the Customer Submissions into the needed XML structure. The Translate block defines how the submitted data is processed by combining the operations defined in the DSL of the Interpreter Tool. The definition of the translate blocks need to be done only once for a whole product family and only need to be adapted if the corresponding Process Model was changed. For this particular example, one possible solution could be that the interpreter tool offers a store-data and an install-application operation. The store-data operation could be used to write the IP address of the web-server to the correct memory location, as well as the encryption key and the according setting to enable the encryption.

Listing 1. Generated XML based on the Order Entry. The Translate blocks need to be edited manually by a developer calling operations defined in the XSD schema.

```
1   <?xml version=" 1.0 " encoding="UTF-8" ?>
2   <Functions>
3     <Function id="Web-Server  Configuration"
4                minOccurs=" 1"
5                maxOccurs=" 1">
6       <Configuration>
7         <Parameter name=" IP  Address" type=" ipAddress" />
8       </Configuration>
9       <Translate> ... </Translate>
10    </Function>
11
12    <Function id=" Encryption"
13               minOccurs=" 0"
14               maxOccurs=" 1">
15      <Configuration>
16        <Parameter name=" Key" type=" hexstring" />
17      </Configuration>
18      <Translate> ... </Translate>
19    </Function>
20
21    <Function id=" Custom  Application"
22               minOccurs=" 0"
23               maxOccurs=" unbounded">
24      <Configuration>
25        <Parameter name=" Binary" type=" fileUri" />
26      <Configuration>
27      <Translate> ... </Translate>
28    </Function>
29  </Functions>
```

Listing 2. Exemplary generated Configuration file based on customer submissions. Two different versions are shown. The first example illustrates a "Version 1" product and the second one a "Version 3" product.

```
1   <?xml version=" 1.0 " encoding="UTF−8" ?>
2   <CustomerOrder>
3     <WebServer>
4        <Connection>X.X.X.X</Connection>
5     </WebServer>
6   </CustomerOrder>
```

```
1    <?xml version=" 1.0 " encoding="UTF−8" ?>
2    <CustomerOrder>
3      <WebServer>
4         <Connection>X.X.X.X</Connection>
5      </WebServer>
6
7      <EncryptionKey>
8         <Key>0x01020304 ...<Key>
9      </EncryptionKey>
10
11     <Custom Application>
12        <Binary>file://orderXYZ/app1.elf</Binary>
13     </Custom Application>
14
15     <Custom Application>
16        <Binary>file://orderXYZ/app2.elf</Binary>
17     </Custom Application>
18   </CustomerOrder>
```

Additional restrictions are domain depended and could contain in that example the following checks: Verification that the submitted key is of reasonable strength (e.g. AES key with a minimum length of 16 Byte); that the submitted applications are protected by a signature of the customer, to ensure that they are not replaced by a malicious third party; Verification that the'Custom Application' feature is only used if encryption is activated.

To trigger the generation process, the filled order entry forms (i.e. customer submissions) are converted into a configuration file which calls the specific functions of the Functions XML (see Fig. 7). For example Listing 2 shows the generated Configuration file for a "Version 1" product (the configuration on the top) and a "Version 3" product (the configuration on the bottom). Based on this configuration, the Interpreter Tool is able to generate the ordered product in an automatic way. The result of this process strongly depends on the intended use case; examples could be a binary file which can be directly flashed to the sensor nodes during productions, or script files which are executed for every individual node to configure the nodes.

5   Industrial Case Study

In this section an overview over our industrial case study is given. The implemented business processes of our industrial partner are controlled by an SAP infrastructure and are designed with the BPM-Tool Aeneis. Further, pure::variants is used as SPLE tool to manage the variability of the business processes. Thus, our implemented prototype is based on pure::variants and Java.

The investigated products are smart objects designed for the Internet of Things (IoT). One possible application is the use in smart home environments to automatically control the temperature of the rooms.

5.1 SPLE-Tool: Pure::variants

pure::variants is a feature oriented domain modelling tool which is based on Eclipse. As such, it can easily be extended based on Java plug-in development. It supports family models which was one of the fundamental tool requirements identified in Sect. 4.1. During the implementation of this project, five different plug-ins where developed:

- An extension to the import plug-in which was developed in our previous work. It assists the Process Designers in modelling cross functional requirements and providing the needed information for the code generators.
- An extension to the internal model compare engine for comparing different versions of created feature models with each other.
- An extension to the internal model transformation engine to convert the feature selection of the process model into the according order entry form. This also generates the back-end to trigger processes for internal stakeholders.
- Additions to the internal model check engine to model and create only valid processes (e.g. checks related to the feature selection, the consistency of the feature model, etc.)
- Generator Tools which are able to generate the skeleton of the schema file (as described in Sect. 4.3) and the order entry form (a generated Web-Interface). Additionally, converter tools were written which are converting the generated forms and received submissions into the related XML configuration files.

Additionally, the interpreter tool was written within the same development environment to ensure that the feature models are directly reflected in the implementation of the interpreter.

5.2 Implementation of the Interpreter Tool

As mentioned in Sect. 4.4, XML/XSD are used to model the operations of the interpreter tool and to automatically instantiate the requested features. To ease the implementation, the according class hierarchy was generated from the schema file using the tool Jaxb (a Java architecture for XML binding[1]). The generated bare class hierarchy was then implemented by the software developers. Since the creation of the schema file is semi-automatic, our developed framework (implemented in pure::variants) opens a dialogue which hints the domain expert to check the validity of the schema file to ensure that the changes to the processes are always propagated to the schema file. The domain of our industrial case study was the configuration of small embedded systems. The production was done in

---

[1] http://www.oracle.com/technetwork/articles/javase/index-140168.html.

Table 1. Effort measurements and estimations in man-month to develop the system using traditional software development and our presented framework.

	Framework	Traditional
Base System	12	-
Product Fam. 1	1	6
Product Fam. 2	0.5	Estimate: 4 – 5
Product Fam. 3	0.05	Estimate: 1 – 1.5
Overall	14,55	11 – 12.5

two major steps. During the first step, the initial device was produced having the default software flashed to the devices. During the second step, the order individual configuration was loaded to the nodes by applying scripts. This required that the nodes where mounted to a programming device which communicated with the nodes using their standard API.

5.3   Evaluation

The framework was successfully deployed for three different product families which are based on the same Process Model. The third supported product was a revision of the second, where new configuration settings where supported and the underlying hardware platform was changed (endianness changed and additional sensors where added). The time was measured to implement the initial system and the overhead to support the three systems to get an effort estimation which can be compared with a traditional software development. We use the term "traditional software development" for a software development with ad-hoc (or near to ad-hoc) software architecture which means that multiple different systems are designed almost independently. This leads to the situation that only a little code base is shared between each software project since most of the code is optimized for single purposes. However, this code would be reusable if adaptations of the interfaces/implementations would have been considered.

The effort for the traditional software development was based on the real implementation time for the first system and an effort estimation to port the existing family to the new products. These numbers were given by the responsible developers. As illustrated in Table 1, the "traditional" development effort for the third system was about 20–30 times higher than the implementation effort of the new developed framework. This number may seem too high at first sight, but can be directly mapped to the change of the endianness of the underlying hardware platform. With our proposed framework, it was a minor change which required a byte reversal of integer values of the generated outcome. This was done by introducing a post-processing step in every "Translate" block which resulted in integer numbers using already existing functionality. For the traditional development, the responsible developers argued that they would need to search the whole source base to identify the impacts of the endianness change and to fix the according implementations.

As illustrated in Table 1, the break-even point will be between 3 to 4 systems using a curve fitting interpolation. This number also correlates to the typical number presented in relevant software product line publications (e.g. [22]). The break-even point may also be reduced since these numbers do not consider the maintenance of the systems. The maintenance cost can be reduced since fixing problems in one product family will fix this issue in all others as well.

6   Conclusion and Outlook

The reuse of business process models is an important step for an industrial company to survive in a competitive market. But only with an integrated view of the according IT landscape, it is possible to raise the efficiency of the overall business. With this work we proposed a way to combine the benefits of software product line engineering techniques with the capabilities of a business process modelling tool. This work provides a framework for the systematic reuse of business processes and the configuration of software toolchains used during the actual production of the product. The new introduced framework is able to synchronize variable order process structures with a variable software architecture. This means that changes to the processes will automatically lead to software artefacts which need to be implemented by the developers. For that, the framework uses XML data binding to bind specific software features to a specific set of configurable artefacts which need to be submitted by customers (internal and external) during the order process. This is done in an automatic and managed way such that the order interface is always aligned to the software toolchains. This essentially reduces the development costs and time required to react to changes of the market. Moreover, the overall robustness of the software toolchain is increased since the same code base is shared for a lot of different product families leading to a higher customer satisfaction.

In the current state, the presented framework is focused on covering the variability of the order processes. As a consequence, the developed framework is only applicable in similar contexts, where the variability of the process models is mainly driven by the order processes. In a future work, we will investigate the consequences of different contexts and how these changes influences the process models and the according software toolchains.

Further, Future work will address the semi-automatic creation of the schema file which is used to keep the software architecture aligned to the process models. Another point for improvement is the fact that additional restrictions like security requirements are implemented and mapped manually to the according product configurations. In a future work, we will investigate a way to map these security requirements to the according process model which enables an automatic way to bind these requirements to the product families. Thus, additional non-functional requirements can be automatically enforced during the process. This is important especially if a certification of the generated products is intended.

Certification requires, that evidence is provided which ensures that the functional and non-functional requirements are met no matter which valid configuration is used. This requires mature development processes and verification gates to allow an automatic detection of violations.

Acknowledgements. The project is funded by the Austrian Research Promotion Agency (FFG). Project Partners are NXP Semiconductor Austria GmbH and the Technical University of Graz. We want to gratefully thank Danilo Beuche from pure::systems for his support. Further, the authors want to gratefully thank Felix Jonathan Oppermann for his support during the design and the implementation of the industrial prototype.

References

1. McCormack, K.P., Johnson, W.C.: Business Process Orientation: Gaining the E-Business Competitive Advantage. Saint Lucie Press (2000)
2. Valença, G., Alves, C., Alves, V., Niu, N.: A Systematic Mapping Study on Business Process Variability. Int. J. Comput. Sci. Inf. Technol. (IJCSIT) (2013)
3. Willaert, P., Bergh, J., Willems, J., Deschoolmeester, D.: The process-oriented organisation: a holistic view developing a framework for business process orientation maturity. In: Alonso, G., Dadam, P., Rosemann, M. (eds.) BPM 2007. LNCS, vol. 4714, pp. 1–15. Springer, Heidelberg (2007). doi:10.1007/978-3-540-75183-0_1
4. Saidani, O., Nurcan, S.: Towards context aware business process modelling. In: 8th Workshop on Business Process Modeling, Development, and Support (BPMDS 2007), CAiSE. vol. 7, p. 1 (2007)
5. Sinnhofer, A.D., Pühringer, P., Kreiner, C.: varbpm - a product line for creating business process model variants. In: Proceedings of the Fifth International Symposium on Business Modeling and Software Design, pp. 184–191 (2015)
6. Fantinato, M., Toledo, M.B.F., Thom, L.H., Gimenes, I.M.S., Rocha, R.S., Garcia, D.Z.G.: A survey on reuse in the business process management domain. Int. J. Bus. Process Integr. Manage. 6(1), 52–76 (2012)
7. Derguech, W.: Towards a framework for business process models reuse. In: The CAiSE Doctoral Consortium (2010)
8. Gimenes, I., Fantinato, M., Toledo, M.: A product line for business process management. In: International Software Product Line Conference, pp. 265–274 (2008)
9. Hallerbach, A., Bauer, T., Reichert, M.: Guaranteeing soundness of configurable process variants in provop. In: IEEE Conference on Commerce and Enterprise Computing, CEC 2009, pp. 98–105. IEEE (2009)
10. Hallerbach, A., Bauer, T., Reichert, M.: Issues in modeling process variants with provop. In: Ardagna, D., Mecella, M., Yang, J. (eds.) BPM 2008. LNBIP, vol. 17, pp. 56–67. Springer, Heidelberg (2009). doi:10.1007/978-3-642-00328-8_6
11. Reichert, M., Hallerbach, A., Bauer, T.: Lifecycle support for business process variants. In: Brocke, J.V., Rosemann, M. (eds.) Handbook on Business Process Management 1, pp. 251–278. Springer, Heidelberg (2014)
12. Gottschalk, F., van der Aalst, W.M.P., Jansen-Vullers, M.H., Rosa, M.L.: Configurable Workflow Models. Int. J. Coop. Inf. Syst. (2007)
13. Rosa, M., Dumas, M., Hofstede, A.H.M., Mendling, J., Gottschalk, F.: Beyond control-flow: extending business process configuration to roles and objects. In: Li, Q., Spaccapietra, S., Yu, E., Olivé, A. (eds.) ER 2008. LNCS, vol. 5231, pp. 199–215. Springer, Heidelberg (2008). doi:10.1007/978-3-540-87877-3_16

14. Haugen, O., Wasowski, A., Czarnecki, K.: Cvl: common variability language. In: Proceedings of the 17th International Software Product Line Conference, SPLC 2013 (2013)
15. Zhao, X., Zou, Y.: A business process-driven approach for generating software modules. Softw. Pract. Experience. **41**(10), 1049–1071 (2011)
16. Österle, H.: Business Engineering - Prozess- und Systementwicklung. Springer, Heidelberg (1995)
17. Sinnhofer, A.D., Pühringer, P., Potzmader, K., Orthacker, C., Steger, C., Kreiner, C.: A framework for process driven software configuration. In: Proceedings of the Sixth International Symposium on Business Modeling and Software Design, pp. 196–203 (2016)
18. Hammer, M., Champy, J.: Reengineering the Corporation - A Manifesto For Business Revolution. Harper Business, New York (1993)
19. O.M.G.: Business process model and notation (bpmn). version 2.0, pp. 1–538 (2011). http://www.omg.org/spec/BPMN/2.0/
20. Strnadl, C.F.: Aligning business and it: the process-driven architecture model. Inf. Syst. Manage. **23**(4), 67–77 (2006)
21. Kang, K., Cohen, S., Hess, J., Novak, W., Peterson, A.: Feature-oriented domain analysis (foda) feasibility study (1990)
22. Pohl, K., Böckle, G., Linden, F.J.v.d.: Software Product Line Engineering: Foundations, Principles and Techniques. Springer, Heidelberg (2005)
23. Weiss, D.M., Lai, C.T.R.: Software Product-Line Engineering: A Family-Based Software Development Process. Addison-Wesley Longman Publishing Co., Inc., Boston (1999)

Integrated Service E-Marketplace for Independent and Assisted Living – Business and Software Engineering Challenges

Leszek Maciaszek[✉], Wieslawa Gryncewicz[✉], and Robert Kutera[✉]

Department of Information Systems, Wroclaw University of Economics,
Komandorska St. 118-120, 53-345 Wroclaw, Poland
{leszek.maciaszek,wieslawa.gryncewicz,robert.kutera}@ue.wroc.pl

Abstract. E-Marketplaces for services are governed by similar, but not the same business and technology principles as e-marketplaces for products. Additionally, in the particular case of e-marketplaces for senior citizens, service innovation must be requestor-focused. Immobile (residential, fixed) and mobile ambient (sensors, actuators) intelligence devices cover the spectrum of people monitoring (daily living, health status). On the society side, the aim is to enable elderly people, nearing or in retirements, healthy or unhealthy, to live socially-included and economically-active lives. On the IT side, the aim is to provide innovative systems and solutions embracing contemporary shifts of computing paradigm to service science, cloud computing, mobile connectivity, business processes, and societal participation. In this paper the Authors present the service e-marketplace as an ecosystem that is able to utilize the capital of elderly people with the whole added value they can contribute. The special attention is put on integration of elementary e-marketplace systems which provide senior citizens with the specific kinds of services. The importance of the integrator entity is explained and the concept of information system that plays such a role is presented. Selected business and technological implications of embarking on the development of a service e-marketplace platform for independent and assisted living are reported. The Authors discuss also plausible business models, identify major success factors, and present software engineering challenges underpinning development of such platforms.

Keywords: E-Marketplace · E-Service · Independent living · Ambient assisted living · Business models · Service-oriented software engineering · Design science

1 Introduction

Physical and psychological health of elderly people brings concrete social and economic benefits and it is an important enabling factor for the sustained economic growth in the world of otherwise unsustainable-economically demographic change. The increased participation of senior citizens, demanded by the demographic change, is in line with the observed transition to a decentralized and skill-based service economy. The experience, knowledge and wisdom of senior citizens are a huge asset and underutilized

© Springer International Publishing AG 2017
B. Shishkov (Ed.): BMSD 2016, LNBIP 275, pp. 221–231, 2017.
DOI: 10.1007/978-3-319-57222-2_11

enabler of Internet-facilitated service economy of today. The understanding and explanation of these complex relationships constitutes the social and economic background for presented research.

Eurostat's statistics on information and communication technologies (ICTs) show that in 2014 more than one third (38%) of the elderly population (aged 65–74) in the EU used the internet on a regular basis. Over one fifth (22%) of the analysed population made use of internet banking, this was half the share recorded for the total population (44%). A similar share (23%) of the elderly purchased products or services via the internet (Eurostat 2015).

Globally, life expectancy for people born between 2010 and 2015 is 70 years (77 in Europe) and it is expected to keep rising. Moreover, population aged 60 or over accounts in 2015 for 12% of the global population (24% in Europe) and this age group is the fastest growing (3.26% per year) (UN 2015).

The demographic changes have many economic and social implications. On one hand, senior citizens are healthier and more active than past generations. This impacts on the lifestyle needs of senior citizens. On the other hand, longevity is associated with long-lasting medical conditions and disabilities. This impacts on the healthcare needs of seniors. As reported by The World Bank (2015) and elsewhere, the increasing life expectancies and associated healthcare expenditures are becoming unsustainable for world economies. To sustain the pension and healthcare growing costs, there is a need to activate elderly people by providing opportunities for greater economic and social engagement.

From the technology perspective, the first discourse is termed Independent Living (IL), the second – Ambient Assisted Living (AAL). In both cases, the battle ground is to deliver appropriate services to elderly people. At the same time, a service ecosystem should be able to embrace and utilize the capital and contribution that elderly people can give to society. Information technology plays here an ever increasing role, including through provision of e-marketplaces for products and services of interest to senior citizens.

Against that background, enabling business models need to be developed and placed in the economic reality.

2   Service E-Marketplaces

E-Marketplaces for services (such as Booking.com, Airbnb, OpenTable, or BlablaCar) are governed by different value propositions, business models and technology principles than e-marketplaces for products (such as Alibaba, eBay, or MarcadoLivre). The dissimilarity stems from differences between products and services. A requestor of a product request a tangible thing and takes the ownership of that thing when provided by the supplier. A requestor of a service requests an action without taking the ownership of the service.

This said, we must recognize that most services have an element of products in them and vice versa. The dichotomy between these two concepts has been replaced by a service-product continuum (Targowski 2009). On one hand, products are servitized; on the other hand, services are productized (Cusumano 2008).

In the context of R&D reported in this paper, we must distinguish between a service and an IT service. Following the ITIL (IT Infrastructure Library) "a service is a means of delivering value to customers by facilitating outcomes customers want to achieve without the ownership of specific costs and risks." (Aguter 2013, p. 17). Such services can be divided into classic (brick & mortar) services and e-services. The first ones are usually performed locally on the requestor's premises. E-service, on the contrary, can be requested and provided via an electronic channel.

E-Marketplaces differ significantly from traditional e-commerce systems. Firstly, they reinstate the function of intermediaries between the requestor/buyer and supplier/seller (i.e. the function that traditional e-commerce systems can do without). Secondly, and more importantly, e-marketplaces connect actors in many-to-many collaborative networks, in which diverse offerings of suppliers are facilitated by diverse intermediaries and meet with diverse realizations of requestors. Such systems emphasize the appointment coordination process between the three parties. The appointment coordination can be defined as "a process, which leads to establishing time, locations, participants and goal of the appointment" (Biziel et al. 2016). In that process an important role could play the integrator, which provides users with the platform for communication of actors gathered among different systems, that constitutes the integrated ecosystem for ensuring elderly people an independent and assisted living.

3   Integrated E-Marketplace Model

Service innovation is requestor-focused. Requestor market, as the primary driver of service e-marketplace innovation, challenges the way companies innovate and evolve with IT. The innovation ideas need to tap into the phenomenon of consumerization and personalization as the tendency for new IT solutions to emphasize requestor-focused service provision and to emerge first in the personal requestor market and then spread into business and government organizations. Consumerization opens up an opportunity for new business models and ways of value creation.

The shifts to consumerization and personalization underlies next generation service e-marketplace solutions, in which service requestor is placed in the centre of attention, while the service supplier is given enough incentive to use the e-marketplace (and, in most business models, pay for the use of it). The formula of consumer being a core entity in lifestyle engineering domain matches well the traditional marketing principle that "the customer is always right".

What is more, e-marketplaces are more and more fragmented, customized and personalized as service suppliers offer to their customers more specialized services and concentrate on narrow customer segments. Finally many new businesses and businesses participating in traditional service markets appear on the e-marketplace, as entry threshold is still decreasing. Many entities in such a competitive environment have no power to stay on the market on their own because of the limited awareness among customers, small budgets for marketing activities and limited possibilities of investing in IT innovations supporting customers in efficient and convenient service requesting and purchasing. They need to cooperate with other suppliers or exploit opportunities of taking part in bigger e-commerce platforms (service aggregators) to gain access to a larger potential customer base.

That is why modern e-marketplaces should be ready for integration of different IT systems provided by 3rd party market players. This is to enable customers easy access to offers of different kind by providing tools for aggregation of offers from many sources. On the other hand – it can also support and stimulate service providers by enabling them an access to the wider group of potential customers and helping in promotion of their offers in many ways.

The business models need to consider three dimensions: economic, operational and strategic (Osl et al. 2008). The first dimension is focused on the mechanisms of making money, the second – on internal processes to create business value, and the third one – on building the company's market position. The emphasis needs to be put on: key partners, suppliers, resources and activities in the e-marketplace venture as well as on value propositions, cost structure, and revenue streams. The establishment of customer relationships and communication channels to various customer segments are fundamental to the business success.

The models for the use of a service e-marketplace platform involve many actors. Vendors of particular cloud Software-as-a-Service (SaaS) solutions can offer more than one tenant instance to suppliers of concrete e-marketplace systems. E-Marketplace integrator is responsible for aggregating data and providing common functionality from different systems and plays the role of the gate application for users to browse offers, manage them and access authentication mechanism delivering Single Sign On property to all systems (Kutera and Gryncewicz 2016b). Suppliers/intermediaries act as context integrators for interested service providers. A provider enlists service performers as subscribers to a cloud-based service e-marketplace platform. A performer delivers the service to a requestor.

Figure 1 presents actors and revenue streams for the service e-marketplace business case. Requestors (consumers) solicit services of suppliers by using service e-marketplace integrator or directly the particular system. These systems can be loosely integrated with the "gate" system – the market integrator, where at least offer data are being synchronized all the time (an added value is the solution that enables to login once and having access to the integrator as well as all connected systems. Services can be obtained via intermediaries, who have access to service context and information about requestors' standing. They can act as concierge or call centres and can make appointments for services on behalf of providers. Alternatively, requestors can make direct appointments with providers via the service e-marketplace platform. In a typical situation, provider employs performers, who actually execute a service. Volunteers and informal carers can provide their informal services on their own, *ipso facto* playing the role of sole providers who shall not be rewarded financially (only by thanks or barter). They, as well as all market entities supporting the exchange of services between requestors and providers, can be supported by donations coming from public or private capital.

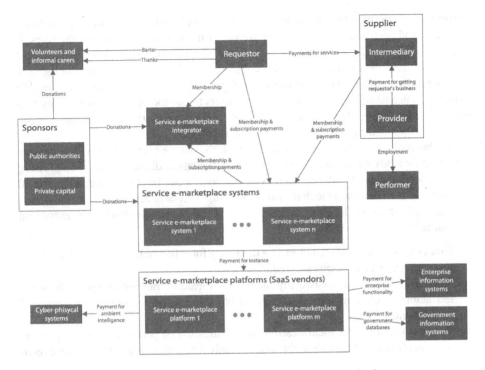

Fig. 1. Actors and revenue streams in service e-marketplace business case.

The intermediary aspect of e-marketplace platform enables human-driven concierge-like appointment coordination made possible by all communication means (Internet, telephone, email, etc.). However, the principal modus-operandi of the platform is to encourage requestors and suppliers to manage appointment and service provisioning with web-based applications using context-aware and purpose-designed mobile and non-mobile devices. In some cases, delivery of services can be auto-activated by sensing/computing/actuating capabilities of cyber-physical systems (Haque et al. 2014). Such systems utilize technologies of IoT (Miorandi et al. 2012) and environments of ambient intelligence (Cook et al. 2009).

4 Business Challenges

A troublesome side-effect of any chosen service e-marketplace business model is the cold start problem. How to entice service providers and performers to pay for and use a vendor's service e-marketplace platform, if there are no requestors yet? On the other hand, how to entice requestors to request services prior to the establishment of a significant presence of providers and performers on the platform with their service offers? That is especially important in the target group of elderly people, where many people could possibly be afraid of utilizing ICTs in their day-to-day operations or have no money for paying for services. One way of alleviating the cold start problem is by creating local communities of requestors, which not only can create "volume" to attract providers and performers, but can even use barter trade to switch between the roles of requestor and provider/performer. What is more, there is an important need to look for social organisations dedicated for helping elderly people. They could provide the new e-marketplace with the significant group of people under their care but also they are able to organize necessary trainings and stimulate users to use the new ICT tools. They also could have the power of engaging providers of local brick&mortar services into moving the part of their selling activities into the e-marketplace.

Technological novelty and attractiveness of a service e-marketplace is a necessary condition for a business success, but it is not a sufficient condition. By observing "rising stars" in service e-marketplaces, such as airbnb.com, it can be observed that the crucial requirement is to facilitate mechanisms of building trust between all actors from both – demand and supply - sides. A coherent trust-building endeavour should concentrate on providing:

1. Guarantees (safeguards to actors in a monetary form for such things as lost business to a performer or damages to a requestor).
2. Safe payment system (trustworthy and reliable means of transferring money between the actors; including refunds, cancellation policies, protection under Terms of Service, etc.).
3. Verification (a proper identification and verification of performers and requestors prior to allowing them to use the system, gathering opinions after a service execution).
4. Community (most services offered via a concrete instantiation of the service e-marketplace platform are "localized", i.e. services are enacted in geographically-closed communities; accordingly the platform must facilitate community building by allowing barter services etc. and permitting the community to evolve the platform).

The main role in developing the whole ecosystem could be played by the intermediary, who usually administers the whole ecosystem or the particular system or just supports it. The intermediary's task is mainly to organise broadly understood assistance for senior citizens, to actively stimulate them to use the IT product, to satisfy their everyday needs, to verify the quality of services and to supervise financial transactions. This is the way of overcoming the barriers resulting from senior citizens' low digital competences and their distrust in technological and process innovations. What is also eliminated owing to the existence of the intermediary is the problem of dishonest service providers, which are monitored by the intermediary and end users (senior citizens) on an ongoing basis. While performing these organic functions, the intermediary can apply different communication channels offered by the IT product (Kutera et al. 2016a).

Intermediaries, as well as other market entities should also promote the e-marketplace by providing tangible evidences of that the platform is working properly and achieves its main purpose of preventing social exclusion among elderly people and supporting them in having an independent and joyful life. That is why the concrete numbers that measure a success of the platform (active users, number of transactions, number of certificated providers and so on) as well as success stories should be communicated to the potential new users.

5 Software Engineering Challenges

Because the IT is an empowerment and enhancer in the service economy and because elderly people are asset and potential engine in the service economy, then there is an obvious need to provide to seniors IT solutions with friendly easy-to-use interfaces. This is a huge challenge because of the "lost in the cyberspace" resistance of seniors to using Internet via mobile and non-mobile devices (Heart and Kalderon 2011). A corresponding challenge is that the delivery of software and systems that are easy to use implies that they are difficult to design and implement. What is more, the growing granularity of systems available on e-marketplace and built on the top of heterogeneous platforms, cause that end users have a problem with effective utilization of their capabilities because they have to learn the navigation scenarios and information architecture. That is why there is a significant need for integrating such systems under the central gate application with the usable interface which enforce the partial unification of basic data flows or even their integration (like signing up or browsing offers). It ensures interoperability – the ability of system to provide services to and accept services from another systems and to use the services exchanged efficiently. In a microscale it is the ability by which the elements of system can exchange and understand the required information with each other (Adams 2015).

In service e-marketplaces, the delivery of services to actors is performed (typically) on Everything-as-a-Service models (Banerjee 2011), in which software, platform and infrastructure are made available in the form of services paid for according to the usage. This creates ubiquitous marketplace where commercial, social, government, health, education and other services are facilitated, negotiated, coordinated and paid for through service e-marketplace platforms.

Some services can be automatically or semi-automatically identified through the process of service matching and selection. This process can be triggered in a way oblivious to a requestor - it can be cyber-physical or concierge/intermediary initiated. It can also be activated and negotiated directly by a requestor. Service order and execution can flow from service matching and selection. In all cases, a requestor will be directly involved in ordering and execution of a service. The process itself can be advised by experts (suppliers and other professionals) and by social networks.

On the integrator level, the user is able to browse unified offers from different sources in a common catalogue, search for or filter them and perform any additional actions that help to organize them (e.g. via marking as favorites). User could also create an account or manage personal data and in a perfect case use this account to login once and have an access to all systems connected by the integrator. These actions are usually handled similarly in most systems, so their unification to an established standard should not be an extensive effort. However business logic of individual systems for particular service types can be significantly different. Short-term services could require different actions comparing to long-term ones, similarly one-time or recurrent ones. The nature of a service type may enforce specific steps of requesting the service (negotiations, necessity of direct meetings, offer customization etc.) that could not be easily covered by standard processes and have to stay within the domain of particular systems dedicated for supporting the special process.

If full integration is not possible (because of circumstances mentioned above), at least loose integration should be ensured (on three levels):

1. User interface (UI) integration – to ensure the rich and seamless user experience from using an integrator as if the users are using single and compact application, not only the gate for an individual system.
2. Backend (web services & data) integration - the integration on a deeper level, concerning the possibility of utilizing data flows from connected systems in common data views. Thus all connected systems need to provide the integrator with APIs / data services delivering the needed information in a standard format (e.g. JSON). Moreover the gate application should convert these data, decorate it in a proper way and display to the user in a particular form (catalogs /map markers).
3. Security integration – the integration on the identity management level, where a user can log in once and have access to all components of the platform. It should utilize popular secure mechanisms of user authentication and allocation of permissions within the whole ecosystem.

While the first level is related only to front-end adaptations within a particular system in compliance with the given standard, the two deeper levels depend strongly on data exchange and communication between client systems and the integrator. That is why all the systems should be implemented by taking into account the contemporary software development approaches.

The established discipline of software engineering (e.g. Maciaszek and Liong 2005) advocates architecture-driven forward-engineering processes. Modern practices challenge such processes. They also challenge the rigid top-down development epitomized in three consecutive phases of systems analysis, design and implementation.

While the architectural patterns, principles, and frameworks remain a valid software engineering objective for development of a service e-marketplace platform (ref. e.g. Maciaszek et al. 2015a; Maciaszek et al. 2015b), the ways of achieving that objective have changed in modern practices. Main practices that underlie this trend are DevOps and microservices.

DevOps is an approach for merging development and operations (Huttermann 2012). On the level of user interface and web programming, DevOps is supported by approaches known as responsive development, progressive enhancement, and graceful degradation (Overfield et al. 2013).

The microservice architectural style is "an approach to developing a single application as a suite of small services, each running in its own process and communicating with lightweight mechanisms, often an HTTP resource API" (Lewis and Fowler 2014).

Together, DevOps and microservices allow for an agile development while not jeopardizing such important software qualities as adaptability (i.e. understandability, maintainability and evolveability) and interoperability. In the ecosystem consisting of integrator ("gate" system) and multiple systems providing data and functionality to end users, these approaches ensure that particular systems are able to provide one API interface. It could be accessible by many endpoints, such as native web frontend, dedicated mobile app and any authorized 3rd party application (in that case – at least the integrator). All these endpoints can communicate with using simple data exchange standards like

JSON. What is more, with DevOps plus microservices at work, a particular service e-marketplace platform could set up many cloud tenant instances for service e-marketplace businesses. Service e-marketplace system is then a cloud instance of a generic Software-as-a-Service platform. These systems could be linked directly to the integrator and use the same API for that purpose. Customization and variability of instances is based on the technology of multi-tenancy and uses the emerging principles of Service Line Engineering (SLE) (Mohabbati et al. 2013; Walraven et al. 2014). It is most important for organizations which provide similar services to their end users (in the context of functional shape of processes and data logic) and do not have enough financial assets to spare on developing an individual IT solution. Using a cloud limits costs significantly.

6   Conclusions

The research on service e-marketplace needs to focus on the dedicated science and engineering for designing software systems and applications supporting provision of e-service solutions in general, and specifically for independent and assisted living of elderly people. By centering on consumerization, personalization, and collaborative context-dependent value creation, the R&D into service e-marketplace shifts towards what Brenner et al. (2014) call user, use & utility research (or 3U research, to use another parlance).

The research agenda must include both fundamental and pragmatically-minded research along the design science principles (Hevner and March 2003; Hevner et al. 2004; Niederman and March 2012; Oesterle et al. 2010). While design science is the preferred scientific method for much of information systems research, it becomes the necessity for R&D into service information systems, as per three convincing arguments identified by Boehmann et al. (2014).

1. Service systems cannot be meaningfully validated in laboratory experiments. An external validity in real-world contexts (piloting of innovation) is necessary.
2. Novel service systems can only emerge with actors' acceptance and involvement (through participatory design and action research).
3. Service systems engineering develops software models and artifacts and is, therefore, design-oriented by their very nature.

From business perspective e-marketplace for independent and assisted living should provide a wide range of opportunities for supporting and engaging elderly people. That is why there is a strong necessity for joining efforts by multiple providers and building an integrated e-marketplace. In such a fragmented environment the policy for ensuring the quality of provided services should be built by various mechanisms of ensuring trust (initial verifications, personal reviews or certifications, testimonials and facts about successes of the marketplace). An important role is played in that case by the intermediary, whose responsibility is not only to managing the marketplace, but also boosting its intensity by gathering new providers with complementary and competitive offers and encourage new end users.

The consequence for software engineering is the necessity of utilizing the DevOps and microservices concept to build a flexible and interoperable environment where all systems can exchange and synchronize information. In a more fundamental sense, any contemporary service e-marketplace platform for seniors is a realization of what Gregory Abowd calls the fourth generation of collective computing that integrates the cloud, the crowd, and the shroud (Abowd 2016). In this collective computing scenario, the cloud delivers endless and always available resources, the crowd contributes collective intelligence of connected humans, and the shroud offers cyber-physical computing of connected immobile and mobile devices. While the cloud and the crowd have broader applicability, the shroud is particularly important in application domains such as personal health and wellness, and therefore in the platforms for independent and assisted living.

References

Abowd, G.D.: Beyond weiser: from ubiquitous to collective computing. IEEE Comput., pp. 17–23 (2016)

Adams, K.: Non-functional Requirements in Systems Analysis and Design, vol. 28. Springer, Heidelberg (2015)

Aguter, C.: ITIL® Lifecycle Essentials. Your Essential Guide for the ITIL Foundation Exam and Beyond, IT Governance Publishing, 375p (2013)

Banerjee, P., et al.: Everything as a service: powering the new information economy. IEEE Comput., 36–43 (2011)

Biziel, G., Franczyk, B., Slowik, J.: Efficiency of the Appointment Coordination Process' Model in the Emerging Business. In: Sixth International Conference on Business Intelligence and Technology, BUSTECH 2016 (2016). (Manuscript Accepted for Publication)

Boehmann, T., Leimeister, J.M., Moeslein, K.: Service systems engineering. A field for future information systems research. Bus. Inf. Syst. Eng. 6(2), 73–79 (2014)

Brenner, W., et al.: User, use & utility research. The digital user as new design perspective in business and information systems engineering. Bus. Inf. Syst. Eng. 6(1), 56–61 (2014)

Cook, D.J., Augusto, J.C., Jakkula, V.R.: Ambient intelligence: technologies applications and opportunities. Pervasive Mobile Comput. 5, 277–298 (2009)

Cusumano, M.A.: The changing software business: moving from products to services. IEEE Comput., 20–27 (2008)

Eurostat: People in the EU – statistics on an ageing society (2015). http://ec.europa.eu/eurostat/statistics-explained/index.php/People_in_the_EU_%E2%80%93_statistics_on_an_ageing_society#Economically_active_senior_citizens

Haque, S.A., Aziz, S.M., Rahman, M.: Review of cyber-physical system in healthcare. Int. J. Distrib. Sens. Netw. 217415, 20p (2014)

Heart, T., Kalderon, E.: Older adults: are they ready to adopt health-related ICT? Int. J. Med. Informatics 82, e209–e231 (2011)

Hevner, A.R., March, S.T.: The information systems research lifecycle. IEEE Comput., 111–113 (2003)

Hevner, A.R., et al.: Design science research in information systems. MIS Querterly 28(1), 75–105 (2004)

Huttermann, M.: DevOps for Developers, Apress (2012)

Kutera, R., Gryncewicz, W.: Single sign on as an effective way of managing user identity in distributed web systems. In: The Actgo-Gate Project Case Study, Business Informatics. Publishing House of Wroclaw University of Economics (2016b). (in reviews)

Kutera, R., Gryncewicz, W., Leszczynska, M., Butryn, B.: The model of delivering an IT product designed to activate and support senior citizens in Poland. In: Ganzha, M., Maciaszek, L., Paprzycki, M. (eds.) Position Papers of the 2016 Federated Conference on Computer Science and Information Systems, ACSIS, vol. 9, pp. 195–202 (2016a). http://dx.doi.org/10.15439/2016F209

Lewis, J., Fowler, M.: Microservices. A Definition of this New Architectural Term (2014). http://martinfowler.com/articles/microservices.html#CharacteristicsOfAMicroserviceArchitecture

Maciaszek, L.A., Skalniak, T.: Confluent factors, complexity and resultant architectures in modern software engineering. a case of service cloud applications. In: Shiskov, B. (ed.) Fifth International Symposium on Business Modeling and Software Design BMSD 2015, ScitTePress, pp. 27–45 (2015a)

Maciaszek, L.A., Skalniak, T., Biziel, G.: Architectural principles for service cloud applications. In: Shiskov, B. (ed.) Business Modeling and System Design 4th International Symposium BMSD 2014, Revised Selected Papers, Lecture Notes in Business Information Processing LNBIP 220, Springer, Heidelberg, pp. 1–21 (2015b)

Maciaszek, L.A., Liong, B.L.: Practical Software Engineering. A Case-Study Approach. Addison-Wesley, Boston (2005)

Miorandi, D., Sicari, S., Pellegrini De, F., Chlamtac, I.: Internet of things: vision, applications and research challenges. Ad Hoc Netw. 10, 1497–1516 (2012)

Mohabbati, B., Asadi, M., Gasevic, D., Hatala, M., Mueller, H.A.: Combining service-orientation and software product line engineering: a systematic mapping study, information and software technology, 15p (2013). http://dx.doi.org/10.1016/j.infsof.2013.05.006

Niederman, F., March, S.T.: Design science and the accumulation of knowledge in the information systems discipline. ACM Trans. Manage. Inf. Syst. 3(1), 3–15 (2012)

Oesterle, H., et al.: Memorandum on design-oriented information systems research. Eur. J. Inf. Syst., 1–4 (2010)

Osl, P., Sassen, E., Oesterle, H.: A guideline for the design of collaborative business models in the field of ambient assisted living, deutscher AAL-Kongress mit Ausstellung. Berlin, Offenbach: VDE Verlag GmbH, pp. 179–183 (2008). http://works.bepress.com/hubert_oesterle/169

Overfield, E., Zhang, R., Medina, O., Khipple, K.: Responsive web design and development. In: Overfield, E., Zhang, R., Medina, O., Khipple, K. (eds.) Pro SharePoint 2013 Branding and Responsive Web Development. Apress, pp. 17–46 (2013)

Targowski, A.: The architecture of service systems as the framework for the definition of service science scope. Int. J. Inf. Syst. Serv. Sect. 1(1), 54–77 (2009)

The World Bank 2015, Doing Business 2016. Measuring Regulatory Quality and Efficiency. http://www.worldbank.org/en/events/2015/11/11/doing-business-2016-report

UN, World Population Prospects. Key Findings & Advanced Tables. 2015 Revision, United Nations, 66p (2015)

Walraven, S., et al.: Efficient customization of multi-tenant software-as-a-service applications with service lines. J. Syst. Softw. 91, 48–62 (2014)

Author Index

Printed in the United States
By Bookmasters